Transition, Reception and Modernism in W. B. Yeats

Richard Greaves

palgrave

© Richard Greaves 2002

All rights reserved. No reproduction, copy or transmission of this publication may be made without written permission.

No paragraph of this publication may be reproduced, copied or transmitted save with written permission or in accordance with the provisions of the Copyright, Designs and Patents Act 1988, or under the terms of any licence permitting limited copying issued by the Copyright Licensing Agency, 90 Tottenham Court Road, London W1T 4LP.

Any person who does any unauthorized act in relation to this publication may be liable to criminal prosecution and civil claims for damages.

The author has asserted his right to be identified as the author of this work in accordance with the Copyright, Designs and Patents Act 1988.

First published 2002 by
PALGRAVE
Houndmills, Basingstoke, Hampshire RG21 6XS and
175 Fifth Avenue, New York, N.Y. 10010
Companies and representatives throughout the world

PALGRAVE is the new global academic imprint of
St. Martin's Press LLC Scholarly and Reference Division and
Palgrave Publishers Ltd (formerly Macmillan Press Ltd).

ISBN 0–333–74933–2

This book is printed on paper suitable for recycling and made from fully managed and sustained forest sources.

Cataloging-in-publication data

A catalogue record for this book is available from the British library

A catalogue record for this book is available from the library of congress

10 9 8 7 6 5 4 3 2 1
11 10 09 08 07 06 05 04 03 02

Printed and bound in Great Britain by
Antony Rowe Ltd, Chippenham, Wiltshire

For Michelle

Contents

Acknowledgements	*viii*
Abbreviations	*ix*
Introduction	1
1 Problems with Modernism	3
2 *In the Seven Woods*	26
3 From '*The Green Helmet and Other Poems*'	68
4 *Poems Written in Discouragement*	97
5 *Responsibilities*	126
Conclusion	148
Notes	154
Selected Bibliography	175
Index	192

Acknowledgements

My thanks to A. P. Watt Ltd for granting permission on behalf of Michael B. Yeats to quote from the works of W. B. Yeats. Also, in the United States, quotations from *The Variorum Edition of the Poems of W. B. Yeats*, edited by Peter Allt and Russell K. Alspach (New York: Macmillan, 1957) are reprinted with the permission of Scribner, a division of Simon & Schuster. Thanks to A. M. Heath for permission granted on behalf of Anna White to quote from *The Gonne–Yeats Letters 1893–1938: Always Your Friend*, ed. Anna MacBride White and A. Norman Jeffares (Copyright © Anna MacBride White). Material from *The Collected Letters of W. B. Yeats: Volume Three, 1901–1904*, ed. John Kelly and Ronald Schuchard (Oxford: Clarendon Press, 1994) is quoted by permission of Oxford University Press.

My thanks to Liverpool Hope for a semester's research leave to help me prepare this book. I appreciate the moral support of all my colleagues, but special thanks are due to Steve Devereux and Rufus Wood, who read and offered helpful comments on a sample chapter, and to Michael Parker for his insistent encouragement to publish my work. I owe a great debt of gratitude to Warwick Gould for his supervision of my PhD, from which this book developed. He was always generous with encouragement, advice, and practical assistance. My thanks also to Michelle Paull, ever my most stalwart supporter.

RICHARD GREAVES

Abbreviations

Au	*Autobiographies* (London: Macmillan, 1955).
CL1	*The Collected Letters of W. B. Yeats: Volume One, 1865–1895*, ed. John Kelly and Eric Domville (Oxford: Clarendon Press, 1986).
CL2	*The Collected Letters of W. B. Yeats: Volume Two, 1896–1900*, ed. Warwick Gould, John Kelly and Deirdre Toomey (Oxford: Clarendon Press, 1997).
CL3	*The Collected Letters of W. B. Yeats: Volume Three, 1901–1904*, ed. John Kelly and Ronald Schuchard (Oxford: Clarendon Press, 1994).
E & I	*Essays and Introductions* (London and New York: Macmillan, 1961).
Ex	*Explorations*, sel. Mrs W. B. Yeats (London: Macmillan, 1962; New York: Macmillan, 1963).
GYL	*The Gonne–Yeats Letters 1893–1938: Always Your Friend*, ed. Anna MacBride White and A. Norman Jeffares (London: Hutchinson, 1992).
ISW	*In the Seven Woods: Being Poems Chiefly of the Irish Heroic Age* (Dundrum: Dun Emer, 1903).
L	*The Letters of W. B. Yeats*, ed. Allan Wade (London: Rupert Hart Davis, 1954; New York: Macmillan, 1955).
Mem	*Memoirs: Autobiography – First Draft: Journal*, transcribed and edited by Denis Donoghue (London: Macmillan, 1972; New York: Macmillan, 1973).
Myth	*Mythologies* (London and New York: Macmillan, 1959).
UP2	*Uncollected Prose by W. B. Yeats*, vol. 2, ed. John P. Frayne and Colton Johnson (London: Macmillan, 1975; New York: Columbia University Press, 1976).
VP	*The Variorum Edition of the Poems of W. B. Yeats*, ed. Peter Allt and Russell K. Alspach (New York: Macmillan, 1957).
VSR	*The Secret Rose, Stories by W. B. Yeats: A Variorum Edition*, 2nd edn revised and enlarged, ed. Warwick Gould, Phillip L. Marcus, and Michael J. Sidnell (London: Macmillan Academic and Professional, 1992).
YA	*Yeats Annual* (London: Macmillan), followed by number and date.

YP *Yeats's Poems*, ed. and annotated by A. Norman Jeffares with an appendix by Warwick Gould (London: Macmillan, 1989).
YT *Yeats and the Theatre*, ed. Robert O'Driscoll and Lorna Reynolds (Toronto: Macmillan of Canada; Niagara Falls, N.Y.: Maclean-Hunter Press, 1975).

Introduction

This book has as its starting point my strong reaction against a tendency in criticism I had read to locate, see and judge the phase of Yeats's poetry from 1903 to 1914 in relation to what is referred to as 'modernism'. Initially, I was particularly outraged by the attribution of a definite change in Yeats's poetry to the influence of Ezra Pound, an attribution which surfaces still in spite of clear refutation by Thomas Parkinson in 1954.[1] But the centrality of Pound to what is called 'modernism' in literature led me to think further about the nature of the term as it is used in this context, and this is the concern of the first part of this book.

There follows a reading of the three volumes of poetry Yeats published between 1903 and 1916. I aim to offer a different way of looking at the transition in Yeats's work in this phase, seeking to account for it without relying on what John Harwood has convincingly described as the reified edifice of modernism.[2] It occurs to me that academic criticism sometimes overrates the significance and explanatory power of its own categories. The category of modernism can become so central in a consideration of writers and their work that it overwhelms other factors.

Reductive biographically based criticism can give the impression that the task of interpretation is merely to turn imaginative literature back into its raw material, and the reaction against it was necessary. Also, it seems to me wrong to claim that only those with years of painstakingly accumulated knowledge of the poet's biography and historical context can interpret a poem at all. I see reaction against this as part of what drives the New Critics' view of the poem as a verbal icon. I'm a teacher too, and can see the value in saying to a group of students that we can all, at least, work with the words on the page, the poem in front of us. The problem is that this reaction can lead to a sealing off of the poem.

It is, I think, possible to restore connection with life and milieu without falling back into reductiveness. One advantage of trying to do so is that it restores particularity and diversity. I want to see Yeats as Yeats, and not as a partial example – or failed example – of modernism in literature. Professional imperatives in the academic study of literature lead increasingly to a separation of academics' ways of thinking about literature from those of others with an interest in it. Who hasn't heard the comment from a student: 'Oh, I thought that was just the kind of thing lecturers wrote for each other to read'? My view is that the attempt to see the writer's work in relation to his life is a move towards reconnection.

I wanted to see the transition in Yeats's poetry in the context of his life – for instance, his position in Ireland, his relationship with Maud Gonne – not to iron out the particularities of *his* transition by seeing it only as an instance of a retrospectively identified and labelled literary category. I am interested in the ways in which Yeats represents Yeats in his poems, and in the relationship between the construction of the figure of the poet within the poems and the construction of the public figure of Yeats in Ireland. I am also interested in the Yeats constructed in other texts: his autobiographies, letters, essays. The feeding back of the influence of these constructions into the life of the man who writes fascinates me.

To refuse to allow Yeats to disappear into the category of modernism (or even to disappear in being found inadequate to be included in it) seemed to me crucial. In 'The Tree of Life' in *Discoveries*, Yeats claims that the artist must climb free of 'common interests', of the interests of the 'market-place', but not climb *too* high. He establishes a sense here of relinking art and the quotidian world even as he preserves distance and artistic integrity. Seeing in Yeats's idea the figure of the poet owing responsibilities to two spheres which can seem incompatible led me to think of what strikes me as a growing inwardness, reflexiveness, self-concern in literary studies. The figure of Yeats the poet, textually constructed, existing within the work, is, nevertheless, connected with the flesh-and-blood figure. The connection is complex, but it is not non-existent. The figure of Yeats the poet, then, guarantees a connection between the work and the life, between literature and the world.

1
Problems with Modernism

I

There is general agreement that Yeats's work altered considerably in the phase which includes *In the Seven Woods* and *Responsibilities and Other Poems*. Some critics have judged that at some time in this phase Yeats became a modernist poet. But what do they mean by 'modernist'? Matei Calinescu finds the first favourable application of the term to literature in Latin America, by Ruben Dari, in 1888.[1] He notes the difficulty of establishing the use of the term in anything like its current sense in connection with literature in English, but suggests a little magazine, *The Modernist: A Monthly Magazine of Modern Arts and Letters*, published in 1919 (though this magazine turns out to be more political than literary),[2] and John Crowe Ransom's 'The Future of Poetry', published in *The Fugitive: A Journal of Poetry* in February 1924. Ransom claims that it is necessary for poetry to recognize modernism, though '[i]t is undefined'. He does describe the manifestos of the Imagists as modernist.[3] He also refers to 'the Moderns', 'we moderns' and 'modern poets'. The Imagists' 'modernist manifestos' are, for Ransom, partly a declaration of what the modern poet should do. But, as John Harwood points out, Calinescu's understanding of the term 'modernism' seems to be conditioned by its use in literary criticism from the 1960s on. The idea of attempting to trace the history of the usage of the term can be overwhelmed by the attempt to trace the origins of 'a reified construct' projected from one's own time, and that it *is* a construct gets forgotten. The existence of something called 'modernism' (which is also what Calinescu means by it) is inferred from a reference to it by someone who says it is 'undefined'.[4]

R. A. Scott-James, in his *Modernism and Romance* (1908), distinguishes his use of the term from the theological use, and claims to be using it in the sense suggested by Hardy.[5] He believes it difficult for poets to find expression in a scientific, self-conscious and materialistic age which has even infected the English language. But his intention is not to identify and describe as 'modernist' a particular type of poetry, but rather to show the difficulty of writing poetry in modern times. The earliest extensive treatment of modern poetry in English which specifically categorizes some of this as modernist seems to be Riding and Graves's *A Survey of Modern Poetry*, published in 1927.[6] Calinescu claims that by this time, 'the term [modernism] must have established itself as a meaningful – though still largely controversial – literary category'.[7] This seems rather speculative, and a little difficult to interpret, if Calinescu wants to say that the term is meaningful yet there is controversy over *what* it means. He speculates that since 'modern' could be used as adjective and noun and the word 'modernism' had until recently been tainted by pejorative connotations, 'a large number of aesthetic theories, insights, and choices, which today we would not hesitate to describe as "modernist," went on being formulated within the broader framework of the idea of the modern.'[8] The readiness today to call 'modernist' what at the time was called 'modern' indicates what is happening here. Within 'the modern', academic criticism from the 1960s on has distinguished a 'modernist'.[9]

One generalization Riding and Graves *do* make about the poetry they want to characterize as 'modernist' is that the plain reader finds it difficult to understand. This difficulty may make the statement: 'Keep out. This is a private performance,'[10] or it may be a means of demanding the application of a higher level of attention and intelligence on the part of the reader. The potential of the second for academic criticism is clear. Here is poetry the interpretation of which demands an elite of specially trained readers. The idea of poetry as private performance is also significant in relation to what later critics concerned with modernism have to say and in possible sources for critical tenets which fall within the ambit of the retrospectively projected idea of modernism.

Frank Kermode's *Romantic Image* strongly makes the case for the resemblance of modernist critical tenets to those of French Symbolism, though he is careful to point to the parallel track of a similar influence from Blake and Pater.[11] Donald Davie's response to Kermode accuses him of failing to distinguish between post-Symbolist and Symbolist practice, but this kind of distinction is unlikely to be clear-cut, of course, since the degree of transformation that demands the 'post' is a matter for debate.[12]

The chief difficulty that arises with the French Symbolist poetry of Mallarmé in particular is that privacy of performance threatens to become complete; that is to say, the extension of Mallarmé's poetics to their logical limit would create a private language, one without reference to the external world. Kermode was not the first to see Symbolism at the root of some of the literature of the modern period. Edmund Wilson, in *Axel's Castle*, setting out to 'trace the origins of certain tendencies in contemporary literature',[13] heads his opening chapter 'Symbolism'. It is the emphasis on the individual that, for Wilson, threatens to make poetry too much of a private performance, 'indeed ... so much a private concern of the poet's that it turned out to be incommunicable to the reader.'[14]

If Kermode is right in seeing Symbolism as so influential, then the idea of the autonomy of the text, very much a part of the New Criticism which developed at least in part from the critical ideas and theories of Eliot and Pound, can also be seen as a development from Symbolist ideas. Riding and Graves make a concern with the autonomy of the poem one of the distinguishing marks of their idea of modernism. '[T]he important part of poetry is now not the personality of the poet as embodied in a poem'; the poet is to separate the poem from his own personality in order to make it independent, 'a new and self-explanatory creature'.[15] Yeats's 'secondary personality' is very much 'the personality of the poet as embodied in the poem', however problematic the relationship with the biographical figure of Yeats may be. Yeats's 'something intended, complete' is this personality; Riding and Graves's idea of the poem as 'complete' makes it a self-enclosed system. Their 'modernist' poem is a 'rootless flower', detached from the life from which it grows. Their insistence on the poem's own personality implies that it is particularly amenable to a purely textual analysis.

Davie's response to *Romantic Image* indicates how he thinks French Symbolism does not merely use images from the external world to reflect the poet's state of mind. The French Symbolist poet was able to assume that 'the relationships the poet seemed to discover in the world outside were really relationships true only of his own psychological being, and projected on to the external world as on to a screen.' Why then wait for the right screen? The poet can construct his own 'apparently external worlds free of the logic and the structure of the everyday ... '[16] Davie acknowledges the collapse between inside and outside that can occur here, and that some of the resulting poetry is 'entirely solipsistic'. He claims that the work of Yeats, Eliot and Pound has partly, though not yet completely, rehumanized poetry, and that the task to be completed is the rehumanization of poetry that would come with the escape from solipsism involved in the re-establishment of an external world, though without losing the technical advances made through the dehumanization of poetry by the French Symbolists.

The attack he makes on Kermode here points to a problem of cause and effect. Davie judges Kermode's suggestion that Yeats builds the way out of solipsism by 'keeping in mind the claims of the common reader' (468) to be unsatisfactory. His own idea is that once the external world is re-established by the poet in his work, the common reader will be once more accessible to him (or, maybe, the poetry to the reader). This 'which comes first?' kind of dispute indicates a relationship between the difficulty of 'modernist' poetry (that is, the difficulty the common reader experiences in understanding it), and the philosophy behind it. Does the modernist poet deliberately make his poetry hard to understand because he wants to limit his audience, or is the difficulty of understanding it due to what the common reader recognizes as the world, external reality? Both of these possibilities lead to a spiral, are self-feeding, tend to increase.

Difficulty of understanding leads to the forming of an elite audience, and the necessity for explication which members of this elite can supply to neophytes. The connection of this tendency with the rise of the academic study of English is obvious. Second, if the work has no reference to external reality, no reference outside itself, it will demand a special technique of interpretation according to its internal structure. Again the fostering of an elite cadre of interpreters is indicated, and, more damaging, a tendency for literature and criticism to become involved in a closed circle, with no connection with the outside world, to become completely reflexive, marginalised and trivial.[17] Edward Said links the New Criticism and French Structuralist criticism as movements which began with the laudable aim of removing the barrier placed between the common reader and literature by specialists who claimed that large amounts of extrinsic information were necessary to understanding. It is, then, all the more unfortunate that 'an interest in expanding the constituency lost out to a wish for abstract correctness and methodological rigour within a quasi-monastic order.'[18] J. G. Merquior points out that while F. R. Leavis complained of an over-concern with the social contexts of literature, late twentieth-century criticism is 'text-besotted', at the expense of consideration of the social ground of literature.[19] As the textually obsessed criticism that Merquior deplores separates literature from the world, from its social and human context, so it loses touch with – fails to pay genuine attention to – the literature it purports to address. For him, 'the true object of literature is not itself – it is the human experience of the world.'[20]

Criticism which insists that literature refers to nothing outside itself will itself become reflexive and narcissistically trivial.

Davie's awareness of these problems is indicated in his hope for a rehumanized literature, but his dismissal of Kermode's suggestion as to how Yeats might have contributed to such rehumanization suggests partisanship towards Pound. What Kermode's claim for Yeats's work draws attention to is a quality in it that comes from his involvement with theatre. It is not only that Yeats has in his mind the fear of coming to 'chaunt a tongue men do not know', or that he is constantly aware of the need not to ascend so far out of the everyday that he loses touch with people; it is also that Yeats's dramatic sense keeps his eye on his audience in such a way that his performance cannot become an entirely private one. Of course, this dramatic aspect has a figurative element, and it seems unlikely that Pound wrote the *Cantos* purely for his own amusement, that they were not intended to be read by others. But it does seem that Yeats's involvement with theatre led to a greater awareness than Pound had of the sense of relationship with an audience involved in performance.

A later essay of Davie's distinguishes between poets like Yeats who 'see poetry as a vehicle for personality' and others who aim to make their poems 'seem to be a product of language', 'the poet merely a medium through which the language becomes articulate'.[21] There are the histrionic, self-dramatizing poet and the poet who aims at an impersonality which makes the poem a formal construction, impersonal because its elements seem to speak through their relationship to each other. Davie's idea of the poet as medium is, of course, that put forward by Eliot in 'Tradition and the Individual Talent'. Charles Feidelson connects the autonomy of language with modern literature and criticism. Criticism finds the 'structure' it explores in language, 'not *behind* the poem in the writer's mind or *in front* of the poem in an external world.'[22] But Feidelson's comments on Eliot indicate that the nature of the medium rules out the private performance, no matter how difficult the poetry seems. His analysis liberates the poem from the poet, but into the shared world of language. He sees as mistaken Edmund Wilson's view of a trend to extreme individualism.[23]

Poetry as histrionic, as an occasion for self-dramatization, links Yeats's poetry with the concept of poetry as performance. How private this performance is in Yeats's case is problematic, and might be seen to change between 1903 and 1914; but the extent to which private performance is a paradox, the extent to which performance implies an audience, demands attention. Even oral poetry can be performed privately, and we should not forget the contemplative qualities of literature in any reaction against Romantic individualism.[24] But Yeats's theatrical experience and sense of drama direct him to an audience.[25]

II

The idea that poetry can be the vehicle of personality might remind us of Riding and Graves's distinction between the personality of the poet and the personality of the poem, of which the second is supposed to be paramount in the modernist poem. But, especially when considering Yeats, it raises the question of just what personality is. Yeats addressed the issue of self-dramatization in his 1909 Journal (Mem 142). His secondary personality is a construction of himself within and through his work, and this personality is distinct from, though related to, the biographical personality. What then becomes important is the relationship between these two figures. The idea that all personality is role-playing, that to play a part, to dramatize oneself, is, in fact, the way to true self-realization, is common to Yeats and modern psychology.[26]

Stephen Spender, in *The Struggle of the Modern*, claims that modern poetry short-circuits the 'I' which is the writer present within his work in a 'communicating relationship' with the reader.[27] He connects this idea with the poetics of Rimbaud, where the 'systematic disordering of the senses ... cuts out that which is consciously the poet ... who writes "I"'. The poet's brain again becomes merely the medium on which, this time, 'experiences write'.[28] There is a certain similarity to the idea in the opening of Yeats's 'A General Introduction for my Work' (E&I 509), but Spender's idea is much closer to Eliot's catalyst in 'Tradition and the Individual Talent', that is the idea of the poet's mind as a place of confluence for experience, which Yeats would have considered too passive. Spender's distinction between 'modern' and 'contemporary' (for which the current equivalents would probably be 'modernist' and 'modern') groups, on the modern side, imagists with French Symbolists represented by Rimbaud, Eliot (by implication) and Henry James; and on the contemporary side H. G. Wells, Shaw, Bennett, Galsworthy and the Georgian poets. The 'I' of Wells, 'acting as interpreter between Wells's often poetic material and the reader' is the object of particular scorn.[29]

There is something of the twentieth-century cult of immediacy behind an apparent wish in Spender to be rid of the author's mediating presence, as well as the desire to escape from rhetoric (a desire associated with Symbolism). But Yeats's idea of the secondary personality offers another kind of mediating presence. The establishment of the secondary personality within the work is a way in which the poet can escape solipsism while retaining the advantage available through impersonal technique of avoiding egotism, a way in which the solipsism that threatens to result from Symbolist poetics can be avoided. The work retains a measure of autonomy from the poet, since the secondary personality is itself a construction of the work, yet, in dramatic terms, the poem is not a private performance since the 'I' that is the secondary personality maintains the link with the audience, maintains the element of communication. Of course, the potential charge of rhetoricalness returns with the sense that the poem is an act of communication.

The idea of the autonomy of the text, the work which stands free of its creator, was an influential one in criticism and theories of poetry in the twentieth century. We can see a connection with Symbolism in a claim made by the Symbolist painter Gustave Kahn: 'The essential goal of our art is to objectify the subjective (the exteriorization of the Idea)'.[30] Compare George Oppen's comment on the meaning of the word 'Objectivist' in *An 'Objectivists' Anthology*, to which he, Pound and Williams contributed: 'the poets' recognition of the necessity of form, the objectification of the poem.'[31] The poem becomes a thing in its own right, something which stands independent of its author's intention, through form, which allows its constituent parts to function in relation to each other regardless of any value they might have as instruments for the communication of some message from the author. Form, then, frees the poem from rhetoric. It also contributes, according to Davie, to the freeing of the poet from the feeling that he needs to consider his audience. Davie sees 'Objectivism' as leading to a healthy disregard for the poem's audience.[32]

I am attempting to trace here the continuing influence of a Symbolist idea. But it is an influence that the post-1960 adoption of 'literary modernism' has picked up and run with. Erik Svarny, for instance, sees a similar idea of objectification of the poem in Imagism, and also in a phase of Eliot's and Pound's poetic practice:

> This demand for 'impersonal' aesthetic autonomy can be seen to be relevant to Pound's and Eliot's adoption of the Gautier quatrain, for once the writer eschews a communicatory aesthetic and begins to regard the poem as an artefact, it becomes possible that the increased 'detachment' of the poet *vis-à-vis* the poem will encourage him to regard it in spatial terms, as a self-sufficient entity to be

appreciated by the reader in terms analogous to the manner in which a painting or statue is viewed by the spectator.[33]

Although Svarny considers Joseph Frank's thesis on the relation of modernist literature to the concept of spatial form to be insufficiently thought through, we can see in this idea of how the work can be viewed the suggestion of a possibility for literature of the kind of synoptic perception supposedly available to the plastic arts. The suggestion indicates a leaning for Symbolist-influenced aesthetics opposed to the more usual one. Symbolism is usually seen as leaning towards music (an art which, like literature, is time-dependent) because music is purely formal and non-discursive.[34] But the idea of the poem as a self-sufficient entity also suggests the beginnings of something pernicious. The deliberate detachment of the poet, the elimination of the idea of communication, places the work in a world that exists for no-one and at no time. Such an aesthetic invites a purely formalist approach and the consequent separation of literature from life which trivializes literature. We must also ask if this aesthetic invites that separation of the poem from its historical context which would necessarily impoverish our understanding of it.

The efforts of New Criticism to develop an objective approach to literature encouraged a view of the poem as a self-sufficient entity, a closed system which contains everything necessary to exegesis within itself.[35] Whereas deconstruction shows that the idea of a poem as a closed system is unsatisfactory, it does so by indicating that the poem is always in some sense self-contradictory, that it is not entirely self-consistent. The impossibility of establishing an unequivocal relationship between the poem and the world, a definitive interpretation, leads to a concern only with the surface of the work, with the relationship between word and word, with the infinite play of signs.[36] Some critics have taken the arbitrariness of the connection between signifier and signified to mean that language is a self-enclosed system which 'gestures obliquely to a world of objects'.[37] For such critics, Saussurean linguistics has shown 'the essential disjunction between language and reality' and that 'all meaning in every sphere of human activity consists of closed systems wholly independent of the material world'.[38] Although it draws its justification from a new source,[39] this insistence on the impossibility of reference has the same effect of detaching the poem from the world as New Critical dogma and the persisting influence of an idea from Symbolism. The separation of poetry from life and the world by New Criticism and Symbolist-derived poetics delivers poetry over to the purely textual analysis of structuralist and poststructuralist criticism.

If meaning is to be understood as process and relationship rather than something which can be contained by a poem as a vessel contains material, then the poem must be reintegrated with life. The restoration of context in the sense of recreating the artist's milieu is insufficient. It involves Romantic ideas of the autonomy of art and of originality associated with the development of print culture and its effect of dividing literature from lived experience.[40] Nevertheless, the restoration of context assists in restoring the connection between the poet and his work, and resists the notion of the work as an autonomous text.

Yeats himself emphasized the fact that the secondary personality must be both separated from and related to life. Biographical criticism sees only the second part of the equation, but the correction of this blindness must not lead to our seeing only the first part. The secondary personality exists within and is created by the work. The relationship of this figure to the biographical Yeats is an issue for criticism as it was for Yeats himself. The poetic figure resists both absolute identification with *and* absolute detachment from the biographical figure, and so maintains the link between art and life and refuses to allow the work to become a self-enclosed text analogous to an artefact.

III

Hans-Georg Gadamer claims that all reconstruction is the production of something dead and anachronistic:

> Reconstructing the conditions in which a work passed down to us from the past was originally constituted is undoubtedly an important aid to understanding it. But we may ask whether what we obtain is really the meaning of the work of art that we are looking for, and whether it is correct to see understanding as a second creation, the reproduction of the original production. Ultimately, this view of hermeneutics is as nonsensical as all restitution and restoration of past life. Reconstructing the original circumstances, like all restoration, is a futile undertaking in view of the historicity of our being. What is reconstructed, a life brought back from the lost past, is not the original. In its continuance in an estranged state it acquires only a derivative cultural existence ... a hermeneutics that regarded understanding as reconstructing the original would be no more than handing on a dead meaning.[41]

A sense of how a work's original readers read it can deepen our sense of our own reading, though such a reconstruction does not, any more than the reconstruction to which Gadamer refers of the conditions in which a work was produced, constitute an understanding of the work. This is not to say that the past is always isolated from us in an unintelligibility determined by historical difference, sealed in its historical particularity as we are in ours. A sense of historical difference is, indeed, necessary to the perspective which allows genuine understanding. Interpretation is a mediation between its object and the interpreter, not just a repetition: it relies on difference, a space in which it can take place.

Yet Yeats's poetry retains a directness of address otherwise unavailable in an historical interpretation. A communicative aspect of meaning is generated by the presence of the secondary personality within the work. The fact that language does not refer directly and what Gadamer calls 'the historicity of our being' conspire together to allow Yeats's poetic personality to transcend the limitations to which Gadamer refers. The poetic figure, created by and within the poetry, survives to be articulated into new contexts. The openness of language means that this figure cannot be identified absolutely with the historical Yeats; nevertheless, any reading of the poetry demonstrates that the two figures are not unconnected. Approaches which emphasize the autonomy of the text are shown to be unsatisfactory by Yeats's ability both to insist on the attachment of his poetry to his life and to allow it to remain alive and communicative. The complexity of the relationship between his poetry and his life demonstrates that it simply is not the case that unless language can be shown to refer directly, term by term, to things in the world then we must accept that language is a self-enclosed system 'wholly independent of the material world'.

In 'A General Introduction for My Work', Yeats writes of the difference, but also of the link between the flesh-and-blood poet and the poetic personality: 'A poet writes always of his personal life' (E&I 509). The creation of a mythology, a phantasmagoria, through which the poet writes of his personal life, distances from the work the arbitrary nature, the imprisoning causal necessity, of daily life. The projection of the secondary personality into the mythic world of the work is a subjective way of escaping the limitations of daily life. It builds on the subjective way of understanding the world which comes through from Pater, who claims that there is 'a general consciousness ... independent indeed of each one of us, but with which we are, each one of us, in communication.'[42] Each of us is attached to history by what is passed on from the minds of his or her predecessors:

It is humanity itself now – abstract humanity – that figures as the transmigrating soul, accumulating into its 'colossal manhood' the experience of ages; making use of, and casting aside in its march, the souls of countless individuals, as Pythagoras supposed the individual soul to cast aside again and again its outworn body.[43]

The sense of a collective mind to which the individual mind has access is present in *Per Amica Silentia Lunae*. There is a subtle dialectic in Yeats's thought which suggests the necessity of individuality in order to gain access to the collective. Perhaps this might be put as the necessity to become a self in order to gain access to the self; where 'a self' is an individual free of the averaging effect of modern daily life, and 'the self' is the idea of the collective mind.[44]

Pater sought not to reconstruct the past as an object for his contemporaries to contemplate, but rather to perceive it by recognizing elements in himself which proved a continuity from the past into his own time.[45] If we accept Yeats's idea of a collective mind as the store or expression of those elements of the human mind which continue from the past to the present, we recognize its importance to him. It confers on his work a continuity with the past and the possibility of continuation into the future. The paradox lies in the fact that the recognition of one's own historicity is necessary to the placement of oneself in relation to the process of history which renders possible the recovery of the past in any meaningful sense. The reconstruction of the past is not in itself sufficient to its meaningful recovery; meaningful recovery depends on the forming of a link through the recognition of continuity. At the same time, difference needs to be accepted for understanding. Interpretation is not a repetition, which would leave the interpreter nothing to say.[46]

The evident importance to Yeats that there be a man behind the work and his comments on the difference between the poet as a man and the personality constructed within the work, point to a need for a rethinking of critical attitudes to the biographical approach to literature: we need to look carefully at the nature of the relationship between the life and the work.[47] The independence of the work from the life on which the New Criticism tended to insist is undermined by the links with Eliot's life of *The Waste Land*, especially in so far as the New Criticism seems to take up a poetics and criticism defined by Eliot. The emphasis on impersonality, on the autonomy of the work, might be seen as merely a defence against the exposure of painful aspects of his private life.

IV

Modernism, however defined, has come to be seen as the most significant movement in literature during the early years of the twentieth century (though it is difficult to establish an exact starting date for it), and Yeats's own significance makes it difficult for some to see him as peripheral to such a movement. Since literary modernism is retrospectively defined, and something whose definition seems to be subject to revision of an expanding nature, it is perhaps not surprising to find it growing to encompass Yeats. Ezra Pound, Ford Madox Ford and T. S. Eliot are all accepted as theorists of, and eminent figures in, what has come to be called literary modernism, but none of them saw Yeats as part of any movement they were involved in.

Some critics have indicated the involvement of modernism in Romanticism, and so made the definition of modernism more problematic.[48] If we look back to the polemical pronouncements of Eliot, then we might see anti-Romanticism as a defining aspect of modernism. But if we see Eliot as a covert Romantic – and the argument for this is persuasive – then it becomes difficult to exclude an author from the compass of modernism simply because his or her work has a strong Romantic element.[49] Carol T. Christ describes Yeats as 'the most Romantic of the Modernists'.[50] Romanticism and modernism are not, then, mutually exclusive; and Yeats's claim to have been one of the last Romantics is no longer sufficient, even if we take him at his word, to exclude him from modernism. It is possible, and worthwhile, though, to distinguish between the thinking of Yeats and that of, for instance, Pound, Ford and Eliot. The idea of literary modernism tempts rather towards generalization and similarity-spotting.

Some of Pound's early work has been found derivative of early Yeats, and much of it shows characteristics the later Pound condemned as soft in others, part of a decayed Romanticism. We need to distinguish different positions in the developing Pound. Pound acknowledged the great influence Ford had on him, and much of the change in Pound's style, from the outmoded poeticism towards the rhythms of normal speech, can be attributed to this influence.[51] But Ford is also significant in a more philosophical sense. His memory, his biographer tells us, was impressionistic,[52] and his literary theory can also be seen as impressionist. Through impressionism we can see how close the subjective and objective views can come. Ford's impressionism says that art should present the world exactly as it strikes the artist. This is, in fact, an extreme subjectivism. What the artist is to relate are his own impressions. But the aim of impressionism is to present the world as exactly as possible: our sense impressions are the closest the world comes to us. The impressionist can claim, then, to be presenting the world as it really is, since if there were an objective reality independent of our sensory perceptions, this would not be available to us directly.

Ford's retreat to the self as the only source of value has to do with the increasing uncertainty of the age, with the loss of traditional values and certainties.[53] It has to do, then, with the loss of a shared world more real than that closest to the individual; the loss of a shared world which was the source of values superior to selfish values, those drawn from the immediate world of sensory perception.[54] The figure of Pater looms here, as the threat of solipsism emerges from a position which sees only the world of sensory perception as real, since sensory perceptions alone are immediately available to the individual, and are ultimately unverifiable by appeal to anything shared. Pater easily slides Arnold's call for objectivity into a statement of the priority of subjective perception:

> 'To see the object as in itself it really is,' has been justly said to be the aim of all true criticism whatever; and in aesthetic criticism the first step towards seeing one's object as it really is, is to know one's impression as it really is, to discriminate it, to realise it distinctly.[55]

In presenting his impressions, Ford is presenting reality directly: '[T]he real collapsed into the perceived, and the artist began to usurp the place of the world'.[56] There is a confusion of objectivity and subjectivity which comes through into Pound's thinking. 'When Pound praises Ford because he has "expressed himself and mirrored the world," it is unclear whether he thinks Ford has done one thing or two.'[57]

In a letter written to Harriet Monroe in January 1915, Pound calls for 'objectivity and again objectivity, and expression.'[58] Pound's 1937 footnote acknowledges the influence of Ford on the thinking expressed in this letter. Objectivity here relates to directness of expression, the absence of conventional poeticism which would detract from the precision of expression, and so from sincerity. The expression is nevertheless the expression of something subjective, something deeply and personally felt. Objectivity seems to be something the poet should aim at, but only in order to give a particular force to his subjective impressions.[59] Thomas Jackson questions the objectivity Hugh Kenner finds in Pound in a way which makes the situation of objectivity itself a problem:

> Kenner's view of Pound as an unshakeably objective, mimetic artist, though it flies in the face of all I have said about the true nature of

Pound's poetic moments, is in its way true. But what is involved is the mimetic presentation of the inner discoveries of a thorough going subjectivist.[60]

There is a philosophical root to this problem:

> It is problematic whether radical theories of perception do not in fact come full circle to a kind of subjectivism – whether there is not a blurring of the distinction between objective revelation and subjective transformation or re-creation of external reality.[61]

However counter-intuitive it may seem, objectivity and subjectivity are not such clear opposites:

> Governing itself by rule, objectivity tries methodically to eliminate bias, prejudice, and all the distortions that go by the name of subjectivity. This Cartesian endeavour assumes that a methodically purified consciousness guarantees certainty. On one level, objectivity consists in humble self-effacement, but on another, it is marked by a distinct arrogance insofar as it makes individual self-consciousness the locus and arbiter of truth. Though it is by definition not subjective, then, objectivity as an ideal derives from a highly subjectivist epistemology.[62]

Pound's article 'Status Rerum', headed December 1912, links his idea of objectivity with Ford, and contrasts this directly with Yeats, whom he characterizes as subjective. Ford, Pound says, 'believes in an exact rendering of things'.[63] How we interpret 'things' is crucial here. Ford's own aesthetic implies that his idea of the direct rendering of things is the direct rendering of his impressions. Pound, in *Gaudier-Brzeska: A Memoir*, says, 'An *image*, in our sense, is real because we know it directly,' and further, 'It is our affair to render the *image* as we have perceived or conceived it.'[64] Pound seeks to distinguish between the passive reception of impressions and the active conception of the world, but even the active form of perception he refers to seems to be a means of reflecting something exterior, almost a form of radar, 'directing a certain fluid force against circumstance'.[65] Pound takes Yeats to task, apparently for failing to make this distinction between passive and active perception when abusing modern art for its, quoting Yeats, 'want of culture'.[66] Written in 1916, this is an early indication of the trend in Yeats's thought which sees work such as *The Cantos* and *Anna*

Livia Plurabelle as the product of an artist 'helpless before the contents of his own mind' (E&I 405). It is not so much that he is unaware of the distinction that Pound is trying to make, but that he sees even Pound's active type of perception as in his own terms passive. It points also to Yeats's view that personality is necessary to the control of the contents of the mind, perceptions, impressions; and to the role of culture, tradition, in forming the personality. The formation of personality is a safeguard against the excessive closeness of object and subject which can be the result of the subjectivism of Fordian impressionism, or of the attempt at objective presentation. In his essay 'Yeats, Titian and the New French Painting', Ronald Schuchard points out that Yeats 'disliked in Manet the displacement of "personality" by "character".'[67] He claims that Yeats's essay 'The Tragic Theatre' is actually 'about the haunting, irreconcilable conflict of Manet's art and Titian's art in Yeats's mind' (155). Schuchard draws on Yeats's 'Discoveries: Second Series' to demonstrate Yeats's association of Impressionist painting with the 'degeneration of the Renaissance canon' (152–3). He shows that Yeats's response to Manet's work in particular played an important part in the development of his ideas on the division of man from his world, the reflection of this in contemporary art and literature, and the need for an art of personality rather than of character if reintegration were to be achieved.

The recognition of the impossibility of the sort of objectivity associated with a fully shared reality raises the demand for a means of escaping from the extremes of subjectivity.[68] Joyce, clearly influenced by Flaubert, has the artist refining himself out of his work – perhaps, then, creating an illusory objectivity.[69] In his book on Flaubert, Jonathan Culler exemplifies one track of the notion of the autonomy of the art-work from French literature, through 'literary modernism', to structuralist criticism. The idea of the relationship of a work's audience with the work through a process of understanding is replaced by the audience's passive observation of a free-standing object, as Flaubert tries 'to make the novel an aesthetic object rather than a communicative act.'[70] Culler wants to show that 'the communicative model' is based on the discredited 'metaphysics of presence':

> The work tries to express an essence which presides over it as its source and its purpose. To capture the truth of the work is to recover that essence and make it present to consciousness.[71]

I believe that the attempt to discredit the idea of the communicativeness of literature plays a part in its dehumanization and the descent into narcissistic triviality of literary studies to which I have referred earlier. Culler's argument depends on an oversimplification. The communicative model only rests on the metaphysics of presence if we see the work as absolutely defined by and limited to a message that its author sought to convey. The concept of communication as an endeavour to construct understanding between the work and its reader involves the reader in a more active process than the appraisal suggested in the literary-work-as-artefact model. This concept also gives us a communicative model which cannot rest on the metaphysics of presence, since it specifically denies that the reconstruction of the author's mind is sufficient. Understanding implies mediation and distance, the recognition of difference: there must always be a space within which understanding can take place.

Eliot seeks an impersonality which will allow him to escape what he sees as the excessive subjectivity, or egoism, of Romanticism. Pater was a *bête noire* of Eliot's, though Louis Menand notes a similar passivity in the model of the mind in Eliot's argument in 'Tradition and the Individual Talent' and that in Pater's argument in his essay 'Style'.[72] Eliot attempts to correct excessive subjectivity in a way which falls in with T. E. Hulme's final, anti-humanist position, the neo-classicism of Wyndham Lewis and Pound's impressionism in its objective guise. The corrective image of the poet that Eliot offers in 'Tradition and the Individual Talent' is similar to Joyce's idea of the artist refined out of his work. For Eliot, the poet's mind is a catalyst, inert, the means of bringing about the reaction to the world which forms the work yet is not present in the finished work. Eliot's metaphor is rather more elegant than that employed by Pound in 'Affirmations: As for Imagism', but both are of a scientific nature: 'The best artist is the man whose machinery can stand the highest voltage.'[73] Pound is at pains to point out that his view of the artist is not as passive as his metaphor suggests. But the form of *action* he claims the artist to be capable of is of starting his own machinery. The mechanical idea remains, then, along with an idea similar to Eliot's catalyst (the instigator of reaction completely absent from the nature of its outcome, though responsible for the reaction as a whole). Pound, Eliot, Pater all illustrate the difficulty of escaping excessive subjectiveness without leaving the artist passive.[74] I aim to show that Yeats's ideas of mask and *anima mundi*, his refusal of any passive model, and his dramatic sense (his ability to conceive, create and play a role, and his attention – direction – to an audience) enabled him to take up the problem from Pater and achieve a more satisfactory solution than Pound or Eliot.

V

Two problems arise from the inclusion of Yeats within what is called literary modernism: one concerns the term, and the other Yeats's work. To indicate the presence of a Romantic element in even the most (apparently) anti-Romantic modernist, as George Bornstein does in the case of Eliot, is a useful subversion of what may have become a limiting critical polarity. But the literary movements of the modern period which have now been subsumed into the general term 'modernism' established their critical terms via the polemical pronouncements of those involved, such as Eliot and Pound, and earlier T. E. Hulme, another avowed anti-Romantic. The revision of literary modernism which stresses the presence in it of Romantic tendencies moves it further from how those involved at the time would have seen it. Of course, such revision is in itself legitimate. But it is difficult to hold together a recognition of the reactive, polemical nature of what has come to be called the modernist movement, and a recognition of the involvement of that movement within what it reacted against. There is a tendency for the term 'modernism' to slide towards the merely chronological, as it loses the possibility of being defined *against* something other than itself.

The slide from a position which sees modernism as involving covert Romantic elements to a position where a Romantic element can actually be seen as establishing a writer's modernism begins to seem less perverse and increasingly threatening. Modernism is a 'protean' term.[75] Difficult to define objectively, it has tended to become something which is defined by means of the writers it includes. The set of modernists can then be expanded by the inclusion of writers who have something in common with those already included, whether or not these things held in common are the most significant aspects of the new writers included, or those aspects of those originally included which led to their inclusion. The danger then is of the term becoming so all-embracing that it no longer excludes anything other than chronologically.[76] We are, in fact, threatened with a suspiciously circular form of reasoning. For example, Bornstein attacks J. Hillis-Miller's attempt to distinguish between Romanticism and modernism by saying that Miller makes a contrast which is questionable, 'for it is difficult to maintain that distinctions like that between subject and object are more basic to Shelley than, say, to Yeats.'[77]

The second problem with the inclusion of Yeats within modernism, that concerning his own work, is that such inclusion tends to exaggerate the significance of particular aspects of the change in his work between 1903 and 1914. One such aspect is the claimed influence of Ezra Pound. If we see literary modernism in the way it would have seen itself had it been defined at the time, then it is difficult to see how Yeats could be included. If we see it as revisionist critics see it, then we are likely to look for similarities in Yeats's work to that of writers generally accepted as modernist, and to concentrate on these areas for our account of the transition in the period from *In the Seven Woods* to *Responsibilities*. This can only mean the undervaluing, even the elision, of those things which drive the change that are particular to Yeats. The account will be impoverished and slanted.

It is because the work of literature has so much of its life in the medium of commentary and criticism that I am trying to analyse the idea of literary modernism and to consider the effects of this idea on the reception of Yeats's work. Attention to the historical, social and biographical contexts of the work can offer a counter to those interpretations which contextualize in terms of a literary history itself revisionist. For all that the complete recreation of the historical context in which an author worked is made impossible by the interpreter's own historical conditioning, the particular historical context of the work can still be respected. In his essay 'Romancing the Native Stone', Bornstein claims:

> Yeats's celebrated thematic 'movement downwards upon life' after 1906 was matched by a technical one as well ... The new diction and syntax replaced the derivative, strongly English patterns of fin-de-siècle verse with those we now associate with modernism.[78]

The 'we now' is crucial, and the suggestion that the technical movement can be dated from 1906 fails to recognize the beginning of a change in diction in *In the Seven Woods*. Further, the use of 'English' here suggests that the critic has learned from Pound to employ this as a term of abuse.

Bornstein goes on to comment on 'September 1913':

> Here Yeats writes of specifically Irish matters in a language no longer redolent of English romanticism. It is not so much that

phrases like 'fumble in a greasy till' or 'dried the marrow from the bone' belong to Irish speech rhythms but that they no longer echo the diction and cadences of the English romantics. Instead, they belong to literary modernism, and that modernism itself no longer displays an Anglo-centrism. Indeed, Yeats calls up an explicit counter ideal to English romanticism in 'Romantic Ireland,' which he associates particularly with O'Leary. (117)

This implies that whereas early Yeats is English, later Yeats is Irish, and Irish by virtue of the fact that he writes in the language of literary modernism, a term later invented by critics. 'Romantic Ireland', at least in the poem, is opposed to modern Ireland, which seemed to be moving into the materialism Yeats hated. Bornstein finds his own refutation (though without recognizing it as such) in the passage from Yeats's 'General Introduction' where Yeats reminds himself that he owes his soul to Shakespeare, Spenser and Blake.

The association of the English language and literary tradition with the England he hates is something which tortures Yeats because he can do nothing about it. Shakespeare, Spenser, Blake were English. They are linked with Yeats through the English language. In fact, they form a part of him: he owes them his soul. The idea can be traced to Pater:

> [W]e come into the world, each one of us, 'not in nakedness,' but ... clothed far more completely than even Pythagoras supposed in a vesture of the past ... in the language which is more than one half of our thoughts; in the moral and mental habits, the customs, the literature, the very houses, which we did not make for ourselves; in the vesture of the past, which is ... of the race, the species.[79]

This understanding of one's relation to the past through language and a literary tradition connects with the individual's access to the collective mind. Yeats insists that whatever he might change he will always express himself through traditional forms, since by doing this he eliminates the 'accident and incoherence', the merely contingent associated with daily life and so an obstruction to the creation of genuine poetry (E&I 522).

Bornstein's position seems to be that Yeats's change of diction and syntax, which Bornstein retrospectively associates with modernism, marks a break from the English Romantic tradition. Having escaped the excessive influence of English Romanticism, Yeats is then able to capture Romanticism for Ireland. This position is conditioned by the ideas of

Harold Bloom: Yeats appropriates the work of his poetic ancestors and makes it Irish through the association with himself. It might also be traced to Hugh Kenner, who claims that international modernism dispossessed England of the English language and made it its own.[80] Kenner's view is, of course, traceable to Pound, and Bornstein himself quotes Pound's criticism of the state of British verse from 1890 to 1910:

> a horrible agglomerate compost, not minted, most of it not even baked, all legato, a doughy mess of third-hand Keats, Wordsworth, heaven knows what, fourth-hand Elizabethan sonority blunted, half melted, lumpy.[81]

That the English language is now that of literatures other than that of England is undeniable. But some of the assumptions which follow the recognition of this are dubious. It seems that Yeats was better able to realize the necessary historical involvement of the English language with England by way of its development through the English literary tradition. His own development of the language – his own contribution to literature in the English language – has a particularly Irish quality because of its involvement with Irish place, myth and national concerns, his attempt to develop a style related to the English language as it is spoken in Ireland, and the fact that Yeats was an Irishman.

Much of the problem here arises from what we understand by the term 'the English language'. Because of England and Britain's imperialist past, the English language is no longer solely a national language, but a grapholect within which several national versions are identifiable. The concept of the grapholect adequately deals with the language which transcends national boundaries and becomes decentred in its associations. To identify English as the language of international modernism is to assume that modernism was a solely anglophone phenomenon.[82] Political change – the decline of empire, the advent of the postcolonial era – has meant that England is decentred, since it is no longer the political hub of the area covered by the English grapholect. The change since the decline of empire in the status of literature written in England is interesting to observe, but its relevance to the development of Yeats's diction and syntax in the period before 1914 is difficult to see.

Sean Golden's engagement with the idea of modernism as marking a break with tradition and the decentring of England is more interesting:

> The emergence of non-native writers in English in the Modernist period of the first quarter century as the major literary figures of the

period signals the end of the native English literary tradition as the major force in writing in English. Non-English writers used the native tradition and its forms in new ways and integrated them with cosmopolitan traditions precisely because it was an object to them, not a vested interest. Once the tradition was recognized as a 'tradition', once it was capable of definition, it became historical, not living, so that any 'return' to it is reactionary, deliberately atavistic, a conscious choice, not an unconscious working of the same vein but the reopening of a closed mine, a deliberate anti-Modernism. The key here is the idea of an historical period earlier in the century which is post traditional English literature. Modernism is one if its symptoms.[83]

The idea of 'historical' and 'living' being in opposition and even mutually exclusive marks a difference between the view Golden puts forward and my own. For Yeats, to reject tradition was to risk the intrusion of the merely contingent into his work. Though he used Irish material, the language he worked in was, of necessity, his mother tongue, English; not merely because he found Irish to difficult to learn, but because the English language connected him with something larger than the contingent and personal.[84]

In his account of literary modernism, Michael Levenson traces a movement from the egoism (influenced by Stirner and present in the title of an important magazine) of the early stages – which fits well with the extreme subjectivism of Ford's literary impressionism – to Eliot's moves to reinscribe modern literature within a tradition and to eliminate by means of stylistic impersonality the excessive subjectivism he associated with Romanticism.[85]

'Tradition and the Individual Talent' suggests (possibly unintentionally) that the poet's personality and personal emotions will show themselves through the attempt to escape them, since 'only those who have personality and emotions know what it means to want to escape from these things.'[86] This sounds like a cry from Eliot the man, forcing its way into the argument for impersonality put forward by Eliot the critic. It points, perhaps, to the personal nature of much of the material of the work disguised by impersonal technique. But the main thrust of the essay is to stress the nature of the poet's mind as the site of the confluence of emotion not personal to him, and to indicate that this emotion is to be allowed to combine there, and be transmitted as purely, as untainted by that emotion which arises from the poet's personal circumstances, as possible.

Eliot's idea that the poet as a man, that is to say the poet as he exists in relation to the everyday world, should be kept out of the work seems at first to be similar to the idea Yeats expresses in 'A General Introduction for My Work' (E&I 509). Yet this is another of the instances where thinking of Yeats as a modernist poet can lead one away from the most profitable analysis. Thinking about the relationship between Yeats's thought and his poems is not helped by shouting, 'Ah, so Yeats is a modernist then' every time we spot a similarity between his thought and that of Eliot. If we want to construct a narrative where various movements in early twentieth-century literature are bundled up as the modernist movement, which is later captured and institutionalized by Eliot, then we might also tell the story of an escape from the extreme subjectivism brought about by a general change in mindset (the loss of certainty and shared values and so on) and epitomized by Pater.[87] But if we do see literary modernism like this, then the escape has been anticipated by Yeats, and in his own way. Whereas Eliot sees the poet's mind as something to be held open, in order that his personality should remain out of his work, and that the 'significant emotion' available through the tradition should form itself there for him to transmit, Yeats speaks of creating a secondary personality through the work.[88]

Joseph Frank claims that 'modern literature has been engaged in transmuting the time world of history into the timeless world of myth.'[89] His explanation of the removal of narrative logic, the 'juxtaposition of past and present' so that they are 'apprehended spatially'[90] and not sequentially, collapsing time, relates modern literature to the movement towards non-naturalistic style in the plastic arts. If Frank is right, the engagement with myth of his examples, *The Waste Land*, *The Cantos*, *Ulysses*, is part of the depersonalizing technique of later modernism. Yeats, though, seeks to create a secondary personality and project this figure into a mythology itself in part created by his work.[91] While this position may seem close to Eliot's on the need to remove from the work all that is due to the arbitrary necessity of daily life, he does not identify personality exclusively with this necessity as Eliot does. Personality for Yeats is the freedom from such necessity that the artist can create within his work: it is associated closely with style.[92] The connection between 'the bundle of accident and incoherence that sits down to breakfast' (E&I 509) and the poetic personality is problematic, but it is the presence of such a personality within the work (rather than the complete exclusion of personality Eliot claims to aim for) which prevents the poet becoming 'helpless before the contents of his own mind.'

2
In the Seven Woods

I

Yeats's 1910 essay 'The Tragic Theatre' shows how he felt himself at odds with the dramatic criticism of his time, which saw lyric poetry in opposition to character, as a hindrance to action.[1] His meditation on tragedy in this essay indicates that the concern of the drama of his own time is with character, which makes it comedy, rather than the greater, more lyrical form, tragedy. Schopenhauer distinguishes between lyrical and dramatic work:

> Accordingly, as in the lyrical poem the subjective element predominates, so in the drama, on the contrary, the objective element is alone and exclusively present. Between the two epic poetry in all its forms and modifications, from the narrative romance to the epos proper, has a broad middle path. For although in the main it is objective, yet it contains a subjective element, appearing now more and now less, which finds its expression in the tone, in the form of delivery, and also in scattered reflections. We do not so entirely lose sight of the poet as in the drama.[2]

Yeats's involvement with the theatre during the phase of transition in his poetry from 1903 to 1914 was closely tied to the change in his poetics which saw a consciously closer engagement with the world. Yet he did not accept the objective view which contemporary drama critics considered essential to good drama, although their idea was that such objectiveness was necessary to the credible dramatic presentation of life. 'The Tragic Theatre' shows that Yeats's idea of the presentation of life was very different. While subjectivism risks losing touch with what is outside the self and so sliding into egotism and solipsism, objectivism relinquishes the living connection with the world it sees and describes, shunning responsibility in another way. Schopenhauer's description of epic poetry indicates means by which the poet retains a subjective element in his work, but makes epic seem something of a dull compromise, following a 'middle path'. Yeats's dissent in 'The Tragic Theatre' from the simple pairing and opposing of lyrical and subjective and dramatic and objective points to an opposition of his own, that of character and personality. Character is created from observation, externally; it is a representation of the contingent, the accidental. For the poet, personality is that dramatization of himself which projects him into his work: it is his guarantee that his poetry will be a personal utterance, that it can engage with the world without becoming external and objective. Yet because the personality of the poet is something created within the work, his poetry is always more than confessional.

Even a violent reaction by Yeats against earlier moods and ways of thinking does not mean that these can be left completely out of the account as worthless. On occasion, new thought can be a completion of the old by the addition of its opposite, in a way which might appear more of a volte-face than actually it is. His letter to George Russell of 14 May 1903 shows how his thought, and in his view history, can move to its opposite without negation. He does not repudiate the thought of *Ideas of Good and Evil* in this letter, but sees it as only half the story, and feels he now has hold of the other half. He feels that the world has moved from an impulse to escape form to a phase of the 'contrary impulse', one 'to create form'. He relates these phases to Greek ideas of the 'sad and desirious' 'Dionysisic' and the 'joyful and self sufficient' 'Apollonic' (CL3 369). Clearly here Yeats feels himself to have entered a phase of transition.

There are similarities between the thought of Yeats and that of his friend Arthur Symons. Symons's 1901 essay 'Fact in Literature' shows a distaste for journalism and materialism, and traces the beginning of the fall of literature to the invention of printing.[3] His 1899 essay on Balzac looks back to a time of unity of culture, 'where poetry could still represent an age and yet be poetry', whereas now it has been driven into a 'divine seclusion' and a disregard for 'the many voices of the street'.[4] Symons shows here an acceptance of the marginalization of poetry (or at least lyric poetry) which some of Yeats's reviewers seem to seek. The idea of seclusion Symons refers to was something from which Yeats was determined to move on. Symons's preface to the second edition of his collection of poems *London Nights* floats the idea that the visible world is 'a symbol, made visible in order that we may apprehend ourselves, and not be blown hither and thither like a flame in the night'.[5] Perhaps the necessity of self-apprehension and the need to avoid becoming so ethereal as to blow away demand a closer engagement with the world as it appears. Though Symons's thought is close to Yeats, we might see the beginnings of a divergence which illuminates the development of Yeats's poetic. For Yeats, it was insufficient merely to separate poetry from the materialism of modern life, although this was an important requirement. The period 1903 to 1914 marks a transition in Yeats's work during which he sought to relate his work to life in a way which Symons's symbolism and talk of beauty failed to do.[6] He saw a way in which poetry might try to regain some of the advantages of the time of a unified culture to which Symons refers. Yeats's concern with the idea of personal utterance is an influence in *In the Seven Woods*. Personal utterance, the living word, stands in opposition to the word detached from life by the developments of Symbolist poetics as well as by the effects of print culture. Yeats was able to appeal to the high residual orality of Irish peasant culture as a basis for a more living poetry.[7] He was also able to assimilate this to his system of oppositions, relating the living voice and personal utterance to Ireland, and print culture to England and materialism.[8]

The theme of personal utterance and the dramatization of the poet are important to 'The Old Age of Queen Maeve' and 'Baile and Aillinn'. This theme can be related to the pervasive opposition in Yeats's work of life and death, immortality and the ending of life by death which is its limitation but also the source of its intensity. The idea of the intensity of mortal life is complicated by the weariness of old age. This opposition is addressed through the relationship of the quotidian world to another world associated with desires and longings: the intemporal world, the world of what does not pass away. Yeats needed to retain – to keep faith with – this world in his work, in spite of difficulties caused by the events of his life.

In considering the poems of *In the Seven Woods: Being Poems Chiefly of the Irish Heroic Age*, it is necessary to remember the effect on Yeats of Maud Gonne's revelation of her life with the French politician Lucien Millevoye. There was a break in his writing of poetry after this.[9] He wrote to Lady Gregory, 'My whole imagination has shifted its foundations & I am not yet used to the new foundation' (CL2 329, 26 December 1898). The woman whom he had made the imaginative centre of his poetry, or rather had transformed by means of his imagination into such a central figure, had proved to be too human to support such a role. The imagined figure with which Maud Gonne became associated in the poet's mind pre-existed his acquaintance with Maud Gonne herself. John Harwood suggests the complexity of the relationship between the imaginative figure at the centre of Yeats's poetry and the actual Maud Gonne: 'No sooner had *The Wanderings of Oisin and Other Poems* been published than (on 30 January 1889), Niamh became incarnate as Maud Gonne.' Elizabeth Butler Cullingford makes a similar point, though relating the development of Yeats's imagination to the English Romantic poets.[10] Maud Gonne's revelation that she was a mother, with a life completely detached from Yeats, a life intimately involved with another man which she had kept secret from him, led to the collapse of the imagined figure central to Yeats's poetry. The incarnation – the rendering bodily – effected by the revelation overwhelmed Yeats.

Those reviewers who saw *The Wind Among the Reeds* as marking a limit were right, though not in the sense they thought.[11] *In the Seven Woods: Being Poems Chiefly of the Irish Heroic Age*, then, marks the beginning of a new phase; but it is transitional. In this volume, Yeats seeks to re-establish the figure of Maud Gonne in a different way. This figure remains central to the art, but must, because of the events of life, change. Foster indicates that Yeats sought to convince himself that the spiritual relationship Gonne offered in place of marriage was superior: 'Renunciation brought the reward of artistic achievement and continuing inspiration.'[12] Terence Brown believes that Yeats 'probably preferred [spiritual marriage] to the demands of conventional married life with Gonne and her daughter ... '[13] This gives a pragmatist twist to the idea that Yeats's poetic inspiration depended on Gonne's rejection of him. But for all that he may have been retaining his freedom from conventional relationship or shying away from a relationship whose intimacy would be of the wrong kind to be appropriate for a woman so closely tied to fantasy, the reaction in his poetry is one of reaccommodation of the imaginative to the actual.

Brown sees *In the Seven Woods* as 'a book of the body', a move away from the ethereal symbolic dimension of *The Wind Among the Reeds*.[14] Yeats took an interest even in the physical form of the book, produced by his sister at the Dun Emer Press: 'The book, both in its contents and its production, acknowledges the material aspects of human existence.'[15] Brown's insight further marks *In the Seven Woods* as the beginning of a transition in Yeats's work. Embodiment and incarnation take on greater significance. Given that Yeats's poetical imagination conditioned his response to Maud Gonne from the first, as both Harwood and Cullingford suggest, then the revelation of her relationship with Millevoye brought to light an unsustainable distance between Yeats's imaginative world and external reality, forcing him to reforge his imaginative world. The relationship between imagination and life is one in which forces operate in both directions. Harwood's and Cullingford's points draw attention to the impact that imagination can have on events: in affecting our relationship with the so-called objective world, the imagination affects that world. But, at least if schizophrenia is to be avoided, the extraordinary event may demand an adjustment of the imaginative view, and the seeking of a new accommodation of imagination to external circumstances. This volume not only reflects this imperative, but is itself part of the process of change.

II

'The Old Age of Queen Maeve' (ISW 1–7) bridges the gap between the 'Great Plain' of the gods and the mortal world via Maeve, who, though subject to mortality and the wearisome process of ageing, is of an older time when mortals were closer to the gods. The story that the poem tells involves the dependence of the immortals on mortal help. Maeve can be seen as a parallel for the mortal world, which while young was continually in contact with the supernatural, and which, even in age, can be drawn back towards the supernatural by the demands of love. The difficulty of contact between the two worlds and the need the supernatural might have for the mortal is an issue in this poem, and a problem for Maeve. If her question as to how a mortal may help an immortal is answered in the practical task Aengus asks her household to perform, there remains her puzzlement at the end of the poem. The immortal world seems untiring. There is also an implication in the need of the supernatural for the mortal which can be related more generally to the work of the artist. 'Mortal Help' (Myth 9) claims that the people of Faery are too 'shadowy' to engage in physical pursuits without the help of mortals. 'Rosa Alchemica' had indicated the need for mortal help for the gods to become corporeal: 'into the dance! that the gods may make them bodies out of the substance of our hearts ... '[16] More sinister, the narrator feels that in dancing with someone 'less or more than human', that someone is consuming his soul.

This aspect of the relationship between the two worlds addresses the problem of the detachment of art from life implicit in Symons's kind of Symbolist aesthetic. The passions which transcend individual existence, identified with the supernatural world, demand the entry into the dance of the individual human figure in order to attain expression. It is as if the transcendent passions can only achieve expression within the mortal world. The artist, if he is to express these passions, gives himself up to them in a way which consumes his own life, in a way which, perhaps, ruins the potential for normal, individual expression of his individual feelings. The metaphor of the dance is crucial. Dance involves physical movement and allows the absorption of the entire body into artistic form.[17] 'Rosa Alchemica' suggests a fear of dissolution which, from 1903, Yeats's poetics increasingly seek to overcome by insisting on the importance of the personality of the poet, and on poetry's finding again the voice of the 'normal, active man'. Yeats wants to retain a place for the human figure, not to allow it to disappear, Symbolist fashion, into the formal construction of the poem. The figure of the poet as it exists within the poems is part of the work, yet it remains a human figure, forging that link between the work and the human world also made by the dancer, who remains a human figure though indistinguishable from the dance.

The poet laments the passing of a beauty he sees as part of an older, less materialistic world in an early intrusion of his own concerns into the story which hints at the growing importance to Yeats of the presence in the poem, even of the legendary narrative type, of the personality of the poet. A comment in 'Literature and the Living Voice' shows his thinking: 'The minstrel never dramatised anybody but himself ... He knows how to keep himself interesting that his words may have weight – so many lines of narrative, and then a phrase about himself and his emotions.'[18] The kind of strong, fierce, practical beauty he attributes to Maeve in this poem is contrasted with an effeteness he sees in the modern materialism ('the fool heart of the counting-house') which would no doubt class itself as hard-headed, but whose heart can find beauty only in softness. What he criticizes is what he would see as a result of the separation of thought and feeling which comes from a fall away from that unity enjoyed in an age closer to the mythical way of life, life lived by a people who felt close to the supernatural.[19] For the modern materialist, the concerns of everyday life must remain divorced from the stuff of true poetic beauty until such time as his materialism can be sufficiently overcome to restore the unity of thought and feeling.

The poet's next intrusion into his narrative is more dramatic:

> O unquiet heart,
> Why do you praise another, praising her ... (ISW 2)

In telling himself to stick to the story of a great queen of two thousand years ago and not slip into his own, the poet makes the previous contrast even more obviously one between the age of Maeve's youth and that the poet lives in. Introductory lines which dramatize a poet reciting the poem are a later addition. In 'Literature and the Living Voice' it is envisaged that poems will be recited by someone in costume. The addition of the first few lines (for the *Collected Poems*, 1933) moves the reciter into the printed version of the poem, shifting from the idea of an audience actually physically present to an audience implied by how the poem appears in a book. Yeats is also introducing his own great love-affair, and comparing Maud Gonne with Maeve. For the poet's heart, for his deepest level of feeling, there is no other tale but its own. The later intrusion, where the poet addresses Maud Gonne – 'Friend of these many years' – deepens the significance of this idea that there is but one tale:

> For there is no high story about queens
> In any ancient book but tells of you ... (ISW 6)

The manner of the relation of legend is one that links the poet with the legendary. Maud Gonne and his own great love are put on a par with Maeve and her story. But also, these lines make Maud Gonne all the queens of legend: she is a type, not in what Yeats would classify as the mistaken modern literary sense of a personified average, since this would be a mere representation of an abstraction, but rather an embodiment of human passion, the forcing of life itself into expression.[20] This idea helps to show why the over-simplified biographical approach which identifies the Maud Gonne of the poems absolutely with the actual person can be misleading: what appears in the poems is a mythical and intermediary figure identified with Maud Gonne and expressed by Yeats via this identification. Of course, he and his love for her take on a similar dimension through the poems.

The thought, 'She will grow old and die and she has wept!' (ISW 6), is given the appearance of forcing itself into the narrative as it forces itself into the mind of the narrator. The effect of the mythical arising from the narration of the legendary is to force into consciousness a fundamental concern of human life: the ultimate unhappiness and death of the beloved which limits human love and makes us anxious over its adequacy. The universality of the thought is lent by the relation to the mythical, but it retains the immediacy given by personal expression, personal expression whose vividness is enhanced by its bursting into the narrative as it bursts out of the poet's attempts to rewrite it:

> And when I'd write it out anew, the words,
> Half crazy with the thought, She too has wept!
> Outrun the measure. (ISW 6)

The actual words, 'the words ... outrun', contain the emotion expressed, and yet run over the lineation. It is possible to see the climax of the poem suggested here, running clear of the poet's capacity to express, before he forces himself to take up the narrative once more. The consummation of love, assisted by the mortal world, brings peace to the immortal, but Maeve's final question touches the problematic area which remains an issue in 'Baile and Aillinn', and re-emerges in 'The Grey Rock' and 'The Two Kings': 'O when will you grow weary[?]'

Maeve retains the potential of youthful spirit, and even her body is revivified by contact with the supernatural, the contact recalling to her aspects of her youth. But she is ageing, weary of body, regretful of the loss of that youth which seemed, together with her sense of destiny, to give her divinity. The association of Maud Gonne with Maeve takes into account the poet's new knowledge of Maud Gonne's life. It suggests a rather healthier image, in spite of the regret. The regret is also associated with Maeve's lover, Ailell, who ages with her, stressing the importance of the limitation on love which mortality confers. The white calf notebook which Maud Gonne presented to Yeats in 1908 records a vision she had of herself and Yeats as Maeve and Ailell,[21] but this identification is not something merely drawn from Yeats's poem. Maud Gonne signs herself 'Maedbe' in a letter of August/September 1902. She had chosen this as her Inghínidhe na hÉireann name.[22] The description of Maeve as 'great bodied and great limbed, / Fashioned to be the mother of strong children' (ISW 2) may seem reductively male chauvinist,[23] but appears less so if we see the poem as part of Yeats's attempt to come to terms with Maud Gonne's changed status. For a while at least (though this picture of her seems not to have lasted), the image of Maud Gonne as a Maeve-like maternal figure would have been helpful to Yeats. It is also possible to see what begins as a description of Maeve modulating into a description of Maud Gonne, as the poet, dramatized within his poem, proves unable to stick to what is supposedly his task, is unable to keep his own concerns from forcing their way into the poem. Reading like this heightens the impression of the poem as performance. The effect is created of a departure from a supposed text.

Cullingford describes the story of 'Red Hanrahan' as 'the thinly disguised account of Yeats's failure to win her [Maud Gonne] for himself.'[24] 'Red Hanrahan' does indeed replace an earlier story at the head of the Hanrahan stories, but the earlier story, 'The Book of the Great Dhoul and Hanrahan the Red', can also be linked with the 'failure to win' Maud Gonne. In this story, Hanrahan rejects Cleena of the Wave when she becomes mortal. In its even earlier version, 'The Devil's Book' (1892), the peasant poet, here called O'Sullivan the Red, also rejects the faery woman when she becomes mortal.[25] His concern with the fact that having become human she will age looks forward to the concern with Maud Gonne's ageing in the poems of *In the Seven Woods: Being Poems Chiefly of the Irish Heroic Age*.

Deirdre Toomey indicates the complexity of the relationship between the poet's work and his life, and that the forces which operate between imagination and life run both ways. She sees Yeats as having failed to 'win' Maud Gonne in 1898 by failing to respond positively to a confession that was a sign of her availability to him. Yeats's failure, it seems, was due to the entanglement in the 'aesthetic of frustration and defeat' established in *The Wind Among the Reeds*.[26] Yeats does indeed seem later to question his motive for not responding more positively, more warmly, to a confession that may well have been an overture.[27] The question that arises here concerns to what extent conscious choice was involved in the rejection (if rejection it was) of Maud Gonne's advances, and to what extent Yeats's response was constrained by a force which was the product of his own imagination. The supernatural figure which Yeats had constructed in his imagination, and to which he had assimilated Maud Gonne, was rejected when she became mortal, just as his imagination demanded, as indicated by 'The Devil's Book' and 'The Book of the Great Dhoul and Hanrahan the Red'. A noticeable difference between the stories written before 1898 and their 1903 replacement is that in the earlier stories the supernatural woman is positively rejected, whereas in the later story Hanrahan is incapable of response and Echtge must remain asleep.[28]

The expression of *ennui* was so well achieved as to impose on the life of the poet the conditions on which that *ennui* depended. Life imitated art; the work forced its way into the life. Maud Gonne's revelation disrupted the condition of mutually supporting imaginative and emotional paralysis. This disruption may have exposed the 'psychic impotence'[29] paradoxically essential at that time to his creativity, but in forcing the regrounding of his creativity, the regrounding of his imaginative work, it also had a positive effect. The enforced realization (on whatever level of consciousness) of the connection between the will-less quality of the work and an inability to act in life, led to the realization of the power available to the poet who deliberately exploited the relationship between imagination and life. Yeats's pamphlet *Is the Order of R. R. & A. C. to Remain a Magical Order?*, addressed to his fellow members of the Golden Dawn, describes the magical power of the imagination:

> The central principle of all the Magic of power is that everything we formulate in the imagination, if we formulate it strongly enough, realises itself in the circumstances of life, acting either through our own souls, or through the spirits of nature.[30]

III

'Baile and Aillinn' (ISW 7–15) takes up the issue of the desirability of immortal love in a slightly different aspect. Aengus has a more indirect role, not himself a lover but 'Master of Love'. As representative of the supernatural, he claims for his own world what in the natural world approaches ideal love. Once more the supernatural province of immortality is termed 'the Great Plain', but in this poem there is an emphasis on its association with death from normal life. That a love separated from the life of this world is to be idealized is clear from the beginning of the poem as the poem's lovers escape the impingement on love of worldly cares and the wearying of love with physical ageing.

The rubric passages (italicized in later editions) dramatize a singer for the song, suggest a recital, in a way which maintains the presence of the poet, prevents the reader's complete absorption into the narrative level of the poem and obliviousness of the level of the narrator. The typographical distinction of levels was not always appreciated. H. W. Boynton, in his review of *In the Seven Woods*, thought the form 'deliberately queer', and did not see the need for rubrication. Boynton plays the frankly baffled, plain man, who would like to be indulgent, but whose patience is sorely tried.[31] The poem's consequent narrative deals with the contact of the supernatural and natural worlds, and the poem as a whole raises the issue of the effect of the existence of the idealized supernatural world on the everyday world. This issue is emphasized by the link the storyteller forms between the narrative and its audience, or reader.[32] But it is something within the natural world that recalls the story to its narrator, something natural for all that it might seem disembodied: the cry of the curlew and the sound of the wind in the rushes.

The link that these sounds establish with the legendary and mythical[33] is not necessarily to the advantage of the world, since it can lead only to dissatisfaction with what is not ideal, though it may be that the supernatural world is called into existence only as an expression of this dissatisfaction. The link is most present to those who are closest to the birdcall, to the wind among the reeds, rather than to the action demanded by the modern world, and the compromise that happiness within the everyday world demands. The sense of the closeness of the narrator's world to that of the narrative is heightened in the search for terms to describe the condition of the two lovers who have died of their love. The nearness to the real and the attempt at precision and clarity of image – fish, mice, apple-boughs – recall Yeats's comments on how free of vagueness was the supernatural for those who retained the unity of thought and feeling he believed existed in the Irish peasantry. In a letter in May 1900 to George Russell, he wrote, 'All ancient vision was definite & precise' (CL2 522). Following these natural images by likening the lovers to 'the two strings that made one sound / Where that wise harper's finger ran' (ISW 13) relinks the lovers to the world of song and reminds in another way of the presence of the singer.

The presence in the mind of the supernatural can be a cause of sadness. Within the narrative itself is the indication that ideal love does not belong in the ordinary world: the strains of love are so great that in an ideal case they will exhaust the mere flesh and blood of the body.

There is a double comparison within this poem which parallels that of 'The Old Age of Queen Maeve'. Baile and Aillinn, who have become immortal, are held up to the normal world, but the legendary, mortal Deirdre and Naoise are also introduced, first into the narrative, then into the narrator's interpolation. As with Maeve, Maud Gonne does not suffer by comparison with Deirdre – 'you are more high of heart than she' (ISW 15) – but Baile and Aillinn, and the condition they have attained, are a different matter. Description of where they are supposed to be recalls Maeve's description of the province of the immortals, where 'nothing troubles the great streams' (ISW 14). The pairing of sun and moon in the description in 'Baile and Aillinn' suggests the completion of perfection. The otherness of where they are is indicated in the withering of the material. Common to both descriptions is the sense of an even flow in this supernatural region, untroubled by what troubles the movement of life in the natural world. This region represents an escape to tranquillity, as suggested by the disguised Aengus's description of Baile's death.

'Baile and Aillinn' does not, though, rest with quite the same sense of ambivalence towards lovers together for eternity. The poem closes with its narrator's regret that he must be reminded of Baile and Aillinn and so of the imperfection of any love available in this world. And yet the sound of the birds and the wind only take him where it is natural for the Irish storyteller to go. According to Yeats's preface to Lady Gregory's *Cuchulain of Muirthemne*, the Irish storyteller 's interest would constantly take flight from the everyday to Tir-nà-nOg, referred to here as 'the land of Promise', showing its association with the difference between what is and what the human mind wants to believe possible. The Irish storyteller 'only feels himself among solid things ... when he has reshaped the world according to his heart's desire.'[34]

The conflict of temperament between subjective idealist and objective materialist which comes to light in some reviews of Yeats's work of the time is reflected in this quotation.[35] Charles Tennyson, in 'Irish Plays and Playwrights', finds unreality and inhumanity to be traits of Irish literature. His article is not unsympathetic; by 'inhuman' he means tending to mysticism. He stresses the mismatch between Yeats's idealist, mystical temperament and the needs of effective drama, which is 'the most material of all forms of art'.[36] It is my feeling that Yeats wanted to move towards a poetry in which temperaments like Tennyson's could recognize humanity, but without compromising his distance from materialism. For the storyteller, what is solid is what he most believes in, and strength of belief, for him, relates to some sort of emotional necessity: there is a need for the world he believes in to reflect his desires.

Perhaps, in finding the greatest reality within himself, the storyteller might recall Browning's idea of the subjective poet:

> Not with the combination of humanity in action, but with the primal elements of humanity he has to do; and he digs where he stands,– preferring to seek them in his own soul as the nearest reflex of that absolute Mind, according to the intuitions of which he desires to perceive and speak.[37]

Browning's comment on the subjective poet and the pictorial aspect of poetry indicates his sense of a human communicativeness in the subjective poet's work, an aspect which renders the presence of the poet within his work an essential part of it, and which links understanding of the poetry to an understanding of this projection of the poet as human figure into his work:

> He does not paint pictures and hang them on the walls, but rather carries them on the retina of his own eyes: we must look deep into his human eyes, to see those pictures on them.[38]

It is crucial to address here the imperatives, creative and emotional necessities, which make the relationship of natural and supernatural worlds, of mortal and immortal love, such an issue for Yeats, as well as the form of approach through the narrative poem whose subject is drawn from Irish legend. If the approach is mythic, it is not that it seeks to impose an order on the flux of the modern world,[39] but rather that it looks back to legendary material to find a means of addressing an attitude to life felt deeply within the poet's mind. The external manifestations – empirical, objective – become unreal if they are not related to his feelings; it is within his own mind that the poet seeks an ordering that will make sense of his experience. The return, through legend, to a time when the gods were closer to the people improves the chance of success. It also unites personal expression to tradition. Yeats's 1899 article 'The Literary Movement in Ireland' indicates a wish for Irish literature to rediscover the tradition of the people and also a wish to reconcile the spoken and the written traditions, to benefit from the inspiration of the peasant imagination *and* 'the inheritance of cultivated men'. It also claims that 'a writer who wishes to write with his whole mind must knead the beliefs and hopes, which he has made his own, with the circumstance of his own life.'[40] This kneading metaphor for Yeats's idea of projecting himself into a mythology and tradition is one he returns to and the idea is an explicit part of his thinking on his poetry at the time of *In the Seven Woods*. To say the gods were closer, more real, to the people is a way of expressing the unity of feeling and intellect which might otherwise be expressed as understanding one's emotions, of sensing the uniting humanity that all possess at a level deeper than the abstracted mechanical, logical thought of rhetoric and journalism which divides people.[41] The contrast is between a subjective and an objective approach.

IV

Critics writing slightly later, when they have the *Collected Works* (1908) to refer to, often find Yeats's particular abilities unsuited to drama. The distinction between lyrical and dramatic parallels that between subjective and objective, as Schopenhauer suggested. Francis Bickley's view in 'The Development of William Butler Yeats' (1910) is similar to that of Charles Tennyson. He maintains that Yeats is so suited to lyrical poetry as to make drama the wrong form of expression for him, though he shrewdly notes a transition in Yeats, a movement towards a greater humanity which he associates with his theatre work.[42] For Bickley, it is Yeats's 'subjective realism' that contributes to the perfection of his lyrics. Bickley's phrase shows a significant difference from the approach of Lytton Strachey. Reviewing volumes I and II of the *Collected Works* (1908), Strachey opposes ordinary life and reason to what he views as extreme Romanticism in Yeats.[43] In Yeats's favour, Strachey claims that there is a lyrical beauty in, for instance, 'Innisfree', which means the absence of 'certainty of design' is unimportant. His point seems to be that Yeats's strength is in his lyrics, where his weaknesses are insignificant. He seems even to suggest that these weaknesses are almost a part of lyrical genius, so suggesting a natural separation of lyrical poetry from life.

Strachey's comments on dramatic verse illuminate an attitude with which Yeats found himself at odds philosophically. Yeats's verse does not have the psychological realism and intelligible motivation of character that Strachey believes it needs to be dramatic and human. Strachey prefers the narrative to the dramatic verse, but finds 'The Wanderings of Oisin' incoherent: 'its structure is essentially unreasonable, because it depends on no causal law'. Strachey wants art to give him the opportunity to exercise his reason (though he makes an exception for lyric poetry); he wants to be able to trace action back to motivation via a train of logical thought. The phrase 'causal law' is crucial: logic is absolute and explains exhaustively; for every effect, the appropriate cause, and vice versa. To Yeats, it is this kind of thought that is inhuman because it is mechanical. The thinking behind Strachey's argument is that realism is 'objective' realism, that is to say that the empirical manifestations of the world that all ordinary men see, that are verifiable by the senses and logically related by causal laws, constitute reality. Bickley, on the other hand, validates the expression of things as they appear to the artist, though pointing out that the subjectivity of Yeats's ideas makes them poetic not dramatic material. This mismatch indicates a tension, in the view of these critics, between the essentially subjective, imaginative province of the lyrical and the essentially objective province of drama. Yeats's view was that the objective approach led to a concentration on what he called 'character' in drama, so that modern drama tended to comedy rather than tragedy.

The anonymous review of volumes I and II of the *Collected Works* (1908) in the *Saturday Review* finds Yeats temperamentally suited to the use of 'Keltic' material.[44] Yeats is a genuine poet, but his work lacks the 'body and sustenance' for perfection. There is a sort of double bind here. If Yeats continues to work with the kind of material to which he is suited, he will be a true poet, but will be unable to achieve the highest form of art, as this reviewer sees it, simply because the misty material in which he works is unlikely to survive hard realization.[45] Bliss Carman, in his 1907 *New York Times* review of the *Collected Works of William B. Yeats*, shows a similar attitude in suggesting that there is a happy medium between the excessive imagination which renders poetry unintelligible and a poverty of imagination which renders it banal. The rational faculty must be engaged in transforming the material supplied by the imagination into finished poetry if it is to have a relation to real life, and so be of interest to readers who do not share the poet's highly developed and mystical imagination. It seems that readers of Carman's type have an aspiration towards the imaginative which needs to be satisfied, but which is not free of the rationality which ties them to the material and the intellectually logical.

These four reviews indicate the growing problems for poetry early in the twentieth century. The old metaphysical certainties guaranteed by shared religious belief had broken down. A growing scientism, a tendency to think in terms of an objective world, and to demand objective proofs, rendered the subjective expression associated with Romanticism, a now decayed Romanticism, unsatisfactory. Poetry must bring self-expression to terms with the modern world, if it were not to become merely solipsistic.

Yet the banality of the compromise suggested by Carman is in itself enough to indicate the difficulties of self-expression in a society which increasingly believed in an objective reality. Yeats was not prepared to compromise. He never adopted the position on the fence which Carman advocates for the poet ; rather he recognized the claims of the world of imagination *and* those of the social world. But Yeats was able to recognize the claims of the social world without accepting an objectivist philosophy. In fact, objectivism is something he defined himself against. Objectivism abstracts the factors common to the experience of different individuals and reifies them. Yeats was committed to the complete expression of personal experience. His doctrine of personality is crucial. Rather than expressing views and opinions in his poetry, which would then become rhetorical and an incomplete expression of himself, he sought to create an image of himself in his work. In doing this he could fulfil his own criterion of expressing himself completely. Ford Madox Ford's *Outlook* article of 1914 shows the effectiveness of this form of self-expression in communicating with a critic hitherto far from sympathetic.[46] Further, it was the evidence of the relationship of the personality of the poet with the Yeats who was involved in everyday affairs which swayed Ford. It was through the doctrine of personality, then, that the reintegration of art and life could be begun, and the separation of the stuff of lyrical poetry from the concerns of everyday life be healed. The same sort of knowledge that allowed Elizabethan poetry to speak to Yeats can allow his own poetry to speak to *its* audience.

The poet's own experience, speaking biographically, is of an unhappy love-affair, which he knows, nevertheless, is a great one in terms of the depth and strength of his passion for its object. His younger life, too, was characterized by an unhappiness, a feeling of yearning which he found difficult to attach to any specific referent in the objective world. These are concerns which the poet is able to approach in these poems. The poet's attitude towards the world beyond death, the world where eternal love is possible, is disturbed by the demonstration of the actual Maud Gonne's flesh-and-blood humanity, and hence mortality. This is not a *problem* which can be solved here in a way which could only be reductive, but an issue in the poet's psychic life which he needs to express.

For Yeats, it is these issues which are most deeply felt (which are, we might say, out of proportion) which give true life, life as it is rather than a representation of an average drawn from observation of empirical manifestations. Such manifestations are, for him, only the accidents of life:

> Poets have taken their themes more often from stories that are all, or half, mythological, than from history or stories that give one the sensation of history, understanding, as I think, that the imagination which remembers the proportions of life is but a long wooing, and that it has to forget them before it becomes the torch and the marriage-bed.[47]

Further, for Yeats, there has been a shift in modern poetry, under the influence of the increasing complication of thought by its attention to external, material things, towards the explication rather than the expression of passion, which misses the point of what poetry is. The gathering together of people in an urban civilization leads to discussion which makes of the world a 'painful' riddle. Modern poetry is dominated by this: 'It is full of thoughts, and when one is stirred by any deep passion one does not want to know what anybody has thought of that passion, but to hear it beautifully spoken ...'[48] Yeats wants poetry to be from the Tree of Life, not from the Tree of Knowledge. It is nearer to life, to fullness, to express the emotional attitude as a whole, rather than to abstract from it some intellectual problem which can be explicated and resolved. Consolation can still be drawn, can only be drawn in the case of those for whom reason alone is insufficient, from the beauty which comes of the adequacy, the completeness, of expression of the emotion. For Yeats, the poetry which he advocates brings an expression of life more real than poetry which deals with 'the common doings and reasonable thoughts of ordinary men'.[49]

In *Samhain* 1904 it is evident to what extent Yeats's anti-materialism involves both ethical and creative considerations. The opposition of subjective and objective is suggested in his feeling that reality is grounded centrally, as he criticizes the modern world for believing the opposite: 'How can we create like the ancients, while innumerable considerations of external probability or social utility destroy the seeming irresponsible creative power that is life itself?' (Ex 150) Yeats shows his consciousness of the extent to which language expresses the instrumentalist, 'good-citizen' ethics that he sees as prevalent in his own time in describing that creative power unconcerned with social utility as 'seeming irresponsible'. For Yeats, to represent externals, the flux, is not good art: it is the removal of the personality of the artist which will separate art from life and leave only a reflection of illusion. The immediacy of an older poetry, the closeness of expression to what it expresses, comes from the directness of the poet's experience of the world. That the absence of intervening theory and generalization allows the life centred in the poet its proper expression is the point Yeats wants to make in this article. The increasing abstraction in language, its move away from such direct expression, renders it lifeless:

> What the ever-moving, delicately moulded flesh is to human beauty, vivid musical words are to passion. Somebody has said that every nation begins with poetry and ends with algebra, and passion has always refused to express itself in algebraical terms. (Ex 167–8)

The actual physical expression of language is also significant for Yeats. Life is linked to sound ('vivid musical') and the living word to the evanescent flesh. The expression of beauty, if it is to be alive, is transient, unfixed. A letter to Robert Bridges indicates the importance to Yeats of writing with the progression from word to word always in mind. He mentions his and Florence Farr's verse-speaking project:

> We had great difficulty even with Keats & though we got a passage which is splendidly vocal we had to transpose a line because of a construction, which could only be clear to the eye which can see several words at once.
>
> I shall be altogether content if we can perfect this art for I have never felt that reading was better than an error, a part of the fall into the flesh, a mouthful of the apple. (CL3 91–2, 20 July 1901)

The idea of the flesh here is clearly different from what is meant in the *Samhain* article; in this letter, it is a metaphor for materialism. The letter stresses Yeats's sense of speech as somehow relating more closely to lived experience in time since it is a progression. Speech denies the possibility of objectification that the printed word offers via the eye.

T. E. Hulme also saw poetry as a defence against algebraic language, and what he thought of as 'counter' thinking, where words were substituted for things and manoeuvred according to rules. This he condemned as a distancing of thought from reality.[50] Hulme's emphasis is always on the visual. For instance, 'We replace meaning (i.e. *vision*) by words.'[51] He seeks immediate expression, but seems to lack any feeling for the shaping of the world by the artist. Further, his visual insistence implies a belief that the true reality is what for the idealist is only its empirical manifestation. Alun Jones claims that Hulme's visual insistence has mostly to do with his means of expression.[52] The question is, *why* does he express himself like this? His views are a strange mixture. His Bergsonism suggests that he believes there is a more 'real' reality which is available only to intuition. This visual quality in Hulme's thought also suggests the objectivizing tendency associated by Frank Kermode with Symbolism and by Walter Ong with print culture.[53]

A remark by Yeats on Poe in *Samhain* 1904 might lead us to think of the uncanny, what is at once strange and familiar, but also makes completeness of expression crucial. Poe confronts us with the microcosm that 'mirror[s] everything in universal Nature' (Ex 144). Comments on Poe and Crashaw in *Memoirs* (Mem 166–7) suggest that Yeats thought that in older writers the microcosm better reflects the macrocosm. Presumably he would have attributed this to a more unified society, a clearer 'common' mind from which the writer's images are drawn.

Abstraction from the microcosm will remove the universality which makes it recognizable in spite of its difference. The mythic approach expresses emotion directly. When it does so through character, it produces a type which is not a personified average, a collection of empirical characteristics held in common by numbers of people, but the singular expression of a particular emotion. So for Yeats, Shakespeare's Richard II was 'a good image for an accustomed mood of fanciful, impracticable lyricism in his [Shakespeare's] own mind.'[54] Shakespeare's Richard II gives us knowledge of something in our own minds, and makes the historical Richard seem of much less significance.

Yeats's 1910 lecture on the theatre makes the link between incomplete expression of personality, abstraction from life, and the materialist, mechanistic society which this kind of art both appeals to and represents. For Yeats, Galsworthy's play *Justice* interests itself in the 'vast play of circumstance' rather than in life, and does this because the time for which it is written is interested in 'business' and 'commerce'(YT 19). Yeats's understanding of truth to life clearly differs from that of realism. Following Shelley, he believes that true art works against the materialism which is the foundation of realism, and in an opposite direction to the art which is an expression of a materialistic society:

> The cultivation of poetry is never more to be desired than at periods when, from an excess of the selfish and calculating principle, the accumulation of the materials of external life exceed the quantity of the power of assimilating them to the internal laws of human nature. The body has then become too unwieldy for that which animates it.[55]

Yeats's sense that the separation of the external and internal forms of life leads to the paralysis of one and the attenuation of the other is clear in his comment on the body of Ireland having become a stone and its soul a vapour.[56] For Yeats, it is the breath of the spoken word, of personal utterance, that is needed to reanimate poetry. Poetry as the embodiment of personality can reforge the link between internal and external necessary to the genuine life of both.

V

The themes of another world, its relationship with this world, and the ageing within this world of the beloved continue in the lyrics of *In the*

Seven Woods. In the arrangement of the poems first used in the *Collected Works* (1908) the continuity from 'Baile and Aillinn' is emphasized by the similarity in how 'Quiet' (a figure, of course, from *The Wind Among the Reeds*) is introduced:

> They eat
> Quiet's wild heart, like daily meat ... ('Baile and Aillinn', ISW 14)
> ... Quiet
> Wanders laughing and eating her wild heart ... ('In the Seven Woods', ISW 1)

The proximity of these phrases binds the lyric poems to the preceding narrative poems despite the removal of the narratives from the 'In the Seven Woods' frame. Yeats's letter to Robert Bridges of 20 July 1901 indicates the interconnectedness he envisaged for the volume. He wants to give life to 'a whole world of little stories ... to a romantic region':

> The old Irish poets wove life into life thereby giving to the wildest & strangest romance, the solidity & vitality [of] the *Comedie Humaine* & all this romance was knitted into the scenery of the country. (CL3 91)

Lady Gregory's books of Irish myth, the first of which is mentioned in this letter, may later have provided much of the foundational web Yeats was thinking of weaving when he wrote to Bridges. The letter introduces also, though, the idea of the placing of the poet within a tradition. In a way similar to that of the Irish poets to whom this letter refers, he seeks to establish an audience whose memory of his work will condition their response, who will respond with recognition, who will feel themselves and the poet projected into a mythical world.[57] The web weaves together the lives of imagined characters, but also weaves real life into imagined life. Attaching the real world to the imagined world gives the latter the essential connection with life, but also enhances the status of that part of the real world chosen – Ireland – with the aim of freeing it from materialism.

The continuity from 'Baile and Aillinn' is marked in 'The Arrow' (the following poem in the original arrangement) by the apple blossom complexion of the youthful beloved, recalling the resting place of the young Aillinn's body.[58] The emotional disturbance of thought which caused words to 'outrun the measure' in 'The Old Age of Queen Maeve' is here in the 'arrow / Made out of a wild thought' (ISW 16). Apple blossom hides the body which Aillinn escaped by her death and transformation. In 'The Arrow', apple blossom concealed, in the sense of distracting attention from, the inevitability of ageing, the draining away of perfection in the mortal world. Now no-one can see Maud Gonne in quite that heroic light which made her seem part of another, more perfect world, since she has been touched by the signs of ageing, the mark of the imperfect, mortal world. Her beauty is mellower, suggests a sympathy, but sympathy suggests growing humanity, and humanity is doomed to age and die. The mellowing of her beauty is due to something which the torturing thought within the poet revolts against. The poet can no longer see Maud Gonne as he saw her before her revelation of her relationship with Millevoye. Her beauty is kinder in the sense that it is no longer the fatal beauty of the supernatural woman.

Terence Brown notes the consciousness of the physical in 'marrow', in which the arrow of the 'wild thought' is embedded.[59] There is also a sense of connection between the mental and the physical, the remembered and the bodily here. Adding to this physicality is the literal presence of the word 'arrow' within the word 'marrow'. Helen Vendler gives 'The Arrow' as an example of Yeats's use of words which contain the word with which they rhyme. She wants to suggest that Yeats is indeed a magical poet:

> The incantatory power of reduplicative language (learned in part from Swinburne but not abused) served Yeats as an index of magical writing all his life. [Through his early experimentation,] the visual and auditory presence of individual words, rhymes, stanza schemes, and syntactic parallels took on for Yeats an almost palpable shape and solidity.[60]

Compare the more contemporary thoughts of Joseph Hone:

> [Yeats read] Paracelsus, Lull, Flamel, and those alchemists who, believing that spiritual truth could be demonstrated by logical formula with the help of mathematical figures, sought to erect universal systems of knowledge. Mr. Yeats' interest in magic did not spring, as some would have it, from literary impulse; but he dares assert that the magic of poetry is a real magic, and his youthful dictum, 'Words alone are certain good,' takes on in the light of his occult beliefs a concrete significance. The poet with his symbols should do for us moderns what the priest with his magical rites did for the ancients.[61]

The connection through the physicality of words of the emotional – even the spiritual – and the bodily, the making real of magic and symbol through the palpability of words, is what the combination of the insights of these critics draws attention to. It seems to me that Yeats's genuine belief in a connection between symbols and something else, something real, checks the slide into solipsism and epistemological scepticism that can result from Symbolist thinking.

'The Folly of Being Comforted' continues the theme of the ageing of the beloved. The comfort offered is that the pain of frustrated love will surely be eased by the ageing of its object. The implication is that the wisdom of resignation to giving up frustrated love will be made easier as the object of love loses its desirability. The heart's response is to reject this, since the nobleness of the beloved transcends time's effects. There is that about her now which is but the more clear for the passing of the transient beauty of youth. In a sense, then, this poem seems to contradict its predecessor, 'The Arrow', but the contradiction is merely apparent:

> O heart O heart if she'd but turn her head,
> You'd know the folly of being comforted. (ISW 16)

The particular comfort offered is one that twists the knife of the knowledge that the beloved has aged and will die (and reopens the wound of how the realization of the mortality, the humanity, of his beloved has been forced on the poet). Yeats had written in this poem of 'little crowsfeet' around Gonne's eyes, but altered this to 'shadows'. She told him to alter it or people would think he meant Lady Gregory. He commented, 'That was the first time I knew she was human.'[62] Maud Gonne's youthful beauty, as perhaps Helen of Troy's, was the expression of a noble nature, and that nobility would in time find similar expression again because it was a fundamental human passion: once more the treatment of Maud Gonne is mythical. But the transience of her youthful beauty, beauty's worldly manifestation, points to the limitation of love within the mortal world, the concern which tortured the poet in both 'The Arrow' and 'The Old Age of Queen Maeve', and which causes the narrator of 'Baile and Aillinn' to wish he need not be reminded of the ideal, immortal love that the dead couple find in that other world which is, because of the contrast with our world, an expression of the emotionally felt shortcomings of our world. Again, the disruption of his imagination by the emphatic establishment of her humanity by Maud Gonne's revelation of December 1898 distances the poet from the world of the unattainable perfect love, rendering it painful to think of in a new way.

'Adam's Curse' (ISW 18–19) again involves Maud Gonne. In 1940, Eliot noted the move towards the sense of the poet as a man present in his work in both this poem and 'The Folly of Being Comforted': 'By the time of the volume of 1904 there is a development visible ... something is coming through, and in beginning to speak as a particular man he is beginning to speak for man.'[63] Eliot's comment shows his consciousness of the necessity for the poet to express his personality in order that there might be in his work those things shared by all personalities which form the common root of human life. His comments recall Wordsworth's description of a poet as 'a man speaking to men'.[64] The method finds subjective expression for the aspects of human life, passions, which manifest themselves in outwardly different form in each different example of human life. In bringing these aspects to expression in his work, the poet finds the truly typical. The ordering of the flux of the modern material world by 'manipulating a continuous parallel between contemporaneity and antiquity' that Eliot sees in Joyce's *Ulysses*[65] is a project more suited to the side of philosophy opposed to that of Yeats. The type of mythic method Yeats uses, and which Eliot's comment on him suggests, is a subjective one. The type of mythic method which Eliot suggests Joyce uses, and which he claims was 'adumbrated' by Yeats, can be described as objective. The manipulation of a continuous parallel suggests that the two ages are seen side by side. This implies a viewpoint outside lived experience, a looking on from outside, an objective view.

Michael J. Sidnell claims that though Yeats may be 'manipulating a continuous parallel between contemporaneity and antiquity', '[f]ar from imposing order on anything, the parallelism between the myth and actuality discloses a tragic separation between the lyrist who suffers and the narrator who re-creates.'[66] Warwick Gould suggests that Eliot may have been referring to the poems and notes method of *The Wind Among the Reeds*. He claims that Eliot's analysis is in any case anachronistic, since it depends on Yeats's taking a post-war attitude to modern times. He also points out that myth had a reality for Yeats.[67] Specifically, myth had a reality for Yeats as an *Irish* artist. Note this from the report of a Yeats lecture on Watts's pictures in 1906:

> Here in Ireland they had still myths and beliefs among the people. They had still left some of the element of the middle ages, and he thought if Watts had been an Irishman he would not have painted these allegories but would have devoted himself to the celebration of the national legends and heroes. (UP2 342–5, 345)

The use of myth is a means by which the artist can appeal to an audience of the common people, and in a way dependent on what remains in such a popular audience of a more unified sensibility. The implication of what Yeats says is that the English common people have fallen too far into materialism, whereas in Ireland there is still a chance of success for an art that uses the common resource of myth. Yeats's attempts to come to terms with the disruption of the imaginative foundation of his poetry and to re-embrace orality also need to be taken into account. The presence of the poet's own concerns in the poems is essential to both of these projects. The poet must not be absorbed into his story, but foregrounded, in order to dramatize a recital. The issue that the poem addresses is a personal one, and the poet must retain his personality.

In Eliot's suggestion of an objective view we can see the spatializing tendency that Joseph Frank associates with literary modernism, the wish for a synoptic view.[68] Even in thinking about music, seemingly inextricably time-bound, Eliot's spatializing, or synoptic, tendency is evident: 'Ideally, I should like to be able to hold the whole of a great symphony in my mind at once.'[69]

Yeats's 'The Literary Movement in Ireland' (1899) claims that the old poets 'saw the golden age and their own age side by side like substance and shadow',[70] and that art might again be moving towards this conception. Yeats looks back to a time when he believes that the world of myth was present to the common people, built up and kept alive by a tradition of legends and stories. This belief enables him to see the possibility of the existence of the timeless world within the temporal world, once the temporal world can be rid of its materialism. The folk tradition can bring a reality to symbolism, which makes the eternal world present within the temporal:

> [A] change of thought is making us half ready to believe with Ecclesiasticus, that 'all things are made double one above another,' and that the forms of nature may be temporal shadows of realities.[71]

The mythic method suggested in this article involves the projection of the poet and his own concerns into the world that has been built up by local legend. The participation of all of society in the imaginative life of art is essential to the recovery of both society and art, according to the view Yeats expresses in 'The Literary Movement in Ireland'.

The effect of Eliot's and Pound's 'modernist' attempts to have poetry treated seriously was the opposite of the aim Yeats suggests here. That

Eliot and Pound had absorbed some of contemporary society's assumptions is indicated by their inclination to scientific metaphor.[72] Their efforts also helped to encourage or support the move towards the professionalization of poetry and criticism which led to elitism and the marginalization and trivialization of poetry and criticism.[73] Poetry becomes something taken seriously only by a small group (and possibly there will be those within that group who take it seriously only for professional reasons, or, at best, address only their fellow professionals). Such efforts were an understandable attempt to eliminate the amateurish air surrounding poetry and criticism which set it apart from the main current of society, what people would take seriously. Yeats's project could only see this as a compromise with a society which had its values wrong.

The obtuse response to 'Adam's Curse' of H. C. Beeching's 1906 review of *Poems 1899–1905* indicates what Eliot and Pound were up against, and the separation of poetry from what their time took seriously which they attempted to heal by making poetry once more something serious. 'Well, it is perhaps not wise of a poet to make much of the labours of his art, if he wishes "the bankers, schoolmasters, and clergymen" to give him credit for inspiration.'[74] According to this view, the poet relies on something which distances him from the part of society whose prestige is increasing:

> [B]y the early twentieth century, the ideology of professionalism had established itself to the extent of making anything that smacked of amateurism look second-rate. Insofar as art still banked on the unprofessional side of its reputation, the artist was therefore beginning to lose vocational ground; for to the professional view, 'inspiration' will seem like self-indulgence.[75]

Ford, though so often a spokesman for the claims of the modern age, asserts the importance of poetry in a way which invites its marginalization by the everyday world. 'Outside my young friends he [Yeats] seems to me to be the one poet that matters in a world where only poets matter.'[76] The mere assertion by poets and critics that only poetry is important will just lead to the dismissal of their opinion by a world to which other things clearly *are* important. The difficulty is in retaining the special quality of the poet's view while not allowing it to become *merely* the poet's view, to be ignored by non-poets.

Yeats aligns himself with the Irish language movement by trying to appeal to what lies behind the attempt to revive dying languages. The integrated oral culture of a rural Ireland largely free of the influence of the English language is one where the life of the imagination is inextricably involved with the life of everyday: 'The life of the villages, with its songs, its dances and its pious greetings, its conversations full of vivid images shaped hardly more by life itself than by innumerable forgotten poets.'[77]

The oral community's sense of itself depends on the continuity that comes of formalized speech, such as 'pious greetings', and a tradition of stories and legends. Such stories gain reality through being set in the world their hearers see every day, and bind their hearers into a community because they are spoken, not printed in books. 'When a speaker is addressing an audience, the members of the audience normally become a unity, with themselves and with the speaker.'[78] The importance of the theatre to Yeats's project of re-creating an idealistic Ireland, free from the influence of English materialism, is indicated in a comment from a 1902 lecture:

> Victor Hugo said once that it is in the theatre that the mob becomes a people. He meant I suppose that it is the theatre which takes up the traditions of the past and shapes them into such a form that they can become the ideals of the present and the substance of the future.[79]

Yeats's theatre is one where the spoken word is of first importance. The theatre can be the vehicle of the restoration of imaginative community by working through the unifying medium of speech. In a letter to John Quinn, Yeats indicates his belief that within the type of national theatre he is trying to create, the audience has a central commitment and emotion to which the playwright can appeal. Modern culture, he feels, is too diffuse, so that 'in the ordinary theatres ... the audience has no binding interest, no great passion or bias that the dramatist can awake' (CL3 389, 28 June 1903). One *can* read elitism, even a growing Nietzscheanism, in Yeats's increasing sense that the popular audience cannot be his. But it is tinged with regret: 'My work is I am afraid too full of a very personal comment on life, too full of the thoughts of the small sect you and I and all other cultivated people belong to ever to have any great popularity'(CL3 389). Also, the thought in his mind is of Keats's lines on 'how Homer left great verses to a little clan'. He will forgo great popularity if he can inspire those of 'keen and subtle' imagination 'to think of Ireland as a sacred land' (CL3 389). There is a snobbish rhetoric here – 'cultivated', 'keen and subtle' – but also significant is the need Yeats perceives for a sense of integration with the thought of his audience. In addition, the reference to Ireland as 'sacred' distinguishes his and his desired audience's imagined Ireland from the modern materialist world. His perception of the 'ordinary' theatre is that it must cater for a modern audience of diffuse interests and so contribute to the fragmented culture of the modern world.

It is because the returning emigrant Yeats speaks of in his lecture 'Friends of My Youth' expresses his feelings so personally, so accurately gives himself, that Yeats found what he wrote moving, and determined to make his own poetry 'the absolute speech of a man' (YT 30). Yeats again aligns himself with Browning's subjective poet when he insists on the necessity of there being a man behind the work:

> A poet is by the very nature of things a man who lives with entire sincerity, or rather the better his poetry the more sincere his life; his life is an experiment in living and those that come after have a right to know it. Above all it is necessary that the lyric poet's life should be known that we should understand that his poetry is no rootless flower but the speech of a man.[80]

Yeats first wrote about the importance of personal utterance in an 1897 review.[81] In a lecture given in 1902 he uses a phrase similar to that of Wordsworth, after quoting Archilogus:

> Well, we cannot write with that simplicity, that sincerity, for we live in a more complicated and a less friendly world. We have to hide our lives from one another, but we can at least write passionately, not as mere scholars, mere spectators of life. We can at least speak as men to men, out of our own experience, out of our own passions, though we may have to change the circumstance.[82]

Wordsworth's preface to *Lyrical Ballads* is echoed again here, as it is in 'The Watts Pictures':

> [P]oets were men who were content to express the sensations and experiences which they themselves received, being face to face with the world. They were men of finer sensations, and more settled experiences than others, and they gave us simply those sensations and experiences. (UP2 343)

Wordsworth has: 'He is a man speaking to men: a man, it is true, endowed with more lively sensibility.'[83]

Yeats indicates the necessity of the involvement of art with life and a necessary limitation of that involvement, for which he holds the lack of simplicity of the modern world responsible. The disengagement involved in Yeats's move to a more elitist position is a defence against the qualities of the modern world which he deplores. The preposition, 'men *to* men', which Eliot changes to 'for' in *his* borrowing from Wordsworth, shows how Yeats seeks to recapture the directness of address he associates with the spoken word. The detachment of art from life is associated with the move away from oral culture:

> It is because of the written book, in which we speak always to strangers and never with a living voice to friends, that we have lost personal utterance. Hardly anyone now puts himself into his book; hardly anyone dramatises himself, and instead of it all we have got the abstract poet, living nowhere, a man wandering in the void, in the indefinite, a philosopher and scholar, a saint, even, anything you will, but not a man full of passions, not incarnate life. And it is because of this loss of the sense of personality that we have lost drama. When man cannot dramatise himself, he cannot dramatise anybody. (YA8 91)

Another 1902 lecture emphasizes the connection of the artist's work with his life. It also indicates that the artist should aim to live the sort of life which will give him the necessary material for his art:

> The dramatist, if he is to set passions upon the stage, must become himself passionate, he must learn to love intensely, and to hate intensely, he must learn to cry out in his bitterness and to quench the cry in silence or to speak it as the cold precept of art requires. (YA8 96)

Letters from Yeats to his father again refer to the idea of personality:

> The doctrine of the group [the Rhymers' Club], or rather of the majority of it, was that lyric poetry should be personal. That a man should express his life and do this without shame or fear. Ernest Dowson did this and became a most extraordinary poet, one feels the pressure of his life behind every line. (L 548, 16 February 1910)

> I probably get the distinction from the stage, where we say a man is a 'character actor' meaning that he builds up a part out of observation, or we say that he is 'an emotional actor' meaning that he

builds it up out of himself, and in this last case – we always add, if he is not commonplace – that he has personality. (L 549, 23 February 1910)

The implication of the last comment is that the actor must possess unusual qualities as a person, that is to say in his own life, if he is to have the resources to build his role in the subjective way the letter associates with tragedy and values more highly than the objective way in which the 'character actor' builds his role. In the comment on Dowson, and that from the 1902 lecture on the dramatist, there is the suggestion that the life must be such that it is barely contained by the form of expression: the material must make its passion evident almost in spite of the form. The idea of the containment of heat within coldness is one associated by Lionel Johnson with Parnell: 'What miracles and marvels of self-repression must have been his, who, with this fire of feeling in him, was so long its master, that the world thought him austerely cold and hardly human!'[84]

Yeats's lecture tour of the United States between November 1903 and March 1904, efficiently organized by the New York lawyer John Quinn, was a tremendous success. A letter of 27 November 1903 to Lady Gregory tells of an overflowing audience in Philadelphia, though he believed he 'spoke only fairly well' (CL3 476). Another of 8 December tells of a packed hall at Bryn Mawr College (CL3 482). A letter to George Brett of 8 March 1904 notes that he spoke to over 64 colleges and literary societies on the US tour. The estimated audience for his last lecture, at the New York Academy of Music, was four to four and a half thousand, and Quinn's estimate of the total audience figure for the tour was twenty-five to thirty thousand (CL3 555). The tour earned Yeats $3,230.40.[85]

Foster notes also the effects of the tour on Yeats's personality, that it increased his self-confidence, helped him to become an orator.[86] The tour was demanding, but Yeats rose to the challenge. He also reflected on his performance and his lecturing style. Letters to Lady Gregory and to his sister Lily on 2 January 1904 indicate the thought he put into his style and his recognition of the different demands of different sized audiences (CL3 506 and 511). A letter to John Quinn of 19 January 1904 shows his sensitivity to audience, his recognition of differences in responsiveness (CL3 525). Evident in his letters while on the tour, along with the self-consciousness of the public speaker working at his craft, is the enormous enjoyment of engaging the attention of an audience and moving it. It seems to be his form of acting.[87] This is a perspective to add to Eliot's perspective of Yeats emerging to speak as a man to men. Yeats's theatricality, his sense of audience, his capacity for self-dramatization were put to service, practised and developed on the tour. As his self-confidence grew he rose to meet the approbation of his audiences. The tour helped Yeats to develop the power to create himself as an increasingly self-dependent, strong individual. Ernest Crosby, co-editor of the *Whim*, commented that he did not seem smaller than his work and had 'something of the magician in his person as well as in his pen' (CL3 552n3). This is a poet who has developed presence as a public speaker. That presence projects the public poems of *From 'The Green Helmet and Other Poems'* and *Responsibilities*. It also adds to and interacts with the figure of the poet created within the poems.

'Adam's Curse' (ISW 18-19) begins with a dramatized conversation, and brings the poet as a man into his work by making that conversation one that concerns the nature of his work. Further, it brings the idea of the poet's work into relation with the everyday world's idea of work as it addresses the mistake the world makes in believing poetry to be a matter of inspiration without labour. The shape of the poem reflects the emergence of beauty, the poetic image, from the more mundane level of the poet's labour as a man. It is as if there is a reversal of the stereotyped idea of inspiration flowing effortlessly into the poet's mind from some Platonic realm of beauty, the poetic material then to be rendered concrete in the act of forming complete poetry.

The concern which emerges at the close of the poem relates once more to the limitation of love in its mortal aspect, the passing away in this world of what had seemed perfection. Even the labour of 'the old high way of love' is not enough to save mortals from weariness. The moon as an image of love is worn away by the effects of time, as a shell by the movement of the tide. But the moon is also a symbol of the longing, incapable of satisfaction, for the perfection of the supernatural world where love is not limited by mortality. The contemplation of the image and symbol that the moon is leads to the emotion expressed in the poem's final stanza. This emotion blends the regretfulness at the impossibility of perfect love with a sense that if perfect love were possible, then somehow it would lose its desirability by the very fact of becoming attainable. Arthur Symons's comment on Dowson is apposite:

> In the case of Dowson, however, there was a sort of virginal devotion, as to a Madonna; and I think had things gone happily, to a

conventionally happy ending, he would have felt (dare I say?) that his ideal had been spoilt.[88]

According to Eliot, some romantic poetry involves consciousness of the necessity of hopelessness:

> Indeed, in much romantic poetry the sadness is due to the exploitation of the fact that no human relations are adequate to human desires, but also to the disbelief in any further object for human desires than that which, being human, fails to satisfy them.[89]

The limitation of the temporal world is as fundamental a curse as that of labour. Yeats's own view in the 1899 article 'The Literary Movement in Ireland' was: 'It may be that poetry is the utterance of desires that we can only satisfy in dreams, and that if all our dreams were satisfied there would be no more poetry.'[90] But maybe Yeats saw himself as escaping from this sense of hopelessness in the early years of the new century, even if this escaping Yeats was one constructed in later autobiographical writing:

> I think Dowson's best verse immortal ... but he was too vague and gentle for my affections. I understood him too well, for I had been like him but for the appetite that made me search out strong condiments. Though I cannot explain what brought others of my generation to such misfortune, I think that (falling backward upon my parable of the moon) I can explain some part of Dowson's and Johnson's dissipation: –
>
> > What portion in the world can the artist have
> > Who has awakened from the common dream
> > But dissipation and despair? (Au 312)

Eliot's comment that 'Adam's Curse' marks a moment of transition in Yeats's work, a moment when Yeats begins to *speak* as a man speaking for man draws attention to the growing importance to Yeats of orality. 'Adam's Curse' indicates the paradox involved in the modern poet's attempt to re-embrace orality. The conversational tone and the dramatizing of the poet *as* poet (actually at work) present the poem as personal utterance. This method of presentation attempts to give the living word via the dead medium of print. The poem also associates the fine old tradition of love with books. Of course, these are 'beautiful old books', works of art in their own right, not the mass-produced books of a print culture. Nevertheless, an aspiration of Yeats's poetic is suggested in this poem. He seeks to capture the sincere, personal utterance, the life of the spoken word, in a book. The paradox of death and life as represented by the two worlds raises itself again here. The spoken, living word can only survive as long as the exhalation of the breath in which it is spoken: it is transient, a dying word. As Walter Ong puts it: 'Sound exists only when it is going out of existence.'[91] Ong comments on the pressing of flowers in books:

> The dead flower, once alive, is the psychic equivalent of the verbal text. The paradox lies in the fact that the deadness of the text, its removal from the living human lifeworld, its rigid visual fixity, assures its endurance and its potential for being resurrected into limitless living contexts by a potentially infinite number of living readers.[92]

This takes us back to Baile and Aillinn, whose mortal love-affair became an eternal love with their death. The penultimate verse of the poem about them strengthens the idea of a connection between the eternal love available after death and the writing down of love-stories by poets. The poet participates in the immortalization of love. In balance with this, the immortal world of art demands the participation of the mortal world. The work draws on material supplied by the life. The presence of the poet's own mortal life in his work is what gives it passion, and the poet's life is forfeit to the demands of art: he must put his life at the disposal of his art.

VI

The marking by a 'lunar influence' of the lyrics of *In the Seven Woods* shows them to mark in turn a particular phase in Yeats's development. He comments on the symbolism of the sun and the moon in his 1904 preface to Lady Gregory's *Gods and Fighting Men*:

> Old writers had an admirable symbolism that attributed certain energies to the influence of the sun, and certain others to the lunar influence. To lunar influence belong all thoughts and emotions that were created by the community, by the common people, by nobody knows who, and to the sun all that came from the high disciplined or individual kingly mind.

while speculating on a sad longing associated with the moon:

> Is it because all that is under the moon thirsts to escape out of bounds, to lose itself in some unbounded tidal stream, that the songs of the folk are mournful, and that the story of the Fianna, whenever the queens lament for their lovers, reminds us of songs that are still sung in country-places? Their grief, even when it is to be brief like Grania's, goes up into the waste places of the sky.[93]

The linking of a further thought on lunar symbolism to sexual attraction in *Memoirs* carries a sinister suggestion of the fatal supernatural woman:

> All our lives long, as da Vinci says, we long, thinking it is but the moon that we long [for], for our destruction, and how, when we meet [it] in the shape of a most fair woman, can we do less than leave all others for her? Do we not seek our dissolution upon her lips?[94]

'Under the Moon' (ISW 21) maintains the tone of unhappiness continued from the narrative poems. Though he finds no happiness in his dreams of mythical lands, the poet claims initially that these 'seem too dim to be burdens on the heart'. His dreams are pervaded by the stories and talk of women from these lands who were disappointed in love. These dreams are manifestations of an emotion which Yeats thought was also expressed in many of the songs of the country people, an emotion which longs for dissipation in some vast space. The title of *Poems 1895* was to have been *Under the Moon*.[95] The negative implication of the poem 'Under the Moon' indicates that the link with his earlier poetry suggested by the title is, in a sense, established in order to be broken. The connection with Maud Gonne's revelation of her life with Millevoye seems strongest in this poem. Though this connection is disguised by the apparently nonsensical reference in later versions of the poem to 'the famished horn / Of the hunter's moon' (VP 210) (a hunter's moon is full), the version in the Dun Emer *In the Seven Woods* reads 'Because of a story I heard under the thin horn / Of the third moon ...'(ISW 21). Deirdre Toomey points out that the moon was in its third quarter on 8 December 1898, when Maud Gonne made her shattering revelation.[96] The dream on which so much earlier poetry was founded is no longer bearable. The woman who had been identified with the supernatural women to whom this poem refers had revealed herself, in what she told Yeats on that night in 1898, to be incontestably flesh and blood.

'The Withering of the Boughs' (ISW 17) was the first poem Yeats wrote after the break caused by Maud Gonne's revelations. The hint of Keats's 'La Belle Dame Sans Merci' in this poem indicates the presence of the former imaginative associations from which Yeats needed to shift his poetry, particularly that of the faery woman who lures mortals into the world of death or incapacity for action. Once more the theme is of the world in a sense parallel and opposite to this one, and of the effect of knowledge of such a parallel world on the inhabitants of this one. The poet longs for the birdsong absent from Keats's poem. In 'Baile and Aillinn', birdsong evokes the other world. The attitude to the other world is ambivalent. It is associated with a longing that, at some level of consciousness, the poet wishes to escape.

Also in the first stanza of 'The Withering of the Boughs' is the suggestion that the other world is evoked by weariness and dissatisfaction with this world, that it is, in effect, an expression of the emotion associated with such dissatisfaction and weariness. 'The Queen and the Fool' from *The Celtic Twilight* helps elucidate the poem's refrain:

> There is a war between the living and the dead, and the Irish stories keep harping upon it. They will have it that when the potatoes or the wheat or any other of the fruits of the earth decay, they ripen in faery, and that our dreams lose their wisdom when the sap rises in the trees, and that our dreams can make the trees wither, and that one hears the bleating of the lambs of faery in November, and that blind eyes can see more than other eyes.[97]

It is as if the desire manifested in the dream that calls into existence an otherness which could satisfy what the world is not sufficient to satisfy, is itself a cause of the wasting of the temporal world.

In its last stanza, the poem recalls 'Baile and Aillinn':

> I know of the sleepy country, where swans fly round
> Coupled with golden chains and sing as they fly,
> A king and a queen are wandering there, and the sound
> Has made them so happy and hopeless, so deaf and so blind
> With wisdom, they wander till all the years have gone by;
> I know, and the curlew and peewit on Echtge of streams. (ISW 17)

The singing that symbolizes the immortal love of Baile and Aillinn brings a wisdom divorced from the senses which give us knowledge of the world of appearances. In the final stanza of 'The Withering of the Boughs' this sort of wisdom is coupled with a hopeless happiness, another seeming contradiction, which perhaps means a happiness removed from the temporal consideration of what might happen in the future. The king and queen here are to exhaust time, rather than be exhausted by it, to 'wander till all the years have gone by'.

As the birds whose natural cries the poet longs for have been silenced by the moon's murmuring, so the poet has been silenced – though he begins his recovery in this poem – by his knowledge of the timeless world where an endless love is possible. His claim to know of this 'sleepy country' recalls the narrator of 'Rosa Alchemica':

> I repeated to myself the ninth key of Basilius Valentinus, in which he compares the fire of the last day to the fire of the alchemist, and the world to the alchemist's furnace, and would have us know that all must be dissolved before the divine substance, material gold or immaterial ecstasy, awake. I had dissolved indeed the mortal world and lived amid immortal essences, but had obtained no miraculous ecstasy.[98]

It is possible to see the poet of 'The Withering of the Boughs', and of 'Under the Moon', as a similar figure; one who has detached himself from the material world and yet failed to find satisfaction in the immaterial world into which he has projected himself. Yet Echtge is also the place where the poem was written in 1900. Echtge is the sleeping woman in the story of Red Hanrahan, but Echtge is also the mountain, Slieve Echtge, where Lady Gregory had a shooting lodge. The use of place is a means of the poet's tying himself into the mythology he both refers to and helps to form. Place links the poet with the other world of which he tells, and the poet himself constitutes the link between the material and immaterial worlds. The close connection of place and mythology prevents the detachment feared in 'Rosa Alchemica'. In a letter to Lady Gregory of February 1903, Yeats writes of advice he had received that his 'inspiration was from the moon' and that his work was becoming 'too full of those little jewelled thoughts that come from the sun and have no nation' (CL3 321). Lady Gregory had helped him to understand country life again, and more deeply, by gathering for him and going with him to gather stories from the local people, including those of Slieve Echtge.

The sense of completion which goes to make up an impossible perfection is given in 'The Rider from the North' (ISW 23–5), later renamed

'The Happy Townland', by coexistent pairings of gold and silver, red and brown beer, sun and moon. In a way, this poem's townland is a step beyond even the faery world, since its seasons are not merely opposed to those of this world but the seasons of fruit and flowering last all year. It is, though, a counterpart of the world. Reading 'bane' in the Blakean sense suggested by A. Norman Jeffares's note (YP 530), we might think of the townland as the manifestation of an energy reciprocal to the energy of which our world is a manifestation. Curiously, the force of the moon, earlier associated with longing for another world, is holding back the poet in his journey towards impossible perfection, plucking at his rein. The poem marks the possibility of the *vision* of impossible perfection in a way which fits with the sad longing, under the lunar influence, which characterizes the volume. The effect of knowledge of a world of impossible perfection on the material world of action is again treated here:

> It is lucky that their story
> Is not known among men.
> For O the strong farmers
> That would let the spade lie,
> For their hearts would be like a cup
> That somebody had drunk dry.[99]

The emptying effect of such knowledge recalls the hollow moon. But the overall effect of this poem is to mark the end of the volume with a note of cheerfulness, though as if the tone of sad longing were acknowledged rather than dismissed.

The sun here presents a joyful and positive image, which might lead us to look back at the opening poem, 'In the Seven Woods', to examine how it qualifies the tone of the volume. The poem suggests recovery from a mood of depression. Indeed, in January 1902 Yeats wrote to Lady Gregory of an improvement in spirits.[100] Hopeless revolt and disgust at vulgar materialism can be set aside because there is tranquillity to be found in the Seven Woods. We might say that, in the calmed and quietened mood the poem suggests, the emotion evoked in the tone of the rest of the volume can be valued without excessive nervous strain. But, more than this, contentment is deepened by the promise that the figure closing the poem seems to hold:

> while that Great Archer,
> Who but awaits His hour to shoot, still hangs
> A cloudy quiver over Parc-na-lee. (ISW 1)

Jeffares's note offers, 'Sagittarius, a hint of some revelation to come' (YP 525), for the 'Great Archer', but I think that the figure can be related to sun symbolism and so to the development of the poetry along with Yeats's mood at the time. The bow is the favourite weapon of Apollo, the sun god. The notes on Yeats's vision of the archer in *Autobiographies* (Au 576–9) connect Apollo, Sagittarius and trees. The notes state, 'Sagittarius. The symbol is an arrow shot into the unknown. It is a sign of Initiation and Rebirth.' This suggests an air of expectancy in 'In the Seven Woods' of a new phase for the poet. Recalling his twenty-second year, Yeats speaks of a message that he still does not understand, telling him that woods 'concentrate the solar ray' (Au 371). A quiver is part of an archer's equipment, but 'a cloudy quiver' also suggests a concealment, about to be broken, of the sun.

In terms of the life of the poet's psyche, we can see the opening poem as showing an awareness of the possibility of recovery, and the darker-toned part of the volume as the essential working through to expression of deep sadness. Yeats notes in the Dun Emer volume *In the Seven Woods: Being Poems Chiefly of the Irish Heroic Age* his sense of the change coming into his work, which he felt while thinking out the play *On Baile's Strand*. 'The first shape of it came to me in a dream, but it changed much in the making, foreshadowing, it may be, a change that may bring a less dream-burdened will into my verses' (ISW 25). A letter of his to John Quinn, dated 15 May 1903, repeats what he wrote to Russell of his view of *Ideas of Good and Evil*, and mentions the change of influence:

> I feel that much of it is out of my present mood. That it is true but no longer true for me. I have been in a good deal better health lately and that and certain other things has made me look upon the world I think with somewhat more defiant eyes. The book is, I think, too lyrical, too full of aspirations after remote things, too full of desires. Whatever I do from this out will, I think, be more creative. I will express myself so far as I express myself in criticism at all, by that sort of thought that leads straight to action, straight to some sort of craft. I have always felt that the soul has two movements primarily, one to transcend forms, and the other to create forms. Nietsche, to whom you have been the first to introduce me, calls these the Dionysic and the Apollonic respectively. I think I have to some extent got weary of that wild God Dionysius, and I am hoping that the Far-Darter will come in his place. (CL3 372)

Yeats's preface to *Gods and Fighting Men* is concerned with the symbolism of sun and moon in a way which is suggestive of the Apollonic and

Dionysian influences on art, and also of a Nietzschean political attitude:

> But in supreme art or in supreme life there is the influence of the sun too, and the sun brings with it, as old writers tell us, not merely discipline but joy; for its discipline is not of the kind the multitudes impose upon us by their weight and pressure, but the expression of the individual soul turning itself into a pure fire and imposing its own pattern, its own music, upon the heaviness and the dumbness that is in others and in itself.[101]

The sense of a reconnection with the inspiration of the moon through the reconnection with the folk that he refers to in the February 1903 letter to Lady Gregory is balanced here by an acknowledgement of the importance of the solar influence: the individual's disciplined crafting and joy. A later letter to Russell marks even more clearly Yeats's determination not to become bogged down in the sentimentality which he has come to realize threatens those who are excessively preoccupied with a mood of subjective sadness. It is possible for the best subjective poetry to rise:

> above sentiment to a union with a pure energy of the spirit but between this energy of the spirit, & the energy of the will out of which epic & dramatic poetry comes there is a region of brooding emotions full of fleshly waters & vapours which kill the spirit & the will, ecstasy & joy equally. Yet this region of shadows is full of false images of the spirit & of the body. I have come to feal towards it as O'Grady feals towards it some times & even a little as some of my own stupidest critics feal ... I cannot probably be quite just to any poetry that speaks to me with the sweet insinuating feminine voice of the dwellers in the country of shadows & hollow images. I have dwelt there too long not to dread all that comes out of it. We possess nothing but the will & we must never let the children of vague desire breath upon it nor the waters of sentiment rust the terrible mirror of its blade. (CL3 577, April 1904)

A similar embarrassment and impatience to that expressed in 'A Coat' in *Responsibilities* at a form of poetry that he considers himself to have moved on from is evident here. As in an earlier letter to Lady Gregory, he feels his work has become more masculine (CL3 303, 14 January 1903). Although this *could* be seen as part of a 'modernist' reaction against the feminization of poetry, Yeats seems to me driven by events in his own emotional and psychic life. I don't see the assimilation of this change to a retrospectively applied literary category as helpful. Notable too in the letter to Russell is the comment on his critics: Yeats is sensitive to the reception of his work. He may sound here dismissive of the stupid critics, but their suspicion of the mood represented by this region of shadows and brooding emotions is one he has come to share.[102]

W. K. Magee, who wrote as John Eglinton and with whom Yeats enjoyed rather stage-managed controversy, reviewed Yeats's *Ideas of Good and Evil* in 'The Philosophy of the Celtic Movement', which appeared in the *United Irishman* on 27 June 1903 (CL3 342n3). Magee notes Yeats's opposition of reason to imagination and the arts. He also notes: 'The breach between poetry and modern life [Yeats] holds to be absolute and permanent.'[103] The modern world treats poetry with indulgence rather than seriousness, Magee thinks:

> the poet, who represents in a nation far on into its full maturity, its early beliefs and make-believe reality, shuns in these days the paths of actuality, and seeks the twilight haunts of memory and shadows. And thus poetry, though treated with indulgence and consideration, falls in our own time into some contempt: the poet insisting that these memories and shadows are the only real, or at least the most real things, and the ordinary man, when the poet is out of earshot, allowing his opinion on the matter to explode in noisy and good-humoured merriment. (45)

Yeats's letter to Russell shows that he was not deaf to the warning for poetry that Magee puts forward here. I don't want to suggest that Yeats falls into line with Magee's view, but rather that he is sensitive to it.

> Yet there are realities hidden away in the life of each man; and unless the poet can resolutely fix on these, affirming to those who prefer the excitements of the market-place to the dreams of the study, a reality deeper than either, he must seem to the practical man much as a child floating bulrushes on the duck-pond to the mariner whose 'beard in many a tempest has been shook'. (45)

Yeats's sense in *Discoveries* of the need to ascend from the thoughts of the marketplace, but not too far, is different, but shares a belief in maintaining a level of inclusiveness. Magee looks to poetry to appeal to something deeper in the materialist rather than alienating him by pure difference. Yeats looks to carry with him into his personality as a poet some of his personality as a man engaged with the world. In his difference with Magee he is able to find something which helps him clarify to himself the transition in his own thinking.

Some critics attribute much of the development of Yeats's work to the influence of Nietzsche.[104] The argument for a particularly significant Nietzschean influence tends to depend on an initially strong reaction by Yeats to his reading of Nietzsche at the time John Quinn helped awaken his interest, during and immediately after his visit to Coole in the late summer of 1902. Towards the end of that year Quinn sent Yeats copies of *Thus Spake Zarathustra*, *The Case of Wagner* and *The Genealogy of Morals*.[105] Quinn's own account of the visit indicates Yeats's interest in Nietzsche: 'I remember how interested he became in a volume of Nietzsche that I had with me, and how in reading out from it he quickly pointed out the resemblance of some of Nietzsche's ideas to Blake.'[106]

Quinn's article was written in 1911, and, although immediately after this passage he recalls that Yeats had just written 'In the Seven Woods', much of the article has an iterative tone, suggesting that more than one visit is in his mind. It seems likely that after the passage of several years, different meetings and conversations and correspondence with Yeats had become confused in his memory; the article is not sufficiently reliable to fix Yeats's first direct encounter with Nietzsche in the late summer of 1902. Quinn's wondering in his letter to Yeats mentioning that he has mailed him some Nietzsche whether Yeats was acquainted with Nietzsche's work supports this view. In any case, Yeats *had* read Thomas Common's translation of the first part of *Thus Spake Zarathustra* before receiving Quinn's copy of the complete translation, but this contains only 36 pages.[107]

The argument of critics who detect the sudden appearance of Nietzschean influence in Yeats's work in 1902 is undermined by the fact that Havelock Ellis wrote three articles on Nietzsche for *The Savoy*, a magazine in which Yeats's work also appeared.[108] The magazine's editor, Arthur Symons, shows the sort of thinking which is in part reflected in Yeats's eventual move towards a more aristocratic position:

> The world is becoming more and more democratic, and with democracy art has nothing to do. What is written for the crowd goes to the crowd; it lives its bustling day there, and is forgotten, like to-day's newspaper to-morrow.[109]

Yeats's own comments on the transience of immediate popularity indicate that, at least in 1902, he did not intend permanently to limit his audience to a few:

> He [the serious artist] appeals to a small appreciative audience which gradually grows larger and larger until perhaps one sees his picture or his book in the window of a hundred shops. He is proud of this slow certain winning over the public mind, and perhaps contrasts himself with those painters and novelists with less serious aims who come into an immediate popularity and are soon forgotten. (YA8 92)

Yeats sought with his verse-speaking project to appeal to a growing number of people, over the head of the popular products of English-influenced, mass-society art. His increasing detachment from the mass nationalist movement, and his disillusionment with what he saw as the increasing materialism of Irish society were to drive him into an increasingly isolated position, and a greater identification with the aristocracy.[110]

The presence of ideas too readily accepted as exclusively Nietzschean in writers such as Blake and Pater, with whom Yeats was extremely familiar, and the availability to him of Nietzschean ideas through the *Savoy* articles go a long way towards explaining his enthusiastic reception of Nietzsche in 1902.[111] What is more, it seems likely that he would have found Nietzsche congenial to his particular mood. The element of brutality, of the 'Yahoo', in Nietzsche may well have appealed to a mood generated by the attempt to recover from low spirits, and a determination that such recovery was possible.[112] Yeats's references to Nietzsche are not sufficient demonstration of the extent of influence sometimes claimed. His comment to Quinn that he did not 'go all the journey with [Nietzsche]' suggests to me that the critic should be cautious, rather than defensiveness in Yeats due to anxiety of influence. The eclectic thinker is selective, taking and assimilating what appeals to, and fits with, the growing pattern that forms his personality. Analysis of the development of Yeats's work in this period will be misleading if it treats too much in isolation any of the impulses which drive, or the influences which affect, that development.

When Maud Gonne detected the influence of Nietzsche in a 'Celtic rite' Yeats had read to her, she objected in a way that comments astutely:

> *for Neiche is not Celtic*, though his intense individualism & his rushing fiery paradox & his impatience & his contempt for the *banalité* & smallness of the many useless ones, appeal to us – Neiche's central thought seems to be to do away with the Gods, &

to reverence & to recognise nothing greater than himself, this is most contrary to Celtic thought. (GYL 169, 7 May 1903)

There is a bracing ferocity in Nietzsche which is inspiriting, even for those who cannot 'go the whole journey'. Yeats's fellow-Rhymer Ernest Rhys shows a similar reaction to Yeats's:

> [B]ut at that time – in the disruptive nineties – Nietzsche took his place with Wagner, Ibsen, Whitman, William Morris, and Tolstoi as among the rousing revolutionary influences. We did not necessarily accept his ideas, but we felt their powerfully stimulating challenging effect.[113]

Gonne's description of Nietzsche's central thought recognising nothing greater than himself is most pertinent. If Yeats were successfully to oppose a subjective way of thinking to the objective materialism of his age, and to work to heal the separation of poetry from life by the restoration of personality to poetry, then the necessary subjectiveness of his poetics must not be allowed to slip into mere egotism or solipsism.

The presence of the poet dramatized within his work, the presentation of the poems as personal utterance, recognizes the importance of an audience, of reaching out beyond oneself to others, of communication. Further, Yeats's commitment to traditional forms as a means of distancing himself from the merely contingent shows his conviction that personality is the key to personal expression that marks common humanity rather than celebrating difference as character does. The importance of the dramatized poetic figure guaranteeing the presence of both quotidian and imagined worlds within the work would become yet clearer in *Responsibilities*. The relationship between the two worlds and the claims of the imagined world and its effect on the quotidian world are a special concern of *In the Seven Woods*. This symbolizes the immanence of the intemporal within the temporal of which Yeats felt his own society was unaware. The infusion of the world associated with desire and longing into the temporal world marks a conviction that the world in which we live must not be allowed to become an object, but must be connected with our longings and desires – animated by them – if it is to remain capable of sustaining genuine, passionate life, rather than merely material existence.

3
From 'The Green Helmet and Other Poems'

I

The poems in this volume were originally presented under two subtitles: 'Raymond Lully and His Wife Pernella' and 'Momentary Thoughts'. This division draws attention to the private–public dynamic of the volume. The first subtitle is esoteric, restrictive. This restriction is a matter of audiences; there is an audience of insiders who will understand. Indeed, Maud Gonne pointed out to Yeats that he had mistakenly used Lully's name when he meant Nicolas Flamel.[1] This section contains poems which mark a renewed closeness in Yeats's relationship with Maud Gonne when their spiritual marriage was restored. The alchemist Nicolas Flamel's wife Pernella, herself an adept, was supposed to share his skill. The story told of the couple is that both, after their apparent death, faked funerals, and were reunited to live on for the thousand years that is the usual span of the adept.[2] The paralleling by Yeats of his relationship with Maud Gonne with the marriage of Flamel and Pernella suggests that this relationship has a significance to him greater than that of the ordinary life contained within the normal span. The naming of this section is, then, a way of projecting the poet and his ideal partner into legend. This is done rather secretively, through reference to an obscure, occultist couple. The poet's expression of himself is guarded, the allusion restrictive, reflecting his sense of the need for a greater discipline in expression and a narrowing of his audience. This shows Yeats's consciousness of the increasingly marginalized nature of his position in Ireland at this time.

Yeats's use of Flamel and Pernella can be traced back to 1891, the time of Maud Gonne's initiation into the Golden Dawn, the Rosicrucian society of which he was a member. He almost always refers to her by her Golden Dawn initials, P.I.A.L. (*Per Ignem Ad Lucem* – through fire to the light), and does so in the journal he kept at the time he was writing the Flamel and Pernella sequence of poems, even though she was only a member of the order for a short time, leaving because she perceived links with Freemasonry.[3] In 1891 she needed consolation after the death of her son Georges.[4] Yeats felt her need of his friendship and thought that this would become love. The tone of his draft autobiography makes his talk of Flamel and Pernella and the steering of Maud Gonne into the Golden Dawn seem part of a strategy for her capture. 'I had even as I watched her a sense of cruelty, as though I were a hunter taking captive some beautiful wild creature' (Mem 49).

In using the partnership of Flamel and Pernella, Yeats had taken up the desert theme of an earlier dream of Maud Gonne's, in which she and Yeats, in a previous incarnation, were brother and sister 'somewhere on the edge of the Arabian desert, and sold together into slavery' (Mem 46). Yeats wrote a poem about the dream, 'Cycles Ago: In memory of your dream one July night', in October 1891, and this was copied into *The Flame of the Spirit*, a slim manuscript book which was given to Maud Gonne as a love token.[5]

It is possible to see in this part of the draft autobiography the battle building between Yeats and Maud Gonne over the terms of their relationship. Maud Gonne wanted Yeats's friendship, but introduced the idea of brother and sister. She claimed the depth of a relationship which transcended the ordinary lifetime but in which sex was prohibited. Her reason for not marrying was her relationship with the French politician Lucien Millevoye. Yeats drew on the story of Flamel and Pernella to develop *his* desert idyll of a marriage where the most important of work, the secret art, was shared.

The idea of attaching Maud Gonne more deeply to him through a sharing of occult work, while not exactly a weapon which was turned against him, *was* something to which she could appeal when she needed more attention from him:

> I wish you would write to me – I am doing a good deal of occult work just now & get visions sometimes which I don't understand & which when I have not heard from you for some time & know every thing is well trouble me. (GYL 254, 8 April 1908)

Her letter to Yeats dated 26 June 1908 indicates that she sees a change in their relationship after his recent visit to her in Paris, a change which goes beyond a rapprochement between old friends who had fallen out. There is a note, too, of her sense of the opportunity that their relationship offers, an opportunity associated with occult knowledge:

> I think a most wonderful thing has happened – the most wonderful I have met with in life. If we are only strong enough to hold the doors open I think we shall obtain knowledge & life we have never dreamed of. (GYL 256)

Yeats's side of the correspondence is missing, but it seems that he wanted their relationship to be a physical one, whereas she did not. She seems to have believed that if they could avoid the physical element of love they could avoid the material end of the union caused by death. One could, of course, read this as a kind of staving off of Yeats's desire for physical intimacy. In a letter about William Sharp and Fiona Macleod she comments on the influence on one's work of spiritual force:

> to one's imagination that spiritual force may seem to reflect round or almost incarnate in some individual but I should think any attempt at realising a material union on this plain would destroy everything. (GYL 236, 21 January 1907)

But the relationship is obviously far more complex than the stereotype of man chasing woman for her body, woman just wanting to be friends. Deirdre Toomey's essay 'Labyrinths' provides a useful corrective in indicating Yeats's own possible evasions.[6] The letters hint at a perhaps unconscious fear of losing her poet to another woman who might offer the physical satisfaction she finds so difficult to provide. But she also promotes her relationship with him above any conventional relationship he might subsequently enter into:

> That struggle is over & I have found peace. I think today I could let you marry another without losing it – for I know the spiritual union between us will outlive this life, even if we never see each other in this world again. (GYL 259, December 1908)

Yeats was having a 'vigorously physical relationship' with Mabel Dickinson in 1908.[7] Terence Brown notes that Gonne

> seems to have been able to discern when Yeats was sexually active ... choosing at such moments to engage with him at a level which would give him pause, would keep him in thrall to his idea of her.[8]

Maud Gonne's letter to Yeats of 26 July 1908 tells of an astral experience in which she and Yeats share a union which she is anxious to stress is not at all physical. Her sense of a difference between Yeats's needs and her own is evident in her description of the dream conversation she has with him after the vision, in which Yeats says the vision 'would tend to increase physical desire' (GYL 257). Jeffares suggests that Yeats and Maud Gonne did finally sleep together in Paris in December, though Deirdre Toomey indicates June.[9] The letters can support either interpretation. She refers to something wonderful having happened after the June visit, and, as Jeffares claims, there is a 'change in the tone of Maud's letters' from December on, though the letter written after their parting in December again indicates her emphasis on the spiritual side of their relationship. The attempt to persuade in this letter becomes almost coercive:

> I have prayed so hard to have all earthly desire taken from my love for you & dearest, loving you as I do, I have prayed & I am praying still that the bodily desire for me may be taken from you too. I know how hard & rare a thing it is for a man to hold spiritual love when the bodily desire is gone & I have not made these prayers without a terrible struggle ... (GYL 258, December 1908)

Maud Gonne's idea of a spiritual union with Yeats is her means of coming to terms with the difficulties of their relationship. Her letters show her strong affection for him, and her need of him. The sequence title 'Nicolas Flamel and His Wife Pernella' associates these poems closely with the 1908–9 phase of the relationship, when their spiritual marriage was renewed, and shows evidence of Yeats's own attempts to come to terms with it. This group of poems sets up an iconic figure associated with Maud Gonne, and the allusion of the group title suggests that this figure is complementary to the poet in the creation of his work.

In the sense that she is, for Yeats, his ideal partner, Maud Gonne is a completion of himself. This is something he expresses in astrological terms in the 1909 journal:

> There is an astrological sense in which a man's wife or sweetheart is always an Eve made from a rib of his body. She is drawn to him because she represents a group of stellar influences on the radical horoscope. These influences also create an element in his character and his destiny, in things apart from love or marriage. Whether this element be good or evil she is therefore its external expression.[10]

The image of nobility which Maud Gonne represents for the poet is one that he needs for his work. For him, art should not just reflect reality, but rather reflect onto the real world an imaginative image of what that world might be: an image of aspiration. In this view of the relationship between the artist and the world, the world gives the artist an inspirational figure which he then imaginatively transforms into an image worthy of the world's imitation. The journal points to a connection between Yeats's idea of love between man and woman and the relationship between the artist and the world:

> In wise love each divines the high secret self of the other and, refusing to believe in the mere daily self, creates a mirror where the lover or the beloved sees an image to copy in daily life. Love also creates the mask. (Mem 145)

The idea of the necessity to poetry of the establishment of an ideal image forms a link between this group of poems and the conception of patronage suggested in 'Upon a House shaken by the Land Agitation' in the 'Momentary Thoughts' group of poems: 'Perhaps we may find in the spectacle of some beautiful woman our Ferrara, our Urbino. Perhaps that is why we have no longer any poetry but the poetry of love.' (Mem 156).

Coole, Lady Gregory's house, where Yeats spent so much time, was to become another image through which he could realize the world and express his mind. But much of this first group of poems looks back on the relationship with Maud Gonne and its effect on his work. It moves on in 'Against Unworthy Praise' to allow her to suggest an attitude for the poet to strive to adopt towards the contemptible part of the world, so that he can take strength from a re-envisioning and placing of the past in order to move into the future.

II

'A Woman Homer Sung' (VP 254–5) deals in its first stanza with the youthful poet's feelings towards Maud Gonne, demanding the world's recognition of her beauty, yet loving with an intensity that instantly leads to jealousy. The non-requital of his love leads to its being turned inwards and into his writing, 'I wrote and wrought', so that it intensifies still further. The second stanza deals with the image of Maud Gonne that the maturing mind has created from the intensifying youthful feelings, an image that is given to future readers of the work. The final stanza projects this image back into the actual past to complete the process wherein the figure first given to the poet by the natural world is transformed by imagination and reflected back onto the world through the work. The comparison with Helen of Troy emphasizes that the flesh-and-blood Maud Gonne has been mythologized.[11] The figure that the intensification of his thought has created and projected into the past – created in his memory – promotes the life and the work which celebrate her to the heroic, but to 'an heroic dream': this figure has a reality which throws into doubt the reality of 'life and letters'.

The relationship between the actual and the creation of the poet's imagination is central to this group of poems. As Mark Freeman points out, memories are *acts* not *things*; they are 'permeated by present consciousness',[12] and involve a present act of the imagination which presents (or makes present) the past in a way which makes it intelligible now. According to Freeman, 'Memory ... which often has to do not merely with recounting the past but with making sense of it – from 'above' as it were – is an interpretive act the end of which is an enlarged understanding of the self.'[13] Yeats here is presenting the world with an image of what it has lost. His growing disenchantment with a modernizing Ireland leads to his casting himself – writing himself – as the poet of older values, older consciousness.

'Words' offers a more practical reason why Maud Gonne is essential to Yeats's work, and its earlier title, 'The Consolation', helps explain it. Art may involve an attempt to justify itself to life. Life needs and seeks no such justification, but its indifference to this impulse of art's stimulates the creation of art. Also, the poet's unhappy relationship forms the resistance that it is necessary for life to offer the artist, against which he struggles and so creates art. Maud Gonne's rejection of Yeats's proposal in 1902 shows a rather brutal awareness of this necessary resistance: 'you make beautiful poetry out of what you call your unhappiness and you are happy in that. Marriage would be such a dull affair. Poets should never marry'.[14] However, a letter from her to Yeats in 1911 has a more attractive idea of hers about his poems: 'Our children were your poems of which I was the Father sowing the unrest & storm which made them possible & you the mother who brought them forth in suffering ...'[15] It is the necessity of being understood and the failure to be understood that drive the poet to the level of expression that creates his art. The note of regret evident in the last two lines of 'Words' indicates the tension Yeats sees between art and life:

> I might have thrown poor words away
> And been content to live. (VP 256)

For him, the artist must be separated from life, which is what he celebrates: he cannot be thoughtless and instinctive since art demands sufficient separation from life for the artist to be able to contemplate it.

There is in these poems a sense of acceptance. 'Words', 'No Second Troy', and 'Reconciliation' are particularly closely knit by this. There is a progression of thought that suggests a sequence within the overall sequence of the section. The wistful tone of the artist denied participation in life but allowed the consolation of creativity is followed by the refusal to blame which implies that blame has been considered, and finally by reconciliation.

The opening of 'No Second Troy', 'Why should I blame her ... ?', has something more positive than an acceptance of the sadness caused by the earlier relationship. 'Words' has shown how the nature of the relationship was necessary to the writing of the poetry; 'No Second Troy' presents Maud Gonne as an appropriate poetic image for the modern world, appropriate because she is not natural to it. The solitariness the poet finds in her nature, for instance, does not fit with an increasingly democratic age. Yeats's comment on Burns in his journal makes the point that, for him, art is not a mere reflection of the age: 'When a country produces a man of genius he never is what it wants or believes it wants, he is always unlike its idea of itself' (Mem 223).

The poet of genius will have to wait for, to some extent create, his popular audience.[16] Yeats's real subject in this passage is Synge, who he claims spoke for all that was repressed in the Ireland of his time. 'No Second Troy' makes Maud Gonne a symbol of the nobility of a passed heroic age, and so establishes an image to which the present might aspire, or at least points to a lack within the present age. There is a sense in which both Synge and Maud Gonne (increasingly the poet's creation rather than the flesh-and-blood woman) in their simplicity and solitariness, represent a closeness to life, an instinctive way of living, which has been lost to an analytical, abstracted age. The art that is created by Synge and the art that is created through the use of Maud Gonne as an image point to what the world they are created for lacks, and what that world might strive towards in order to complete itself. Art and the world are complementary here; art fills the space that growing abstraction leaves. Not only was it necessary for Maud Gonne to act as she did, being out of place in the age in which she existed, but, in order for her to fulfil her function as symbol for the poet, it was necessary for her to be so out of place, essentially anachronistic. On a more personal level, perhaps the placing of such an active and violent image of Gonne in the past was a way in which she could be rendered less threatening.[17]

'Reconciliation' indicates that Yeats felt a revivification of his poetic imagination through the renewal of the spiritual marriage and presumably from the introduction of sex to their relationship. Though in his 1909 journal Yeats gives eight lines of this poem, saying that it was written about six months previously, these lines are followed by more composition (Mem 172–4). So although the poem's closing lines suggest particularly strongly that they followed the relationship's becoming physical, counting back from the journal entry is not a reliable way to date the affair. Foster points to 'Reconciliation', whose composition he dates August or September 1908, as indicating that Yeats and Gonne's 'reconciliation went beyond the spiritual.' But he cites good evidence for the pair's becoming lovers in December.[18]

Blame has shifted to become something that others may have considered: 'Some may have blamed you'. Maud Gonne is a living symbol of the age of heroism and nobility for which he has been forced to use dead symbols which can now be consigned to the pit. '[T]he world lives as long ago', that is, the world that died when she went from him is restored. But further, the heroic age that he tried to look back to with the help of 'helmets, crowns, and swords' is brought to life for him by the return of his living symbol for it (VP 257). Yet the poem's closing tone is ambivalent: there is a note of fear that the chilling effect of the lifelessness of the poet's thought while lacking his living symbol has a permanent aspect, irremediable even by her return.

A comment from a letter to Lady Gregory of 6 May 1903 hints at a more personal level to the sense of displacement in time in 'No Second Troy': 'I feal somehow that the Maud Gonne I have known so long has passed away' (CL3 359). This comment is closer in time to the poems of *In the Seven Woods* and relates to Yeats's enforced realization of her humanity and to his recognition of the marks on her of painful experience. 'Reconciliation' suggests the renewal of what was taken away by Maud Gonne's marriage to John MacBride. Together with 'No Second Troy' and 'A Woman Homer Sung', though, it looks back to an even earlier version of Maud Gonne. One might say that this earlier version has been subsumed by the image of her created in the poems. It has also been overtaken by the events of her life. The reassimilation of the flesh-and-blood Maud Gonne to the figure who maintains such a strong grip on his imagination is impossible, no matter how intimate and affectionate the relationship becomes between the Yeats and the flesh-and-blood Maud Gonne who exist in 1908. The movement from celebration to anxiety and sadness in 'Reconciliation' also marks a recognition of the belatedness of the new intimacy in their relationship.

'King and No King' (VP 258) takes up the theme of the nature of love in the temporal world and love after death which is also found in the narrative poems of *In the Seven Woods: Being Poems Chiefly of the Irish Heroic Age* and *Responsibilities*. By her 'faith' Yeats means Maud Gonne's Catholicism, to which she converted shortly before her marriage to John MacBride. But he could be referring also to her conviction that their union, if maintained as a spiritual one, can outlast their physical death. His doubt over what the form of a relationship beyond death might take is shown as he wonders if the chance of such a relationship justifies the sacrifice of a conventionally physical one in this world.

The poem alludes to Beaumont and Fletcher's play, *King and No King*, in which a king falls in love with his sister and then discovers that she is not his sister after all, and is able to marry her. Since the play deals with the prohibition of love because supposedly incestuous, the allusion suggests Maud Gonne's desert dream of 1891 in which she and Yeats, in a previous incarnation, were brother and sister. The poem, then, looks back to 1891 and her refusal of Yeats's proposal. Jeffares suggests that the 'pledge' to which the poem refers could possibly be 'some vow Maud Gonne took not to marry in view of her relationship with ... Millevoye' (YP 534). If so, it would have been this pledge that defeated the chance of happiness with Yeats and led to the subsequent misery of her marriage to MacBride. In a sense, it is this pledge which leads to the failure of their physical relationship of 1908, since this relationship follows the disaster with MacBride and is simply too late. The poem suggests resignation, an acceptance that the possibility of happiness was lost long ago, though such resignation is harder for him because he doubts the superiority of what the spiritual relationship offers in the future compared with what marriage would have offered in the past. This resignation matches an air of fatalism in the earlier poem, 'Cycles Ago'.[19] His spirit was awaiting an incarnation of itself and Maud Gonne's spirit into a world and time where they could be together. Yet the needs of their present incarnations are incompatible, so that the coincidence of their incarnation becomes merely ironic: love passes them by 'unheeding'. From the poet's point of view, the purpose of this incarnation, this world, was to bring the two together as lovers. Her presence brings the world into full existence and at the same time destroys it, since her different needs mean that they cannot be lovers:

> My world was fallen and over, for your dark soft eyes on it shone;
> A thousand years it had waited and now it is gone, it is gone.[20]

'Cycles Ago' and 'King and No King' highlight the incompatibility of immortal and mortal worlds, where immortal love can be defeated by circumstance or, more sceptically, by the fact that the needs and wishes of a real woman may refuse to accommodate themselves to the model required by the poet's imagination.

The pledge relates more directly to Maud Gonne's marriage to John MacBride. As she explained to Yeats later and he relayed in a letter to Lady Gregory, Millevoye had caused her some embarrassment in Paris where people did not realize their relationship was over. He had also visited Iseult (his and Gonne's daughter) with an actress he was seeing. She wanted to 'make a final breach' with Millevoye and also make it impossible for him to visit. This was her reason for marrying MacBride, 'in a sudden impulse of anger' (CL3 356, 5 May 1903). The 'anger' makes a clear link with 'King and No King'.

Yeats had been devastated by her decision to marry MacBride.[21] But Gonne had made clear in her reply to the letter expressing his dismay her wish to maintain their friendship (GYL 166, 10 February 1903). The conventional view of Yeats as constantly in pursuit of the unattainable Maud Gonne and writing out his unrequited love in poems seems unsatisfactory in the light of increasingly available biographical detail. Her affection for him and need of his friendship is evident in her letters to him. As her marriage broke down she called on him for support. Foster's reading of the relationship includes a sense of Maud Gonne's pulling Yeats back to her when at times he was recovering nicely.[22]

Florence Farr's comments, as reported by Nevinson, bring out the irony of Maud Gonne's decision to marry. But they also indicate ambivalence in Yeats. Farr may subscribe to the unrequited love theory of inspiration, but she also suggests that Yeats has a sense of having recovered from something debilitating:

> Told me of Maud Gonne's longing for children, & how she had two by Millevoi, the first dying. How she married McBride to keep Millevoi away from the house; how McB in drunkenness ravished the servants & even the little girl. That great, fair woman! Yeats is

> rather disgusted now at her past. For 10 years he possessed the romantic love – now he shudders at it & is terrified lest it come again. Yet it was the secret of his power.[23]

In her comment on the 1908 affair, Farr again subscribes to the same theory of inspiration, telling Nevinson

> of Yeats & how in Paris lately Maud Gonne had at last given in & told him she had really loved him all these 15 years. That he has made his vain affection the chief string of his poetry, & now he is happy, the string snaps![24]

Even at second hand, one detects in Farr's account the amused irony of someone with a more robust attitude to affairs than Maud Gonne or Yeats, which cautions against relying too heavily on her testimony. Yeats himself believed at this time that Maud Gonne wanted to marry him, but could not because of the unlikelihood of obtaining a divorce, so would settle for friendship, noticing also her sadness. Foster detects 'a certain evasion, reminiscent of their passages in 1898' and adds: 'She was never more attractive to him than in these transient moods of affectionate submissiveness.'[25] She is attractive in these moods, perhaps, because she is less threatening, and because she threatens less to inspire the return of 'the romantic love' Yeats fears. If she has power in the relationship at this time, she has it through showing dependence. Whether she eventually rejected the physical relationship with Yeats only because she could not marry him seems pointless to ask; Yeats has his own ambivalence and equivocation which make the relationship more complex.

The note of regret in 'King and No King' continues into the next poem, 'Peace' (VP 258–9), though with more calm and a more complete sense of resignation. The poem was written at Maud Gonne's house at Colleville. Extending the sequence associated with the visit to Paris we might see 'King and No King' as the response to the failure of a relationship which included sex, and 'Peace' as a fatalistic acceptance of the inevitability of this failure. The first sentence, actually an exclamation, lacking an exclamation mark, becomes more a regretful sigh. The thought in this poem has a similarity with that in 'The Old Age of Queen Maeve', that is, that supernatural beauty and nobility are subject to ageing when incarnated into the temporal world. It also recalls 'The Arrow' (from *In the Seven Woods*) in the idea of the change that comes to such beauty with time. The section in quotation marks gives the younger poet's view of Maud Gonne. We might set the younger and more mature views against another opposition: the Dionysian and Apollonian.

> 'Were not all her life but storm,
> Would not painters paint a form
> Of such noble lines ... ?' (VP 259)

suggests an impossibility of containing the wildness of this figure within artistic form. Age, as in 'The Arrow', has had a humanizing effect, which is a matter for some regret, but nevertheless, in bringing peace to the storm, makes the figure more containable. At least in this poem, the poet sees his muse, humanized by the effect of time, moving with him out of formless Dionysian wildness into the more human expression of Apollonian artistic form.

The last poem in the section, 'Against Unworthy Praise' (VP 259–60), is linked with the first of the 'Momentary Thoughts' section by the use of the 'knave' and 'dolt' and reference to the theatre. The poem's idea of partnership in secrecy recalls the occultist couple, Flamel and Pernella. His muse's nobility is something that the poet can draw on to become noble himself. Again the idea from Yeats's 1909 journal on the love between man and woman is relevant: the reflection of the beloved's expectation as an image to which one aspires can generate increasing nobility. The dream recalls that of the poet in 'A Woman Homer Sung', in that it intensifies to the point where something is created from apparent barrenness (the cry of the wilderness). The essential quality of the work, the intensifying dream, exists between only two proud people. The poem concerns the problem of the relationship of art to the world of ordinary people. If art is addressed to the modern world directly, seeks to please a mass audience of the time, it risks becoming too much a part of that world, a mere reflection of it. With an aloofness of attitude typical of this stage of Yeats's development, this poem seems addressed to an audience of only one. Yeats wants his work to be set above the modern world because of those things in the modern world he despises. Art, for him, needs to create an image towards which the world can aspire.

The poem's second stanza has Maud Gonne as a much more personal image of aspiration for the poet. The self-persuasion of the first stanza has not been completely successful, and he finds himself still hankering for public acclaim. The pride more noble than his own, which he might attempt to imitate, allows Maud Gonne to rise above the abuse of the people who seem unworthy of her dream for them. She can continue on the path which is personal destiny without the internal conflict the poet suffers as a result of his need for the reassurance of public acclaim. Maud Gonne in this poem is '[h]alf lion, half child'. Lion and child have been considered Nietzschean images, but are explicable without reference to Nietzsche. The lion is a traditional image of pride and nobility; the child represents innocence and simplicity. The poet's conception of Maud Gonne is of someone innocent of the intrigue and machination of modern politics. She is also simple in the sense of being something complete, at one with life, intuitively convinced and without the self-doubt of the analytical mind.

This is, of course, Yeats's Maud Gonne. She is appropriated by the poetry. Annie Dillard has commented on writing a memoir that it is like 'cannibalizing your life for parts', and that after you have written, 'you can no longer remember anything but the writing. However true you make that writing, you've created a monster',[26] and a similar thing applies to Yeats's poetry. A poem added to the *In the Seven Woods* volume unit, 'Old Memory', makes the point. James Olney claims that 'In the act of remembering the past in the present, the autobiographer imagines into existence another person, another world ... '[27] The idea in 'Old Memory' that words can be thought to have come to mean nothing is ironic when one considers that it is the textual figure of Maud Gonne, Yeats's Maud Gonne, who has come to be so significant, and the thought he sends flying to her, reminding her that her strength is only half hers, acknowledges the extent to which the Maud Gonne who exists in the poems is the creation of the poems. So is 'he', the poet who exists there.

'Against Unworthy Praise' also addresses the failure of the physical relationship, and offers consolation. The poet considers his strength to have been renewed by the brief sexual affair (or perhaps has decided so to consider). The dream in the wilderness again recalls the desert dream of 'Cycles Ago', and so the idea of a relationship which transcends the normal lifespan; though Yeats's own desert dream of Flamel and Pernella displaces Maud Gonne's dream of brother and sister. Yeats's comments on Maud Gonne's 'dread of physical love', in a journal entry of 21 January 1909, are relevant to the second stanza of 'Against Unworthy Praise':

> This dread has probably spoiled all her life, checking natural and instinctive selection, and leaving fantastic duties free to take its place. It is what philosophy is to me, a daily rooter out of instinct

and guiding joy – and all the while she grows nobler under the touch of sorrow and denial.... Of old she was a phoenix and I feared her, but now she is my child more than my sweetheart.[28]

It seems likely that

> The labyrinth of her days
> That her own strangeness perplexed ... (VP 260)

is the difficulty in Maud Gonne's life that Yeats sees as the result of her aversion to sex. Peace is something she claims in her letters to have attained as a result of overcoming sexual desire. Yeats picks up the word 'peace' in this and the previous poem, but maybe her claim to have found peace was directed at him all along. She sees the possibility of peace for them both only in the overcoming of Yeats's physical desire for her.

III

Ford Madox Ford believed that Yeats's involvement with theatre business drew him into the world as a personality, and gave the world the figure of a man to stand behind the poetry, so making the poetry more real and more relevant to the real world.[29] 'The Fascination of What's Difficult' (VP 260) curses theatre business. The prose draft for the poem is in the journal:

> To complain of the fascination of what's difficult. It spoils spontaneity and pleasure and it wastes time ... One could use the thought of the wild-winged and unbroken colt must drag a cart of stones out of pride because it's difficult, and end by denouncing drama, accounts, public contests – all that's merely difficult. (Mem 229)

A letter to John Quinn dated 27 April 1908 shows how Yeats was haunted over a period of time by the fear that drama took him away from lyric writing: 'I have a new play in my head and when that is written shall go back to lyric work. Indeed, for months now I have had lyrics wandering about in the air, waiting the moment of leisure to get them into words ... ' (L 510). In describing the work he has been drawn into as '*merely* difficult', Yeats is questioning that aspect of himself which he believes makes what is difficult an irresistible challenge. His impatience with theatre business is of a piece with an increasingly intolerant attitude and a move towards aloofness. His involvement with the Abbey is a practical form of pressure which adds to philosophical and political pressures behind this move.

In representing artistic genius by the winged colt the poem emphasizes the difficulty of the relationship between art and life, especially if we look at Yeats's entry on Pegasus in the journal:

> When Adam named the beasts, there was one beast that he forgot to name, or else, taking it for some common horse, named wrongly; and so as time went on men came to have much knowledge of what lives and moves, but of the creature whose name they did not know they had no knowledge, for they could not call it and, having looked at it, speak to one another. That creature permits us to call it Pegasus, but it does not answer to that or any name. (Mem 243–4)

Artistic genius is set apart from the common world and not amenable to its call. Yeats represents in his little story the necessary obliqueness of the representation of life by art. His frustration with theatre business causes Yeats to suspect that he has turned his talent into a less worthwhile channel than if he had devoted himself completely to lyric writing. The poet's theatre work has, as Ford suggests, brought him into closer contact with the world, but closeness can create problems as well as the benefits Ford sees.

There is a way in which Yeats's forcing himself into this closer relation with life in the world has added to the earlier poet, to the pure lyricist, an element which contributes to greater completeness as an artist. Since the aim of the work is personal expression, to express the man, the greater the completeness of the man, the greater the work is. To be set against this is the possibility that such involvement with the everyday world might tend not merely to absorb too much time for the exercise of the lyric faculty, but indeed to destroy it. How damaged is the absolute of thoroughbreds likely to be by working as a cart-horse? The danger must be particularly apparent to anyone who is tempted by the type of mask theory which suggests that one grows into the pose one assumes, grows to fit the role one chooses.

But 'The Fascination of What's Difficult' is a 'Momentary Thought', a moment's revolt against the element in himself which works deliberately against his own ease. An earlier entry in the journal shows that he has already found an answer to the problem the poem raises:

> I cry out continually against my life. I have sleepless nights, thinking of the time that I must take from my poetry, from the harvest of

the Lord – last night I could not sleep – and yet perhaps I must do all these things that I may set myself into a life of action, so as to express not the traditional poet but that forgotten thing, the normal active man. (Mem 181)

It is easy to see how a critic such as Ford would find himself in sympathy with such a statement. It is, in effect, a reaction against the stale poeticism or the decayed romanticism of much late nineteenth-century poetry. Yeats seeks to bring art back into relation with the world (this is not to forget the problems involved with too close a relationship), and if the world and art are subjectively ordered, then the position of the artist as a man is crucial: the artist cannot exist in an ivory tower but must make himself a place in the world. The struggle one might forecast is that of retaining the position of 'normal, active man' and yet recapturing the lyric faculty, in order to achieve a new ideal of completeness, a poetic and personal expression suitable for (though not a mere reflection of) the modern world.

The conflict between life and art gives rise to a second-order conflict where the opposition of life and art is set against art's need to be related to life. Though 'the distinction between biography and criticism has a habit of dissolving when applied to Yeats',[30] the dynamic between life and work is essential to the work. Life and work have a relationship whose reciprocal exchanges make it impossible for the two to be separated, though we need sometimes to be able to see them as opposing forces.

The thought behind a draft for Yeats's lecture 'Friends of My Youth' helps to explain his attraction to drama:

> These men had made their gestures from antiquity and they would copy it and be good actors. Is it not that this mask is half unconsciously created, that there is so often something theatrical in the men of the vastest energy, that Napoleon will invade the east not for State craft only, but that he may copy the career of Alexander? (YT 78)

The poet needs to become an actor, needs the theatrical quality if he is to create the necessary relationship with his audience. The apparent contradiction with the idea in 'Against Unworthy Praise' that the work is sufficient if it seems a secret between two people shows the complexity of Yeats's thinking on personal expression in poetry, on the public–private dynamic, and on the small and large audience. The poet addresses a large audience not to gain their applause, but rather to help create that image of himself which will allow fuller personal expression. The contrary movement towards restriction is a means of intensifying what is to be expressed. The finished talk shows how Yeats saw this theatrical quality as a means of transcending the Paterian passive self,[31] following the culture of the Renaissance in 'the deliberate creation of a great mask':

> Wordsworth was dull as compared with Shelley and Byron, because these men had the theatrical quality which enabled them to project an image of themselves. The image of one who has lived passionately and sincerely is always more important than his thought. (YT 39)

This image is created and presented in the work. The poetry Yeats aims at is not just the poet conveying his thoughts, since this would be only a partial, divided, expression of himself. The artist himself is involved in the precept that art should not be a mere reflection of ordinary life. By trying to live up to the image of himself created in his work, he can create an image capable of generating greater and greater work. The poet's involvement in the everyday world also concerns his work.

James Olney has said that

> it is through that act [that is, of writing] that the self and the life, complexly intertwined and entangled, take on certain form, assume a particular shape and image, and endlessly reflect that image back and forth between themselves as between two mirrors.[32]

The personality through which the poet expresses himself is a pose, a creation of his theatrical sense, but it is not an arbitrary creation: it is an imaginative transformation of the flesh-and-blood poet. The personality as the poetic self is a creation of the artist projected into his work. The personality's interaction with the images that are the subject of his work has an intensifying and expanding effect. But the personality is created from something first given to the poet by life, that is, himself. This phase of Yeats's poetry is one of transition, one of whose elements is a greater involvement with the everyday world. In this sense, his poetry 'withers' closer to the reality in which it is rooted, that is, his life. But his poetry can never be *simply* autobiographical, in the sense of conveying the events of his life, because life and poetry are linked in too complex a way. One must, of course, be aware of the influence on one's own reading of the power of Yeats's voice, but it is in voices that 'Yeats' inheres. His life is absolutely that of the writer. He lives his life as a constantly revised draft, both living and writing his identity into existence.

IV

Yeats's idea of the mask informs both the personal and the public sections of this volume. His increasing leaning towards the aristocracy is shown in 'Upon a House shaken by the Land Agitation' (VP 264). 'Time out of mind' is more than a conventional expression for a long while: it conveys the aspect of tradition which lies deeper than conscious thought and allows the possibility of going beyond what conscious reasoning can produce. Conscious reasoning can work only through the logical train, via the obviously present to that which has immediate utility, and through an abstraction increasingly removed from life. The aristocratic tradition represented by the poem's house maintains 'passion and precision' as one, simply because this is the closest thing to life for its people, something they are born with and to, something which is not a matter for reason. Height can only be built on, the poem implies, by those to whom height is natural (at least, customary), a part of themselves.

The poem's political attitude reflects Yeats's friendship with Lady Gregory. It may also look back to Jonson, whom he studied carefully in 1906 with a view to writing an essay:

> I am thinking of writing something on Ben Jonson, or more likely perhaps upon the ideal of life that flitted before the imagination of Jonson and the others when they thought of the Court. The thought grows out of my Spenser essay which is just out. (L 478–9, 21 September 1906, to A. H. Bullen)

In writing later of Coole, Yeats was to follow the tradition of the country house poem begun by Jonson's 'To Penshurst'. Jonson as a poet of patronage points to much of what Coole and Lady Gregory were to Yeats. The relationship between artist and patron is not merely one of practical finance: the patron class offers an ideal image which the poet holds in his mind.[33] Yeats's visit to Italy and his reading of Castiglione had impressed on him the idea of an ideal state achievable by an aristocracy. This was associated in his mind with the idea of tradition, and with the necessity of the long-term view which is instinctive (and possible) to an aristocracy leisured in the sense of being removed from the immediacy of financial need symbolised by the day's wage or takings. The life of the aristocratic patron offers an image for the artist's work, and also for his life as an artist. The artist must avoid that involvement with the everyday world which short-term considerations of success would bring if he is to create genuine art, art which may only be appreciated much later.

Life at Coole enabled Yeats to set up the ideal image he needed in his mind to counter the influence of the age in which he lived, an image drawn from an actual instance of life which he could see, and not built up as an abstraction in a way which would draw his art into the theoretical thinking he condemned in the age in which he lived. It also assisted his development in that it had a presence which kept his mind from an excessively romantic longing for the unreachable absent. It is rather paradoxical that he sets up as an example of a life free from materialism the life of the establishment which has taken care of his material needs, and his condemnation of materialism from a newfound position of comfort can seem unattractive. But, as Yeats sees it, it is the aristocrats' possession of material abundance that frees them from *concern* with the material, as their patronage frees the artist from the same concern. It is this concern with the material, the need to worry over immediate needs, that is ruinous to art and to the pattern of gracious living.[34] Here, as in his use of Maud Gonne, Yeats constructs an idealized image and ignores historical reality. Patronage also has a basis in the material: 'What the aristocracy gives had first to be taken, and the material independence of the class is not in fact the basis of its service to the community but rather a result of its exploitation'.[35]

The poet of the more epigrammatic poems in *From 'The Green Helmet'* and *Responsibilities* has an easily noticed resemblance to Jonson, but the idea of patronage also connects Yeats's conception of Jonson with the symbol that Coole has become for him. Taking the fear of Coole's demise together with a thought from the essay on Spenser pays the house something of a compliment: 'Thoughts and qualities sometimes come to their perfect expression when they are about to pass away.'[36] This essay, although written much earlier,[37] is connected with 'Upon a House shaken by the Land Agitation' by the reflection in the projected fall of Coole of the historical transition in which Yeats places Spenser, and this transition bears on concerns central to why Yeats felt at odds with his own age. The essay is also concerned with the relationship of England and Ireland.

Yeats sets Spenser at the time of the overcoming of the 'Anglo-French nation'. He uses the concept of an Anglo-French England and an Anglo-Saxon England (perhaps owing something to Arnold) to symbolize a noble tradition overthrown by rising materialism. For him,

Spenser is a personification of the transition between two sensibilities. He was of the Anglo-French nation, but felt the influence of the coming sensibility so strongly that he tried to base his art on it. The Queen was the patron and image of ideal life that the poet needs, but she was also the representative of the state. These are two different ways of identifying the Queen with the country: in the first case she is a living embodiment of the best it can aspire to; in the second, she is the personification of an abstract concept drawn from the notion of its people as they exist collectively.[38] Yeats sees in Spenser's work the image of ideal life before the poet's imagination being replaced by an abstract political concept, as court is replaced in his mind by state, with the result that when he came to write of Ireland, his work had become too influenced by politics to be imaginative art.

Yeats uses Spenser here to express the conflict constantly in his thoughts of poet and politician (or political writer, journalist). He does the same when writing of Shakespeare: Richard II is the poet, the courtier of tradition and ceremony, an Anglo-Frenchman; Bolingbroke is the politician, the rhetorician, the custodian of the state. Yeats finds in Cromwell a culmination of the shift to the Anglo-Saxon: a puritan, a persecutor of Ireland, and a king 'of the mob' rather than of the court, effectively no king at all. In this section of the essay, 'the fall of great houses' is part of that persecution of an Ireland whose writers still 'belonged to the old individual, poetical life, and spoke a language even in which it was all but impossible to think an abstract thought', by 'the Anglo-Saxon nation ... in the service of ideas it believed to be the foundation of the State' (E&I 375). Eventually, 'the old house of the noble' was to be turned into 'the house of the Poor' by Cromwell.[39] The threat to Coole by what the poet of 'Upon a House Shaken by the Land Agitation' sees as the encroachment of the mob on the nobility offers an uncomfortable parallel.[40]

The Elizabethan poetical movement which began before Spenser's death was, according to Yeats's essay, the final flowering of the Anglo-French art. Yeats stresses how important to this art was the image of an ideal life which its creators held before their imagination, and suggests the intensification of beauty arising from a reciprocal relationship between art and the image it celebrates:

> Italian influence had strengthened the old French joy that had never died out among the upper classes, and an art was being created for the last time in England which had half its beauty from continually suggesting a life hardly less beautiful than itself. (E&I 363–4)

The Anglo-French art, Yeats tells us, came to an end with the rise of the merchant class, just as he sees the art of his own time smothered by the rise of the shop-keeping middle class. It is the idea of expediency, the positing of a practical purpose for art, that steps between art and life, and so causes that fall away from immediate expression which marked the older order. Whereas the older poetic imagination could draw on images which were close to it, real to it, the newer art has to recreate figures which are personifications of qualities, abstractions produced by its practical sense of morality. This line of reasoning ignores the practical aspect of the relationship between artist and patron and prefers not to see patronage as itself a system of exchange. Once more Yeats can be seen to draw selectively on the world to construct the idealized image that will be worthy of the world's imitation.

For Yeats, Spenser reflects the fall away from unity which comes about when reason comes between imagination and the world, in a way which is illustrated by the growing distance between people and the supernatural. The capturing by conscious art of the energy of an older art, more instinctively related to its world, gives it new expression, but ultimately destroys the directness of its relationship to life: 'Is not all history but the coming of that conscious art which first makes articulate and then destroys the old wild energy?' (E&I 372–3). Yeats was working on this essay at the time when he first read Nietzsche, and this comment is close to the cycle of Dionysian and Apollonian art much associated with Nietzsche's work. Although *The Birth of Tragedy* was not available in translation until 1909, Havelock Ellis's *Savoy* articles do deal with this volume and *Twilight of the Idols* has a recapitulation.[41] The involvement of this thought with Yeats's complex conception of Spenser suggests that the idea of the movement of art is not one which came to him solely through something he was first reading at the time. The temptation to associate with Nietzsche, via Apollo and Dionysus, any idea involving conflict in art between conscious reason, form, on one hand, and wild energy, on the other, should be treated with caution. Yeats's thought draws on wide reading.[42]

Spenser is placed by Yeats at the moment when division enters the mind of man, so that qualities associated with the unified mind are held in contrast with those of the divided sensibility in which reason has come between man and his former intuitive relationship with the world. Edward Thomas, reviewing Yeats's *Collected Works* (1908), shrewdly indicates that the idea of a dissociation of sensibility is ahistorical.[43] He implies that the time of unity and simplicity which Yeats harks back to is an imaginative necessity for his work rather than an actual historical period: this time is a mythical rather than a historical conception. Yet it is in imagining such a unity that Yeats hopes to contribute to its becoming possible, and that the poetry which is to be his contribution becomes possible.

In the Spenser essay Yeats associates the development of poetry with an ethical and social development. Modern poetry must in some respects be separated from life if it is not to be implicated in that shift in ethics and sensibility which has raised the mass above the noble individual and intruded the logical train between man and his world in a way which leads always to that consideration of consequence which exchanges the spontaneous joy of living for a deferred reward. It is because modern life has moved into materialism and logic, whose spokesman is rhetoric, that the voice of the active man is missing from poetry which would remain poetry rather than lapsing into rhetoric.

V

The problem of a fall into division is also one which exercises Yeats in his 1909 journal. He associates the individualism of Augustus John's art with the prevailing importance of character in modern art. The John etchings at Coole show a break from a canon of form derived ultimately from ancient Greece. In a rather Marxist way (though the influence of Morris is more reasonably detectable – Yeats does not seem to have read Marx), Yeats associates the distortion of the bodies depicted in the John etchings with specialized labour. This labour is labour for a purpose, whereas the bodies the ancient canon strives towards are fitted for the complete labour in which life itself is the only purpose. In the older art Yeats contrasts with that of John, he finds a unity with society, the age, and Nature. Lacking this unity, John's figures become celebrations of division.[44] The journal includes poetry in thoughts belonging to the same stream:

> Supreme art is a traditional statement of certain heroic and religious truths passed on from age to age, modified by individual genius but never abandoned. The revolt of individualism came because the tradition had become degraded, or rather because a spurious copy had been accepted in its stead. Classical morality – not quite natural in Christianized Europe – had become a powerful element of this tradition at the Renaissance, and had passed on from Milton to Wordsworth and to Arnold, always growing more formal and empty

until it became ignoble in our own time – just as classical forms passed on from Raphael to the Academies. Anarchic revolt is now coming to an end, and the arts are about to restate the traditional morality.[45]

Classical morality, having been subverted to its own use by 'commonplace energy', needs to be replaced by something which stands above the average, yet will be accepted by the average person (Mem 181). At the same time, art needs to create that image of the ideal which will draw all the arts together. If a complex of such artistic images can be identified with the people's feeling of nationalism, then the image that the artist needs before his imagination can create a model for national feeling to strive towards.

The loss of unity that has occurred since the Renaissance means that the 'simple moral understanding of life' shared by artist and people is no longer present. Yeats sees his old idea of 'the deliberate creation of a kind of Holy City in the imagination' as hopeless, and has realized, under the influence of Synge, that he 'must be content to express the individual' (Mem 184). It is difficult not to sense despair at this point of the journal, as Yeats finds the Irish people too deep in materialism and the democratic ideal to be able to appreciate, and accept as an image of national aspiration, the noble ideal he wants his art to create. He still finds himself at odds with the taste in literature satisfied by Thomas Davis, a taste he and Lionel Johnson had tried to sophisticate. The death of Synge can only have added to the feeling of despair and bitterness, to the point where it becomes unpleasantly arrogant. Yeats seems at one stage even to have believed that the trouble over Synge's *The Playboy of the Western World* caused his illness.[46] It is at such moments of despair that contempt for the mass of the people emerges from behind the rhetoric which privileges as most vital a cultured (because leisured and exploitative) elite:

> The literature of suggestion, richest to the richest, does not belong to a social order founded upon argument, but to an age when life conquered by being itself and the most living was the most powerful. What was leisure, wealth, privilege but a soil for the most living? The literature of logic, most powerful in the emptiest, subduing life, conquering all in the service of one metallic premise, is the art of democracy, of generations that have only just begun to read. They fill their minds with deductions just as they fill their empty houses, where there is nothing of the past, with machine-made furniture. (Mem 209)

But there still exists in Yeats a belief in the possibility that art *can* create an image for the affections of Ireland. He wrote to Annie Horniman, 'I shall write for my own people – whether in love or hate of them matters little – probably I shall not know which it is.'[47] In *Discoveries* he also points to the way in which art might move towards forging a renewed unity, by freeing itself from too close an involvement in the world of materialism while staying close enough to life to avoid ethereality:

> we should ascend out of common interests, the thoughts of the newspapers, of the market-place, of men of science, but only so far as we can carry the normal, passionate, reasoning self, the personality as a whole.[48]

Yeats sought to make his work the expression of the personality as a whole. This is evident in his idea of the poet 'reborn as something intended, complete' in the 'General Introduction', but also in a commitment to the realities of lived experience.

Jerome McGann comments on Yeats's idea of the poet in the 'General Introduction':

> Perhaps the first time he articulated that imperious conception was in the long recollective essay 'Discoveries' ... There Yeats narrated his 'discovery' that while 'I had set out on life with the thought of putting my very self into poetry', he came to see that he was actually 'seeking something unchanging and unmixed and always outside myself': not the succession of his shifting and quotidian self-apparitions, but his eternal identity, what he called 'the personality as a whole'.[49]

My interpretation of this passage from *Discoveries* is different. Yeats's initial idea of putting his very self into poetry had involved the representation of visions which because they were imagined outside himself filled his imagination with 'decorative landscape and ... still life.' The discovery is this:

> Then one day I understood quite suddenly, as the way is, that I was seeking something unchanging and unmixed and always outside myself, a Stone or an Elixir that was always out of reach, and that I myself was the fleeting thing that held out its hand. The more I tried to make my art deliberately beautiful, the more did I follow the

opposite of myself, for deliberate beauty is like a woman always desiring man's desire. Presently I found that I entered into myself and pictured myself and not some essence when I was not seeking beauty at all, but merely to lighten the mind of some burden of love or bitterness thrown upon it by the events of life.[50]

Yeats contends here that his initial method led to a presentation of something dead and external rather than of the self he wished to present. Only by allowing his work to be a response to the events of his life was he able to picture his living self and not some 'essence', which would be an external abstraction. Yet he does not allow the argument to rest here. He also claims that it is necessary to deceive life a little. This deceit, the necessary distance from the quotidian, is available through 'style'. But the 'personality as a whole' is not only some essential, eternal self; the wholeness Yeats wants to emphasize here includes the self as it is involved in life. In the poet's ascent from the quotidian, he must not climb higher than he can take with him his normal self.

The distance between life and art is problematical; there is a reason for proximity and one for distance. Also important is the idea that artistic expression of the self depends on context. Since the context of the self is its life, the life is inevitably linked with the art. If art is to achieve the expression of the self, then the self must be pictured in action, in relation to its context, its life. 'I ... only cared for those wonderful Elizabethan lyrics when I knew the *imagined* men who sang them, and the incidents in which they arose' (YT 30). The poet as he imagines himself in his poetry communicates with the reader's imagination. At the same time, Yeats seeks to distance himself from the mechanistic type of thinking and language that he associates with journalism. To do this by seeking to create new forms would be idiosyncratic, merely personal and so associated with the quotidian from which he needs to ascend. He appeals instead to traditional forms of expression, which connect him with something greater than the merely personal.

In *Per Amica Silentia Lunae* (Myth 319–69) we find the idea of the pursuit of something seemingly exterior in a more positive light. In its 'Anima Mundi' section, it also indicates belief in a collective consciousness, and it is, perhaps, to this that the use of traditional forms might give access. Another way of putting this would be to say that the Anima Mundi can find expression through the poet who sufficiently detaches his work from the contingency of the everyday world, and that such detachment can be achieved through the use of traditional forms. Yeats's sensitivity to tradition reflects his belief that it passes on a cumulative wisdom or consciousness. This sensitivity is one of the things which suggest that Yeats possessed a particularly oral mind-set. This mind-set is manifested in his spoken verse project early in the century and in the poetry itself.[51] It also marks a significant difference from the thinking of T. E. Hulme – a thinker often associated with what has come to be called 'the modernist movement' – who tended to insist on the visual: 'Each word must be an image *seen*, not a counter.'[52] Walter Ong indicates that print cultures have a tendency to visual analogues.[53] He also claims that what he calls 'hypervisualism', the tendency to equate absolutely seeing with knowing, fails to recognize adequately the importance of the spoken word:

> To become intelligible what we see has to be mediated, in one way or another, through verbal formulation, which as such simply cannot be reduced to a visual presentation ... We generate our certainties not in a solipsistic universe of isolated 'observation' but in a total context which includes verbalization and in which we hope others will believe what we say.[54]

I find Ong's thoughts valuable because they jog me out of my own habitual tendency to the visual analogue, and even a visual use of language (if you see what I mean). It is worth noting the emphasis on communication and mediation in what he has to say because the difference between the kind of thinking he associates with print and that which he associates with orality helps me in placing Yeats in relation to a literary studies which has built on and developed from its own idea of what it calls 'literary modernism'. Yeats was not, of course, part of a pre-literate culture. What is under discussion here concerns residual traces of orality, or an oral tendency which tempered his literacy. It is also necessary to bear in mind the way Yeats sometimes groups print, materialism and England, and his wish to distinguish himself from, set himself in opposition to, this group.

There are other caveats:

> Orality and literacy are not two culture-types that exclude each other, but mind-sets which can co-exist beside each other, which may affect each other, and between which people can also to some extent switch.[55]

Ruth Finnegan cautions: 'The idea of pure and uncontaminated "oral culture" as the primary reference point for the discussion of oral poetry is a myth.'[56] Nevertheless, the visualizing tendency of a predominantly literate culture and the different physical state of a written as against a spoken poem contribute to the objectification of the poem. The poem is no longer the spoken word of the poet, something to be listened to, but something which can be looked at as an object in its own right, a text which can be examined. Ong's claim that print 'effectively reduced sound to surface, hearing to vision' seems to me an overstatement, but does suggest that print may have helped give rise to a tendency to objectify language, to treat the medium of communication as an object in its own right.[57] It is the splitting away of poetry from the quotidian world, from 'life', from human experience that I want to argue against and that I think Yeats argues against in *Discoveries*. Art is not life, yet there is a relationship between the two:

> Art is what is not nature; nature stops where art begins. And yet art is like nature. The best plays are those most like real life (in any of a bewildering variety of ways). Or conversely, nature is like art, at least for human beings. A human being enters into the human life-world by role-playing; a child learns to walk and talk, as a teacher learns to teach or a swimmer to swim, by playing at it until he or she is actually doing it ... This dialectical relationship of life (work) and art (play), however, had not inhibited an earlier tendency to think of art, or more particularly the work of art, as a closed system. This tendency ... marked the distinctively literate aesthetics of the New Criticism.[58]

From 'Upon a House shaken by the Land Agitation' and 'At Galway Races', through to 'Under Ben Bulben' Yeats looks to the past, and to the ideal of life lived by an aristocracy, a surviving example of which he finds at Coole, as the image he needs before his imagination to create an art free of the taint both of modern materialism and an unregenerated canon of form.

Yeats also turns to the aristocracy to provide the continuity necessary to the existence of society as society. The tradition of the common people, the passing on of a culture based in orality, is under threat from the growing influences of modern materialism and the printing press which Yeats tends to conflate. His move towards an aristocratic aloofness can be seen, rather paradoxically, as partly motivated by the vision of a whole society. The near oxymoron, 'written speech', which marks the finest attainment that the accumulation of culture can offer in 'Upon a House', emphasizes continuity between Yeats's wish to see revived the oral culture of the common people and his increasing identification with the aristocracy represented by Coole. Poetry tends to have characteristics associated with oral culture, such as rhyme, rhythm and parallel, additive structures. These were essential to its function as the transmitter of an oral society's culture, the bearer of tradition.[59] Yeats includes a literary form of oral features in his poetry. In 'These are the Clouds' four consecutive lines begin with 'And', the definitively additive word. The fitting in of phrases in parenthesis, as if spoken as they occur in the middle of a train of thought vocalized as it takes place, lends another conversational, oral, aspect to the poems in this volume. 'Where passion and precision have been one / Time out of mind ... ' is one example, from 'Upon a House shaken by the Land Agitation' (VP 264). 'King and No King' has a string of three modifying phrases which trail off:

> Yet Old Romance being kind, let him prevail
> Somewhere or somehow that I have forgot,
> Though he'd but cannon – (VP 258)

The whole of 'Upon a House' is a question. The large proportion of interrogatives in the volume is another means of including the 'oral' in a literary form, constructing Yeats as bearer of both high and peasant traditions.[60] Even a rhetorical question engages its reader more than would a statement, to some extent demands an answer, envisages a reader (or even an audience) in a way which weakens the tendency of the printed work to become an object in its own right, separated from its author.

'An Introduction for my Plays' indicates Yeats's lasting sense of poetry as a spoken art. It also indicates that the individual is only part of the equation:

> 'Write for the ear,' I thought, so that you may be instantly understood as when actor or folk singer stands before an audience. I delight in active men, taking the same delight in soldier and craftsman; I would have poetry turn its back upon all that modish curiosity, psychology – the poetic theme has always been present. (E&I 530)

The implication here is that poetry written for the ear is closest to the life it celebrates. It is so, perhaps, because, although written, it supposes an audience. It seeks to avoid its objectification as text, to avoid becoming a verbal icon, to avoid separation from life. Poetry written for the ear retains a consciousness of the social nature of language. Yeats's poetry supposes not only an audience but a place in the world for poetry, and the supposing of both is a creative necessity for his work.

For Walter de la Mare, in his review of the *Collected Works* (1908), the sense of awareness of and dedication to a destiny justifies the intrusion of the poet's personality into his work, something which he claims might otherwise distract the reader.[61] But in Yeats's case, the reciprocal nature of the relationship between the work and the life means that it is through the work that the personality is created, and that the drive to achieve unity of personality through commitment to a destiny fulfilled in the work is necessary to the creation of the work. Personality here is not something which can be considered separately, not something which can be seen as intruding into the work, justifiably or otherwise; it is essential and integral to the work.

4
Poems Written in Discouragement

I

Yeats wrote these five poems under the impact of the Hugh Lane gallery controversy, the third public controversy to have stirred his imagination.[1] The poems illustrate a shift in Yeats's work in which he is driven in on himself. I have suggested that *From 'The Green Helmet and Other Poems'* marks the beginning of an emergence of the poet as a man into the real world. At the same time, the move towards a more aristocratic attitude and the concern that art should present an ideal to which the world might aspire seem to mark a contrary movement towards increasing withdrawal, threatening eventual isolation. This apparent duality of movement cautions against the simplistic interpretation of the development of Yeats's work in this phase as merely the introduction of an objective realism.

Since these poems form part of an intervention in a public controversy (moreover, one concerning art), the relationship of art with the world is a particular issue for them. Yeats does propound a view of this relationship in these poems, which makes them rhetorical, but there is more to it than this. In taking part in this controversy, Yeats establishes himself as a poet who insists on the right of art to affect the world in the way proper to art. In the poems, and in the rest of his part in the controversy, he aligns himself with the poet, Seanchan, of his own play *The King's Threshold*. Art has the potential to transform reality by maintaining both its difference from and its relation to reality. In dealing with public affairs and yet steadfastly maintaining his personal vision, Yeats understood this potential of art. This is not to say that art should be autonomous in the New Critical sense of the autonomy of the poem.[2]

This stance is, of course, fundamentally undemocratic, and can be said to insist on the right of an elite to dictate to the masses because the elite knows what is best for all. Richard Kearney summarizes the position of Kenneth Burke, John Crowe-Ransom, R. P. Blackmur, Conor Cruise O'Brien, Denis Donoghue and Richard Poirier:

> For artists to claim that we should organize the actual in terms of the ideal is, these critics conclude, merely a rhetorical way of saying that the mindless majority should be ruled by an elite; not forgetting, of course, the all important apologia–'for their own good'. This is why artists, whenever they have crossed the thresholds of art to prescribe some political programme, have almost invariably espoused some form of 'artistic' fascism.[3]

Yeats's later flirtation with fascism can be used to discredit still further his view of art's relationship with the world. Terry Eagleton, for instance, funnels an analysis of Yeats's class position into 'one destination of the organic ideal in literature', that is, fascism.[4] Seamus Deane associates the element in Yeats's thought which was opposed to materialism and mechanistic philosophy with the Romantic view of a Golden Age which saw the world imaginatively, and in turn with fascism. He is conscious enough, it seems, of the evidence that Yeats's involvement with fascist politics was little more than dabbling to qualify the connection he makes:

> This Romantic-aesthetic heritage, with which we still struggle, clearly harbours the desire to obliterate or reduce the problems of class, economic development, bureaucratic organization and the like, concentrating instead upon the essences of self, community, nationhood, racial theory, Zeitgeist. Yeats had demonstrated throughout his long career that the conversion of politics and history into aesthetics carries with it the obligation to despise the modern world and to seek rescue from it. His sympathy for fascism is consistent with his other opinions, although he is, in the end, loyal to his early conception of an aristocratic society dominated by 'some company of governing men'.[5]

Luke Gibbons, editor of the section of the *Field Day Anthology* which includes this passage, adds a note on 'Zeitgeist': 'The spirit of genius that prevails in a given age. It has taken on ominous connotations since its association with national aggrandizement in German idealist philosophy.'[6]

The fascist connection is something which can be used to tie Yeats more closely to Pound and literary modernism. 'Eliot, Pound and Yeats for example each flirted with a fascist movement as political equivalent to his poetic creed.'[7] James Longenbach has also linked Yeats, Pound, fascism and modernism, though pointing out that Pound went further with his fascism than did Yeats with his, ending up in a world of his own.[8] Jerome McGann begins by overstating Pound's influence on Yeats and goes on to suggest that Yeats's poetry romantically shirks the areas Pound's full-blooded modernism takes him into

> Having, against his father's judgement, put himself to school to Pound, Yeats began to cultivate poetical relations with that mistress [Ugliness] whom Jack Butler Yeats saw as the young American's wicked new beloved. 'A terrible beauty is born', Yeats declared as he began to explore his own visions of Prometheus cohabiting with the Furies. But his words – his experience – fall far short of the realities which Pound was bent on pursuing. That elegant oxymoron of 'A terrible beauty' is a Romantic phrase embodying a Romantic judgement; as such, it is wholly inadequate to the contradictions which are brought forth through Pound's *Cantos*.[9]

McGann's seems a particularly perverse way of using modernism as a 'lever' to promote Pound at the expense of Yeats.[10]

A careful consideration of the Ireland in which Yeats was writing at this time, of the view of other parties to the gallery controversy, and of the often hostile reception of Yeats's work in Ireland after the turn of the twentieth century is necessary to a less reductive analysis of his position and the transition in his work. To reduce Yeats's work to an indication of a confused class position is to miss the realities of his difficulties as a nationalist from a Protestant background in the Ireland of this time, and the particular nature of his response; it is also to miss the reciprocal nature of the interaction between Yeats's ethical, aesthetic and political positions. There is an assumption in all such criticism that the critic holds a place outside the field of forces which they see as determining the work under analysis. But the reaction against the implication of fascism will clearly be influenced by the events of World War II. In a way that is not quite so clear, the battle-lines drawn up between Yeats and his contemporary adversaries in Ireland underlie some more recent criticism of him. It is still possible to detect traces of the view of such as D. P. Moran, which we might paraphrase as 'Catholic Irish Ireland wants the English Protestant-Ascendancy art-for-art's-sake poets out.'[11]

The association of three major poets – Yeats, Eliot and Pound – with authoritarian politics tends, for the post-holocaust reader, to discredit their views on society. It can also lead to the feeling that the integration of aesthetic and political thought is an aestheticization of politics, and will lead to the same consequences as the previous such aestheticization, that is, to fascism and holocaust. The Marxist critic supports his claim that it is unacceptably elitist for art to seek to escape determination by material factors by raising the spectre of fascism and holocaust. A connection of politics and literature becomes acceptable (indeed, necessary) for Marxist criticism only if it is granted that society, and so literature as a social production, is totally determined by economics and class-politics. Liberal society, on the other hand, *contains* literature by an acceptance of the artist's right to say what others cannot. The granting to art of its freedom entails its social neutralization: it is entitled to its different view because it is *merely* art.[12] The point here is that both Marxist and liberal politics allow the connection between literature and society only on their own terms. Literature cannot be challenging unless, in the first case, it challenges bourgeois society from the standpoint of Marxist materialism, or, in the second case, it challenges in the way liberal society has declared proper to art, that is, in a way which challenges nothing.

If we reject the economic and political determinism of Marxist criticism *and* the theories of consumption typified by the New Criticism which emerge from the view of literature of liberal politics, then, if we are to reintegrate literature and society, we have to find a way of seeing literature as part of a social process, in which the social position of writer and audience play a part.[13] It is worth noting Donald Davie's point that the awarding of the Bollingen prize to the *Pisan Cantos* in 1949 confirmed American society's recognition of 'an absolute discontinuity between the life of the poet and the life of the man', and that the privilege so extended is 'the privilege of the pariah'.[14] Thomas Kilroy's interpretation of what Irish writing says about the integration of culture and art may be unduly pessimistic:

> What Irish writing has said to us, consistently, what it continues to say to us to-day is that such integration is impossible, that the evolving society in this country has persistently fallen behind the finer perceptions of its artists, that it has been and continues to be unworthy of its own art.[15]

Yeats's thinking suggests that it is part of the function of literature so to indict the society which produces it. As with the role that the individual can imagine for himself and then try to fill, literature can imagine its society's potential.

II

An integrated view of the undoubted change in Yeats's work between 1903 and 1914 must take into account the social context within which that change took place. The debate over whether Yeats became a modernist under the influence of Pound, or of his reading of Nietzsche, for instance, might lead to an over-literary account, to the exclusion of social and political factors which also drove the change.[16]

The foundation of Yeats's work as Irish art is 'The Wanderings of Oisin'.[17] This poem marks an attempt to provide a possible unity among Irishmen, to retain a place for the Protestant Irishman, by an appeal to ancient legend going back beyond the tradition of Catholic piety. Seamus Heaney sees the influence of Samuel Ferguson at work in Yeats's early use of Irish material:

> For it was indeed the spirit of the Unionist, Sir Samuel Ferguson, who moved most influentially through the mind of the young poet, because it was in Ferguson's handling of legendary material that Yeats perceived, consciously or unconsciously, a way of maintaining fidelity to the political and cultural postures of his own class, the middle-class Protestant establishment. At the same time he staked a claim in the very roots of the nationalist Catholic ethos by annexing to himself those native myths and legends and treating them as a unifying rather than a divisive factor.[18]

But the tensions involved in the attempt so to reconcile this fidelity and this claim proved increasingly difficult to sustain. Ominously, the first instalment of Ferguson's 'Hardiman's Irish Minstrelsy' combines an appeal to Protestants to learn about the history of Catholic Ireland with an extraordinary diatribe against contemporary Catholic Ireland. The article includes an arrogant assumption of the superiority of the writer's own class which turns any gesture of reconciliation that may have been intended into mere condescension:

> We address in these pages the Protestant wealth and intelligence of the country, an interest acknowledged on all hands to be the depository of Ireland's fate for good or evil. The Protestants of Ireland are wealthy and intelligent beyond most classes, of their numbers, in

the world: but their wealth has hitherto been insecure, because their intelligence has not embraced a thorough knowledge of the genius and disposition of their Catholic fellow-citizens.[19]

'The Wanderings of Oisin' also establishes the value of the heroic, to be continued through the use of Cuchulain, and sets this in opposition to piety, personified by Saint Patrick. This opposition is one that can be adapted to describe to himself the poet's own position at a later date, when he sees himself alone, other heroes having perished, facing a mass public whom he identifies with a Catholic piety which he cannot hope to defeat. See, for a good example, 'The Grey Rock' (VP 270–6). The change in the nature of Irish nationalism between the shift to cultural nationalism that followed the fall of Parnell and its repoliticization and shift towards a mass movement before 1916 forced an adaptation in Yeats, since the nationalism through which he founded his identity altered, and effectively squeezed him out. The process through which this adaptation occurred, the process of Yeats's reorientation to the world, is one which is reflected in, even carried out through, the work.[20]

Yeats's view that the nationalist movement turned away from politics to culture after the fall of Parnell is one that has been widely accepted, but is not uncontentious.[21] John S. Kelly claims that Yeats 'chose to ignore the political motivation of much of this new literary enthusiasm, or supposed that it could be easily transmuted into a national quest for a finer and deeper culture.'[22] Cultural nationalism is, of course, more in tune with the view of politics Yeats held increasingly from the turn of the century on. The artist is bound to have a more significant role than the politician in what is a cultural nationalist movement rather than a political one, the poet a higher place than the rhetorician. Yeats claimed to have recognized under the influence of Synge that his art must aim to express the individual.[23]

A 1913 lecture by Yeats on the poetry of Rabindranath Tagore makes clear that, for Yeats, the idealism necessary to art is not possible in politics:

> If you deal with the crowd, if you try deliberately to convert, you compromise. You no longer speak your own thoughts; you speak the things that you think will please other men. That is what made some of us here turn away from politics. I saw that when you are attempting to speak high things and sincere things, and at the same time carry on a political life, sooner or later you give up the sincere things and high things, and you speak expedient things. Do not

> think I am condemning politics. They are necessary for Ireland ... but my meaning is – different men for different tasks. For those whose business it is to express the soul in art, religion, or philosophy, they must have no other preoccupation. I saw all this years ago, at the beginning of this movement, and I wrote the 'Countess Cathleen' to express it. I saw people selling their souls that they might save the souls of others.²⁴

For Yeats, then, the values of the artist are bound to tend towards the solitary rather than the crowd, to the elite rather than the popular. The appeal of traditional politics seemed to have reached a nadir after the fall of Parnell, and, as represented by the Irish Party at Westminster, to have become 'prose plus Committee Room 15',²⁵ and too much associated – as machine politics – with the British system to appeal much to nationalists.²⁶ Yet the pressure of nationalist feeling among numbers of Irish people was bound to force itself into popular expression eventually. As popular expression it tended ultimately to the sort of political form that Yeats criticised.²⁷

Catholicism in Ireland was something which offered a centre for solidarity for any mass nationalist movement, a centre which had the added attraction of providing a difference from Protestant England. In the view of the journalism of D. P. Moran, Catholicism was almost a prerequisite of being truly Irish.²⁸ The Protestant Irish were, for Moran, merely the agents of British rule in Ireland. He saw the attempt to achieve unity by the appeal to ancient legend which formed part of the Literary Revival as an attempt to block the way forward for a modernizing Catholic nationalism, and treated it with scorn:

> The 'poor old woman' symbol for Ireland is too greenly sentimental for us. Vigorous Ireland has told the old weeping wailing creature to move out of its way; but the 'poor old woman' has gained admittance to the scented drawing-rooms where they take a little green sentimentality with their coffee and gossip. 'Kathleen ni Houlihanism' makes Irish patriotism quite harmless, if not even 'respectable'... Let who will simper and sigh about 'the poor old woman' and her chanting; give us a modern man with a heart and a head and a strong hand, and make a play – not a Yeatsonian chant – about him.²⁹

Note the class-based element of Moran's attack here, and the accusation aimed at writers of forwarding only their own interests in this from *The Philosophy of Irish Ireland*:

> Beyond being a means of fame and living to those who can supply the demand, what good is the 'Celtic Note' in English literature to the Irish nation? What good is it to any, except the owners of them, that Irish names figure largely in current English literature?[30]

Not only, then, was the nationalist movement becoming repoliticized (despite Douglas Hyde's efforts to stem this tide in the Gaelic League[31]), but there was a growing tendency within it to marginalize the Irish Protestant nationalist.[32] The controversies over Synge's plays, offensive to the militantly Catholic part of Irish nationalism which insisted on a pious image of Ireland, further identified Yeats with a perceived anti-Catholic, anti-'true Irish' feeling explicable by his, and Synge's, Protestant descent.[33]

The increasing identification of nationalism with Catholicism had a polarizing effect in that it drove the marginalized Yeats into an increased identification with Protestant patriotism and the Anglo-Irish. This is evident in the naming of Fitzgerald, Emmet and Tone in 'September 1913', and his conception of the heroic Anglo-Irish of the eighteenth century. Augustine Martin cautions against oversimplification on this, pointing out that the poem attacks not so much the middle classes as 'the present times', and that O'Leary, himself Catholic and middle-class, is 'the poem's touchstone of "aristocratic" heroism and generosity'.[34] I agree. It is the Catholic middle classes of the present times whom Yeats wished to attack; O'Leary's exile helped Yeats to see him as representative of a different time, different values. The *Leader* used Yeats's British pension to tie him more closely to the enemy and also to undermine any attempt by Yeats to identify himself with Protestant Irish patriots: 'The Pensioner is, of course, a pure-souled patriot: in payment for his patriotism Emmet got the rope, but Pollexfen Yeats, the author of "Cathleen ni Houlihan", gets three pounds a week from the British Government.'[35] *Sinn Fein* was similarly scathing, considering Yeats to have deserted the cause of Kathleen ni Houlihan, and to have 'died ten years ago'.[36]

Later, Yeats was to identify himself with the race of Grattan and Burke in his Senate speech on divorce. The combative tone of this speech recalls his speech on persecution reported in the *Irish Times* of 25 January 1913: 'If [Irish Protestants] could not fight for their own through any form of persecution known to modern times and win, they were poor creatures, and the country would be well rid of them.'[37] Thomas Kinsella's comments suggest the extent to which the eighteenth-century Protestant Ireland Yeats identified himself with concerned a placing of himself, a justification of his own values:

> You might feel that Yeats created this brief Anglo-Irish tradition for himself, by special selection, and then projected his own values into it. But it is still a coherent entity, at a graceful elegiac height above the filthy modern tide.[38]

Kinsella also believes that Yeats, at least in part, *chose* to be isolated. It is difficult to tell sometimes if Yeats is constrained by circumstances or if he enjoys reacting to them. It seems to me that part of Yeats's rhetoric – its persuasive power aimed at himself as well as others – is to claim power over circumstances by reacting as if they were to his benefit. Increasingly he 'exults' in his isolation.

One of the bases for Irish nationalist hostility to Yeats indicates the difficulty for the poet of maintaining the necessary distance from the world. The response to his work is something over which he does not have control, though he may try to manipulate it. If his work is to be vital, it will touch on social and political realities, and people will respond in terms dictated by these, refusing, as they would see it, to allow the licence demanded by the artist. One anonymous writer, for instance, considered that Yeats and his friends were hijacking the Irish National Theatre for their own purposes, and that the tolerance Yeats asked for should not be granted: 'We can neither admire the grace of the wild animal nor the less artless motions of the poet unless they are under restraint.'[39] The relationship between Ireland and England was not one of equals, and so an Irish nationalist movement seeking to establish an Irish identity not determined by England was sensitive to images of Ireland which seemed to fall in with stereotyped English views. Moran's *Leader* articles indicate a strong feeling that Yeats was peddling a form of pseudo-Irishness to an English audience. As early as 1900, Standish O'Grady indicated to Yeats his fear that Ireland was being used as material for the entertainment of the English:

> You are at one with me about the iniquity of the tourist movement and the exploitation for commercial purposes of the beauty of our country. Yet holding such opinions you bring us all – we who in some poor way stand for Ireland – over to London and trot us round for the delectation of your clever London friends whose favourable opinion we don't want and can do very well without.[40]

As a writer who built so much of his life in London, Yeats was vulnerable to this kind of charge.

'Imaal' (J. J. O'Toole) in the *Leader* of 26 September 1903 pointed to a difference between Yeats's claimed idealism and the reality of his commercially motivated practice in reproducing in *Ideas of Good and Evil* articles previously published in London reviews. Part of his complaint is that Yeats was accepted abroad as representative of Ireland. His article refers to a review of *Ideas of Good and Evil* in the *Saturday Review*:

> It is not at all mortifying to find the giant labours of the Gaelic League not merely ignored, but apparently not so much as known; to find a 'movement' conducted exclusively in the English language, and to no slight degree in the London press, posing and passing as an 'Irish Keltic' movement! This is one of the things that come from having a group of over-adroit literary self-advertisers and 'movement' exploiters frisking about on the fringe of our forces. But an indication like this of the *Saturday* man's has its uses. It teaches us how much is really known about Ireland over-sea, and shrewdly instructs us in a sense of the value of letting Mr. Yeats mix himself up with us.[41]

The kind of view evident in Eugenia Brooks Frothingham's 1904 article in response to Yeats's visit to America, and clearly influenced by Matthew Arnold, makes it possible at least to see 'Imaal''s point: 'The Irishman is a creature of delicious extravagance, who has always cultivated the lovely folly at the expense of the potato patch. May he long continue to do so!'[42]

John S. Kelly notes of *The Wanderings of Oisin* that Irish reviewers 'complained ... of the remoteness of the poems from real life', whereas 'English notices were less concerned with this unworldliness, which was regarded as part of the Celtic element in the book.'[43] The acceptance abroad of Yeats as an Irish writer came to work against his being accepted as an Irish writer by some Irish nationalists.[44]

The difficult relationship of art with the world in which it is produced is indicated in the method of O'Toole's attack. To accuse Yeats of commercial motivation diminishes his claim to credit as an artist. Yeats's own realization of the need of the artist to distance himself from commercial considerations is shown by his comments on the necessity of leisure to art, and his ideas on patronage. Pierre Bourdieu comments on the paradoxical position of the artist: 'The literary and artistic world is so ordered that those who enter it have an interest in disinterestedness.'[45] He distinguishes between different sorts of profit. In the field of artistic production a 'negative relationship is ... established between symbolic profit and economic profit, whereby *discredit* increases as the audience grows and its specific competence declines' ... (330). The imputation to Yeats of commercial motivation in his publishing practice threatened the symbolic capital he had accumulated by his refusal to seek commercial success through deliberately catering for a mass audience.[46] Further, in order to find a large enough outlet for his work (even more of a problem for a writer who shunned the mass market), Yeats was forced to look outside Ireland.[47] To make matters worse, Yeats's interest in the esoteric alienated orthodox Catholics and his campaigning against the Boer War alienated Unionists.

The separation of poetry, especially lyric poetry, from the 'real world', its trivialization as entertainment (probably for the London drawing-room), was a means of marginalizing Yeats which, if he sought to maintain the claims of art dependent on its distance from the imperatives of political expediency, it was difficult for him to defend himself against. F. M. Atkinson, in a 1905 article, associates the Celticism of the 'Celtic School' with an idealism he sees as out of place in the modern world. This idealism can then be made a thing of the past, and Yeats condemned as reactionary as well as out of touch with reality. Atkinson and Moran trump Yeats's Fergusonian appeal to history with an appeal to the need for a new, modern Ireland:

> Modernity disgusts him, he is all for the old high way of things, forgetting the more necessary new high way in which our feet must walk ... This reactionary tendency is the true explanation of his attitude towards religion; he has been charged with every kind of sacrilegious irreverence and blasphemy; he is only flying from another aspect of sordid and ugly modern life and thought.[48]

Atkinson praises Yeats's lyric verse, but his article seems to want to keep Yeats within a certain sort of poetry which can be considered as isolated from the 'real' life which Yeats so clearly dislikes. For Atkinson, engagement with 'real' life involves an accommodation with the imperatives of society as it exists at the time of writing.[49]

The hostility to Yeats in the Irish nationalist press was countered by statements from his allies. His friend Edward Garnett insists in a 1909 article on the closeness of the link of Yeats's nationalism with his poetry. He seeks to show how Yeats's work fits into the tradition of Irish literature, yet is nonetheless modern. Indeed, his contention is that it is in the nature of Irish literature to be able to maintain its traditions and assimilate to itself the concerns of a different age. His source for his theory of Irish literature also indicates the importance of the presence of the story-teller as mediator between the times of tradition and the time of the story's telling:

And Mr. Eoin MacNeill, in 'The Book of the Lays of Finn,' says, 'the legend of the Fiauna remained always modern, not only in its language but in the sense of being entirely the property of each generation of story-tellers and ballad-makers. In this way it retained the power of constantly and freely assimilating new elements'. Substitute for 'the legends of the Fiauna' 'the old Irish sagas and folk-legends' and we have a most curious example in Mr. Yeats of this ever-assimilative yet highly conservative tradition in Irish literature. For the old Irish sagas and folk-legends have retained the power of freely assimilating the new elements in Mr. Yeats' poetry.[50]

Garnett has an answer to those who criticise Yeats for pandering to an English audience:

And let the Irish reader mark that it is that very literature of the invaders (who so long disdained and sought indeed to destroy and root out the literature of the Gael) which is now invaded and conquered by the Gaelic legends reborn in these dramatic songs and sagas. (151)

Garnett stresses the difference between the impatient nationalism Yeats associates with politics, journalism, materialism and the Catholic middle class, and the artist's vision of a national literature which disregards immediate effect in the hope of establishing the basis of a deeply felt sense of nationality.[51] The emphasis here is on the necessary separation of art from the everyday; the equally necessary closeness to the realities of the world is provided by the poet's involvement in the controversy over what sort of art best serves Ireland, and particularly over the theatre and Synge's *The Playboy of the Western World*. Garnett's view of Yeats as somehow more Irish than his critics in the mass nationalist movement depends on his belief that 'Yeats's poetic and patriotic creed is one and indivisible'. The response to Yeats's appeal to a deep level of national feeling will come only when that deep level of national feeling is free of the 'din of political controversy' arising from its battle for liberty. For the moment, national feeling is determined by the realities of its current battle, determined, even if in the negative way which led to the reaction against *The Playboy*, by the English view of Ireland.

The denial to Yeats of his Irishness has continued. Antony Coleman argues that Yeats's claim to be an Irish poet would have been strengthened by the inclusion in his work of the Gaelic tradition. He declares that the sixteenth–century Irish figure Manus O'Donnell would have made a much better exemplar of the man of culture than Robert Gregory. Coleman emphasizes the exploitative roots of the Anglo-Irish 'Big House', 'a symbol which could not be invested with those genial and humane values, the theme of mutuality between *magister* and *minister* which Jonson had hymned in "To Penshurst"'.⁵² Coleman refers with approval to Daniel Corkery's *The Hidden Ireland*, but Foster points out that 'the mentality analysed in Corkery's *Hidden Ireland* is purely that of the Gaelic aristocracy as expressed through their bards … '⁵³ It seems possible that the Gaelic 'Big House' is a countermyth rather than an objective fact.

Michael North also points to the contradiction at the heart of *noblesse oblige*: 'What the aristocracy gives had first to be taken, and the material independence of the class is not in fact the basis of its service to the community but rather a result of its exploitation.'⁵⁴ This is an argument which has force, and could be used against the aristocrat anywhere: the aristocrat merely gives back by his grace and favour a little of what his ancestors appropriated in the first place. Yeats's espousal of the Anglo-Irish 'Big House' in the form of Coole makes him vulnerable to this sort of criticism, and the elitist tone of a poem such as 'Upon a House shaken by the Land Agitation' can indeed be offensive to today's more egalitarian sensibility. Yet there is a strange mixture of harsh pragmatism and idealism in the poem's argument. To divide equally the wealth that Coole has accumulated would spread it so thin as effectively to destroy it; to leave it concentrated makes it, through the art it can foster, a source of cultural wealth for all.

For Coleman, Yeats lacks the roots in the tradition of the Irish people which would have made him an Irish poet, and any use he makes of traditional Irish material is distorted by his own purposes, which 'did not include fidelity to their originating occasions' (YA3 48). His argument seems to develop from those forces which excluded Yeats from nationalism. Yeats was marginalized within the nationalist movement by his Protestant descent, and by the association with the colonial elite (the Anglo-Irish Ascendancy) implicit in this. His reaction may be seen as perverse, but effectively made a virtue of his exclusion from mass nationalism and took isolation as an opportunity. It seems that, for Coleman, such isolation is sufficient to render him un-Irish. On passages from 'My Table' and 'Coole Park 1929', he comments:

> Yeats's is a felt certitude in such value, the value of heroic life, passionate, sensuous, aristocratic living. What he dismisses are the

legitimate felt certitudes of others now engaged in a civil war to establish their own validity. Here lies explanation of his failure to be an Irish, a popular poet: unlike the Gaelic poets of the eighteenth century, he does not express his feelings in the idiom of national events – his mode of consciousness being English, he ignores significant implications in the Irish experience, an experience the stated subject of his meditations, 'Time of Civil War'. (YA3 44)

The equation of 'Irish' and 'popular' implies that Yeats loses his nationality through his separation from the mass of the people, that only a 'popular' poet can be an 'Irish' poet. Theodore Maynard's view in 1919 of Yeats's poetic decline shows a similar tendency to identify Ireland exclusively with the mass of its people. He feels that a more populist nationalism, a more overt espousal of the Irish people's conception of the nationalist cause, would have retained in Yeats's work the freshness and life of his earlier poetry:

> If Mr. Yeats had perceived that his country had real and not seeming needs, the sap would not have dried out of his veins ... The same intellectual aloofness which has driven Mr. Yeats to the narrow tendencies of his poetry has made him an alien in his own country.[55]

Coleman's claim that Yeats's 'mode of consciousness' is 'English' suggests that Daniel Corkery has played a role in mediating to our own time critical attitudes which originated with figures such as Moran and Atkinson:

> This Ascendancy it was that had fixed the moulds of Anglo-Irish literature, if Anglo-Irish it be, those moulds that do not willingly receive the facts of Irish life.[56]

> From the beginning then though we may think of this literature as a homogeneous thing, we cannot think of it as an indigenous thing. Its moulds therefore cannot have been fashioned to express the genius of Ireland in the English language. If in later years certain writers tried to do this, as some have tried, the unnatural homogeneity of these moulds proved their greatest enemy, so inflexible they have ever been. (7)

Corkery's nationalist essentialism does not allow for the back-pressure of experience on language which means that language in use accommodates itself to its users. His view suggests that language determines its users, and so sees only half of a dialogical process.[57] He sees nationality as already a unity, which makes it exclusive, rather than inclusive; divisive, rather than unifying:

> Nationalism is tangible only in its communal pieties. The origin of them, the growth of them, the reverence for them, the homogeneity of them, are the considerations we should keep before our minds. Protestant nationalism will not stand against such tests.[58]

> Nationality is a people's mind's reverential awareness of itself as it finds itself abidingly embodied in the national pieties.[59]

If such a definition is more than circular nonsense, it suggests that national literature can reflect only what is there. There is no place for the imaginary nation of the artist which Yeats saw as an embodiment of the aim of unity, to which the divided society could aspire. W. K. Magee's instinct detected an old sectarianism in the language movement: 'The claim for the Irish language seems to me only a new form of the old impossible claim of one race and tradition to extirpate its rival in this country.'[60]

Yeats's loss of his popular audience is used against him in the continuation of a battle over whether the English language can express Irishness or whether literature written in English can help establish an Irishness for the twentieth century. Maintaining faith with both art and the world becomes impossible for the poet, if, on one hand, art determined by the demands of popular politics cannot be considered genuine and, on the other, it is accepted that the needs of the world are what the mass of its people considers itself to need. To represent the move towards elitism in this phase of Yeats's work as the result of a confused class position is to miss the point. Yeats's aesthetic and political views are too closely tied for us to assume that the political determined the aesthetic in this way, unless we accept the reductive view that all human action and thought is ultimately determined by power relations. Seamus Heaney maintains the artist's view against the political determinists: 'He donned the mantle – or perhaps one should say the fur coat – of the aristocrat so that he might express a vision of a communal and personal life that was ample, generous, harmonious, fulfilled and enhancing.'[61]

The poet creates from something he takes from life an image of what life can become. The distance that the poet seeks to establish between the life he seeks to evoke in the work and life in contemporary Ireland is to stand as an indictment of contemporary Ireland. The use of Coole as a pattern stems from his personal history, rather than the 'facts' of Irish history. As Heaney points out, it is the poetry that emerges from the use of the pattern that should be the basis of our judgement.

Coole provides Yeats with an image, and, in 'To a Wealthy Man' (VP 287–8), Yeats makes the provision of such images the responsibility of the aristocracy. The influence of his visit to Italy and his reading of Castiglione is clear. The wealthy man is attacked partly for his refusal of that element of risk involved in *sprezzatura*, and his care for the judgement of those who are not his equals. He betrays his position as leader by seeking to follow the opinion of the masses who should be led. The anti-democratic note of the poem is one which highlights Yeats's view that democratic art is impossible; it highlights the polarities of art and politics, modern and traditional, mass and elite culture which are also an issue in 'Upon a House shaken by the Land Agitation'. '[W]hat the blind and ignorant town / Imagines best to make it thrive' cannot be what is best for it, since not only is it ignorant, but it is also fallen into the materialism and the seeking of the immediate goal which makes impossible the realization in the future of any goal not currently visible: the exclusive pursuit of the immediately attainable renders impossible the improvement, the transcendence, of present culture through the aspiration towards that imaginative ideal which the best art places before society.

Joseph Hone's *Irish Times* article 'Art and Aristocracy' (11 January 1913), in which he puts forward for Yeats the ideas behind the poem, helps to direct the poem to one of its audiences. The article claims that the struggle to keep the Hugh Lane pictures gives 'the gentlemen of Ireland' an opportunity to show leadership. It appeals to their tradition as one which opposes the 'kind of compliment to democracy [which] is implicit in three-fourths of what is said and written about literary and artistic affairs when these become matters of "public interest".'[62] The article calls on the wealthier classes to show leadership by daring to be different:

> Our landlords and big merchants are ever being told that they might lead the nation if they would but fall in with the political opinions of the majority – a remark which is at the same time both paradox and platitude.

The call to the readers of the *Irish Times* to look to Renaissance Italy for a model of how to behave when political power has been lost is clear:

Ercole d'Este, Duke Guidobaldo, Cosimo de Medici, the greatest patrons of the liberal arts the world has ever known, were more than patrons of the liberal arts. They illustrate for all time an attitude which must be that of aristocracy if the word has any meaning. Deprived temporarily of his political power, Cosimo did not grow embittered, or forget that it was still his prerogative to patronise Michelozzo. Who can say that Mr. Yeats's analogy is impertinent to Ireland today?

This from a 1908 article by Synge shows how ideas concerning politics and the arts can come together with a particularly Irish class position:

Until recently the political affairs of Ireland were directed, to a large extent, by leaders, like Parnell, from the Protestant and landlord classes, but now after the experience of a century the more native portion of the people have reached a stage in which they have little trouble in finding political leaders among themselves. In the arts, however, it is different. Although the Irish popular classes have sympathy with what is expressed in the arts they are necessarily unfamiliar with artistic matters, so that for many years to come artistic movements in Ireland will be the work of individuals whose enthusiasm or skill can be felt by the less-trained instincts of the people. These individuals, a few here and there like the political leaders of the nineteenth century, will be drawn from the classes that have still some trace or tradition of the older culture and yet for various reasons have lost all hold on direct political life. The history of the founding of this new gallery and the work done for it by Mr. Hugh Lane and a few others since 1902 is a good instance of these new courses in Irish affairs.[63]

There is a new twist here on the Yeatsian idea of a switch from politics to culture after the fall of Parnell. Here Synge preserves a role for his own class in a switch from political to cultural leadership.

Roy Foster indicates the effect of Yeats's new social alignments – 'friendships in great houses ... and his assumption into a kind of artistic establishment in England' – on his response to what seemed the imminence of Home Rule.[64] I am interested in the connections between the arguments he developed as a result of his changing social alignments and his modifying nationalism and in how these relate to his poetics, since the creation of himself as a public figure is so much a part of his poetic practice. For Yeats, personality is crucial. For him to have identified himself completely with the mass nationalist political cause (probably by 1913 impossible in any case[65]) would have been to make of his poetry an abstraction, the expression of a cause – the thought common to many – rather than the expression of the individual. Yet by establishing *himself* as a public figure, involved in controversy, and by maintaining the link between himself and the figure of Yeats who inhabits the poems, he was able to mediate between the world of art and the everyday world while retaining the necessary distance between them.

Through his poetry and his involvement in public controversy Yeats created himself as a figure embodying particular values. He had started this process much earlier and as a matter of artistic practice. George Russell noted in 1916 the connection of the creation of personality with that of style and the deliberate connection of work and life:

> He began about the time of *The Wind among the Reeds* to do two things consciously, one to create a 'style' in literature, the second to create or rather to re-create W. B. Yeats in a style which would harmonise with the literary style. People call this posing. It is really putting on a mask, like his actors, Greek or Japanese, a mask over life. The actor must talk to the emotion on the mask, which is a fixed emotion. W.B.Y. began twenty years ago vigorously defending Wilde against the charge of being a poseur. He said it was merely living artistically, and it was the duty of everybody to have a conception of themselves, and he intended to conceive of himself. The present W.B.Y. is the result.[66]

Seamus Heaney indicates the achievement by Yeats of this self-creation when he comments on the difficulties of the Irish writer of the present:

> in terms of the writer conducting himself in a politicized milieu, I think Yeats becomes important within that milieu not so much for what he says as for who he is. Within a culture the most important thing for the poet is to establish authority, and Yeats had the gift of establishing authority: first of all by achievement, but secondly by a conduct which was 'majestic' in some kind of way and overbearing to some extent but based upon a belief in the culture. He could rebuke the culture because he was its most intense representative to some extent. And I think that the poet has to not get caught in a position where he is answerable to the politician but where in some way the politician is under his spiritual gaze. Now that is what is

exemplary about Yeats, but also what is very difficult to achieve for a writer in contemporary Ireland.[67]

The effect of Yeats's poetry is not totally contained within the words on the page. His position as a man in relation to his society (as well as to literary culture) contributes to the effect of his poetry, and since this position was consciously achieved, constitutes part of the work. The difficulty Heaney notices is that which the writer faces in trying to bring the force of symbolic capital to bear outside the sphere of art. On one hand, late twentieth-century and early twenty-first-century criticism is not to be fooled by the artist's claim to disinterest; on the other, the recognition (or is it insufficiently critical acceptance?) of the political element in all social matters promotes politics to a point where art becomes marginal and trivial. At the same time, the discrediting of the concept of authority and leadership by fascist politics and their culmination in the Holocaust renders the authority of the poet suspect, even as an aim.

III

In his 1913 speech addressing the fear felt by Protestants of persecution in an independent Irish state, Yeats indicated his belief that once English dominance was removed, Ireland would find a way forward in which its different groupings would discover common interests and so put an end to factionalism. The belief in the absolute necessity of removing English domination marks a continuity with Yeats's earlier nationalism: 'He was an Irish Nationalist, because he believed since he first gave thought to these things that no country could prosper unless the greater portion of its intellect was occupied with itself.'[68]

But, though he specifically denies a denominational aspect, this next comment shows an attitude easily associated with the ideas of Protestant Ascendancy:

> They were asking nothing but an arena in which the best might come out, and the best might rule. The intolerance which he dreaded was the intolerance that existed amongst Catholics and Protestants, against ideas, against books, against European culture, and he saw nothing that would put down that intolerance but the obtaining of that arena that would teach them how to sift out the best men.

The disclaimer cannot alter Yeats's vulnerability to the charge that elitism is an attitude carried over from the belief of the Protestant Anglo-Irish in their right to ascendancy, and that it must be inimical to the rights of the mass of the people (who happen to be Catholic) since it is anti-democratic. Comments by D. G. Boyce illustrate how vulnerable a Protestant-led cultural movement is to charges of class, or displaced political, motivation: 'a revival inspired by Protestants who hoped to give cultural direction where political control eluded them.' 'Who was Ireland to be saved from? Possibly the Irish; but O'Grady, Yeats and Hyde could hardly come out and say that openly.'[69] The charge of simple anti-Catholicism would be excessive, but it is possible to see a connection between an increasing identification with Protestant Anglo-Ireland and the pressure of marginalization within nationalism on Yeats because he was not Catholic.

In one sense, Yeats was well aware of the reason why political nationalism reasserted itself after the shift to cultural nationalism which, in his view, followed the fall of Parnell:

> Home Rule is essential because all the characteristic Irish public faults come from the absorption of the nation in one subject of political discussion. No Irish movement can succeed till the intellect of Ireland has been liberated from national obsession.[70]

With the Irish mind so obsessed, cultural movements could only be judged by their use to the cause of independence from England. Synge's *In the Shadow of The Glen* and *The Playboy*, for instance, could be charged with putting Ireland in a bad light abroad, with undermining the image of a chaste Ireland so different from degenerate England. Lyons indicates the doublebind in which 'those Anglo-Irish writers who claimed to have no propaganda but that of good art' found themselves:

> As Protestants for the most part, as products of the still distrusted ascendancy, they could have been welcomed into the new nationalism only if, like Parnell, they had turned their backs completely on the tradition that had bred them. This they instinctively refused to do. To deliver up their integrity to the rule of the majority was a sacrifice they could not contemplate. Still less could they contemplate it when they saw what the majority had done to Parnell. It is no accident that in Yeats's poems of alienation of this period that tragic figure reappears as a symbol of rejection.[71]

The appeal which Yeats's artistic beliefs make, then, to the tradition of an elite, patronising art and so bringing forth the best and eventually raising the cultural level of the whole society, is one which can only tie him more closely to what the mass of that society sees as the enemy. His justification drives him further into elitism and the refusal to accept mass values. The image of Parnell, developed further by Yeats from Lionel Johnson's Parnell, the Parnell who said *'Secretum meum mihi'*,[72] is particularly suited to his needs because of Parnell's aloofness, the apparent lack of care for what the mass of people thought of him while still working in their cause, and their ultimate betrayal of him because of what Yeats would have seen as a puritanical piety (and, within the Irish Party, political expediency, since Gladstone threatened to withdraw his backing if it did not repudiate Parnell).

'To a Shade' (VP 292–3) ties together the first and third of the public controversies by which Yeats's imagination was aroused by associating Hugh Lane and Parnell. The idea once more is of what the patron of art can do for the majority of society by placing before it art which might provide an imaginative ideal to which it can aspire. What art can bring works in the veins like blood. By patronising art the aristocrat can lend to future generations of the masses some of that nobility which comes to him through his line of descent. This poem makes even clearer, then, the attack on the wealthy man, who, far from providing this possibility for the masses, seeks only to allow culture to reflect their own existing tastes.

The first part of the poem suggests a valuing of place above society:

> When grey gulls flit about instead of men,
> And the gaunt houses put on majesty:
> Let these content you and be gone again. (VP 292)

There is something which the poet can think of as Ireland, a place, which is not associated with the contemporary Irish society he despises. Once men are removed from the scene, the Ireland that the poet cares for, that Parnell cared for, resumes the dignity society's business strips from it. '[W]hen the day is spent' also suggests a longing for the peace of evening which reflects a dislike of the daily business that typifies commercial society. Gaunt, majestic Dublin is associated with eighteenth-century Protestant Ireland:

> Protestant Ireland had immense prestige, Burke, Swift, Grattan, Emmet, Fitzgerald, Parnell, almost every name sung in modern

song, had been Protestant; Dublin's dignity depended upon the gaunt magnificence of buildings founded under the old Parliament. (Au 418–19)

The recommendation that Parnell's ghost return to his tomb recalls the idea in 'September 1913' that modern Ireland has betrayed the vision of its earlier patriots, though, of course, Parnell lived close enough to the time of writing of these poems to have suffered from those attitudes of middle-class Catholic Ireland personified, for Yeats, by William Martin Murphy, enemy of both Parnell and Lane. The poet espouses the values of the one against those of the many through identification with Parnell and Lane. Both are the noble stag dragged down by the hounds[73] which are the mob set on by the rhetorician by means of the abstracted political cause; both stand on the artist's side of the polarity which is no match, in modern society, for the journalist, the politician, who uses the mob as his tool. Though back in 1904, Yeats had secured a retraction from Arthur Griffith in the *United Irishman* after the paper had implied that Hugh Lane's motivation was solely commercial.[74]

Yeats's discouragement stems from a glimpse of the independent Ireland that is to emerge from the long struggle for freedom. The distinction between state and nation may be a further way of throwing light on how Yeats's aesthetic is tied in with his response to the changing nature of the nationalist movement, at least as he saw it, and his efforts to establish his identity. David Miller suggests that the nation is established as a parallel force alongside the state during the nationalist struggle for independence.[75] We have seen from Yeats's essay on Spenser his view of the state as an abstraction, a political entity replacing that personification of the people in the form of the monarch which is the sign of a more unified sensibility.[76] The Parliament Act 1911 had put an end to the ability of the Conservative Party to use its majority in the Lords to block indefinitely Liberal government legislation for Home Rule. The nationalist movement, with independence almost in sight (though the difficulties presented by the North should not be forgotten), caused Yeats to realize that the function of the state currently fulfilled by the easily hated England was to be taken over by something Irish, once independence could be achieved. The type of ideal independent Irish nation which had long been an aspiration must have seemed as far away as ever under the impact of the Hugh Lane controversy. Irish nationalism itself had become identified with the materialism, the short-term view, the philistinism, which Yeats had always tried to typify as English.[77]

IV

Yeats's thoughts on the theatre in a lecture given in March 1913 illustrate the way in which his particular sort of mind attempts to order the world it observes:

> The uneducated mob now paid the piper and exacted the tune, and all the art movements of to-day were attempts to recover control of the means of expression, the most powerful of which was the theatre, which was also the most debased, because nowhere else had the uneducated mob got so tight a grip. Theatres needed a vast audience to succeed ... Besides, the theatre had its hold on the newspapers through advertisements and notices. They had a combination of the theatre of commerce and the newspapers supporting it. It was a vast vested interest of the ill-educated expressing itself in multitudes of copies day after day.[78]

In spite of the effort he had put into the Abbey Theatre, Yeats had not been able to form the audience he wanted there.[79] A mood of pessimism combined with a tendency to try to see pattern in events to group popular theatre, journalism and commerce within an upsurge of the mass of people which threatened to extinguish the possibility of a high culture in Ireland fostered by the elite bearers of tradition. The sense that the nationalist movement had been taken over by an ill-educated middle class underlies the discouragement in *Poems Written in Discouragement*.

The original title of 'September 1913', 'Romance in Ireland (On reading much of the correspondence against the Art Gallery)' (VP 289–90), stresses the element of comment on a public matter, and foreshadows the ironic note of the refrain. The first stanza attacks the commercial values and mechanical (even mathematical) piety Yeats sees as having become dominant in Ireland, displacing the heroic values he associates with O'Leary. Yeats uses the same image in a speech reported by the *Manchester Guardian* (15 July 1914):

> If Hugh Lane is defeated, hundreds of young men and women all over the country will be discouraged – will choose a poorer idea of

what might be ... if the intellectual movement is defeated Ireland will for many years become a little huckstering nation, groping for halfpence in a greasy till.[80]

He offers the gallery issue as a contest between aristocratic values and the commercial values of the lower middle class. O'Leary found middle-class values unheroic:

> The middle class, I believe, in Ireland and elsewhere, to be distinctly the lowest class morally – that is, the class influenced by the lowest motives. The prudential virtues it has in abundance; but a regard for your own stomach and skin, or even for the stomachs and skins of your relatives and immediate surroundings, though, no doubt, a more or less commendable thing in itself, is not the stuff out of which patriots are made.[81]

That Yeats returns to thoughts of O'Leary in 'September 1913' might lead us to look at the essay 'Poetry and Tradition' (E&I 246–60), though it was written rather earlier, in 1907. As well as O'Leary, there are references to Parnell, to the petite bourgeoisie and its materialism, and lack of education and tradition, and to Castiglione. The essay links O'Leary not only with a romantic Ireland but also with Grattan, and so with the Anglo-Irish conception of an Ireland free of English domination. It points to the difference between the nationalism of O'Leary and the current nationalism, and indicates the change in the Ireland for which Yeats sees himself working from an ideal to an imaginary one. The further difference between the Yeats writing 'Poetry and Tradition' and the Yeats writing in discouragement in 1913 seems to be that, since it proves so difficult for Lane to place before the Irish public the art which might help towards the creation of a future highly cultured Ireland, Yeats's imaginary Ireland loses all place and purpose. The effect of the controversy was to threaten Yeats's sense of an aim for his work.

The O'Leary Yeats first knew was a solitary figure:

> O'Leary found himself isolated as a kind of a venerable crank during the height of the Parnellite excitement, in that lonely time when Yeats first knew him.[82]

It is easy to see that this exile may have had a sort of Rip Van Winkle effect, so that O'Leary, still carrying the credit of his earlier years, still a nationalist hero, was isolated within a movement which had moved on while he was in exile: he had returned from the dead to offer to Yeats the possibility of a living embodiment of the values of dead heroes. This contributed to Yeats's conception of him as a representative of older values which could be opposed to modern ones. Foster's comment – 'For O'Leary, his life was his art'[83] – hints at a further influence on Yeats's poetic of personality, in the significance of the life of the poet and that shaping of the public figure of the poet which is part of the art of the poet. The O'Leary of 'Poetry and Tradition' is an example for Yeats to follow under the pressure of his discouragement:

> The worth of a man's acts in the moral memory, a continual height of mind in the doing of them, seemed more to him than their immediate result, if, indeed, the sight of many failures had not taken away the thought of success. (E&I 247)

Driven increasingly in on himself, it is important for Yeats to establish a set of values within himself to which he can appeal for justification and identity, and which he can claim is an older and more worthwhile set of values than that of the nationalist movement as it currently stands. For Yeats, it is the nationalist movement which has fallen from its right to justify: it has abandoned the older values of nation (rather than political and materialist state) identified with O'Leary and Grattan.

The example of O'Leary as a man acting according to his own set of values, according to what he believes to be right rather than with a view to what might be gained in the short run, is a particularly good one for the artist to follow, as Yeats sees it, since the artist must strive to avoid contemporary values, especially in the modern materialist, commercial age. The values Yeats aligns himself with are those of tradition. He writes of O'Leary's 'Roman courage', of Grattan's generation reading Homer and Virgil. How to live is to be decided not by an appeal to self-created values, according to Nietzschean principles, but rather to traditional values, internalized and opposed to the influence of the values of modern materialism. There is an almost religious feeling to the idea that the actions of a man doing what he believes to be right, without considering success or popularity, somehow raises the level of morality of society. The increasingly isolated Yeats, even if cut off from the imagined view of a goal, an aim for his work, a potential success, can follow the example of the stoical hero O'Leary, and continue to act as he thinks right.

There is a sense in the essay of the necessity of distance from the modern age, which he also applies, in the Lunn interview, to art:

The truth is, I don't know much about contemporary writers, except the poets. Till a few generations ago, writers founded themselves on the classics, and so saw their own age at a distance, and more clearly. But a modern writer, if, like so many of us, he has not the classics, must get his place apart from life by avoiding his contemporaries. I always advise young writers to read the English authors of the seventeenth century. Even Wordsworth, even Keats and Shelley, have the same illusions as us. We are too near to what is worthless in them.[84]

Section III of 'Poetry and Tradition' expounds the theme of a freedom of expression which is not available to the modern artist who is a man of his age, again opposing the values of Castiglione to modern materialism.

No new man has ever plucked that rose, or found that trysting-place, for he could but come to the understanding of himself, to the mastery of unlocking words, after long frequenting of the great Masters, hardly without ancestral memory of the like. Even knowledge is not enough, for the 'recklessness' Castiglione thought necessary in good manners is necessary in this likewise, and if a man has it not he will be gloomy, and had better to his marketing again. (E&I 255–6)

Style is the equivalent in the writer of courtesy in Castiglione's courtier; and it is an excess, something surplus to the requirements of everyday, which Yeats feels is necessary to style. It becomes, then, an absolute expression of the artist's self, something to which he is not constrained by necessity, an expression of that in him which is free, which is not forced on him by the nature of things and the world.[85]

The idea of breeding is prevalent in this section of the essay, emphasizing the link Yeats sees between the place of the artist in an artistic tradition and the place of the aristocrat within a dynasty. The 'recklessness', the 'shaping joy', the *sprezzatura* of the artist come from a quality of carelessness which only the placing of himself within a tradition can give him. This is the equivalent of the high breeding of the courtier, the working of blood in his veins. It is a freedom from concern with the world to which a separation from the modern age, an age obsessed with utility, is necessary. This separation, Yeats says in his interview with Lunn, can be found by studying English authors of the seventeenth century. Yeats himself was at the time of the interview reading Donne, and a comment on Donne, in a letter to

H.J.C. Grierson dated 14 November 1912, makes him an exemplar of the expression of self through style: 'the more precise and learned the thought the greater the beauty, the passion; the intricacy and subtleties of his imagination are the length and depths of the furrow made by his passion' (L 570).

Style is becoming, then, in Yeats's mind the means by which the artist can free himself from the utilitarian, materialist modern world. Driven in on himself by the subsumption of nationalism within the modern democratic type of thinking which is anathema to him, he seeks to establish a value system to which he can appeal. This value system is based on elitism, as opposed to egalitarianism, and the traditional, as opposed to the modern, and accordingly associated with aristocracy and with eighteenth-century Protestant Ireland.

This section of 'Poetry and Tradition' suggests a particular, perhaps paradoxical, capacity of the artist made individual through style to express the universal. The sense of joy available to the artist through the celebration of his individuality in style is one which the use of 'exult' in 'To a Friend whose Work has come to Nothing' (VP 290-1) suggests might be extended from the sphere of art into life. This poem's advice to Lady Gregory shows a similar attitude to that expressed in the 'Closing Rhymes' of *Responsibilities*: that in a world which has no appreciation of honour and the truly fine, notoriety is a badge of honour. Secrecy, the withdrawal into a self which knows its own superiority, is a means of overcoming defeat by rising above the idea of competition, refusing to acknowledge the values of contemporary society in a way similar to the political prisoner's refusal to acknowledge the jurisdiction of a state court. There is also a sense of the necessity of self-overcoming, which is perhaps directed as much at the poet himself as at his friend.

It is tempting to see a Nietzschean link here, as so often when Yeats's work shows such clear evidence of his shift towards the aristocratic. But there is also an appeal to tradition and class value evident in 'Bred to a harder thing / Than Triumph' (VP 291). 'Bred' has clear connotations of pedigree, and the whole phrase carries a note of *noblesse oblige*. The parallel between artist and aristocrat which Yeats draws in the 1909 journal seems still to be in his mind here.[86] 'Exult' recalls 'To a Wealthy Man' (VP 287-8). In both poems exultation is associated with private celebration, an affirmation of the heroic stance of the few, even of the one, against the many. Once more the '*Secretum meum mihi*' of Johnson's Parnell shows through. Yeats takes this image of Parnell as an exemplar of public behaviour.

The isolation of Yeats's political and social position is one which his aesthetic can justify his seizing with joy, or accepting in a heroic way, rather than merely acknowledging that circumstance has thrust upon him. His later occupation of Thoor Ballylee is an instance of his making one of the life and the work which embodies this unifying of aesthetic and ethical values: the tower is a symbol of isolation, representing an isolation from modern Irish society nonetheless rooted in Irish soil. Thoor Ballylee has a necessary solid connection with the world, but is nonetheless transformed, appropriated, by the poet's imagination, by means of his work.[87] Donald Davie notes that *Poems Written in Discouragement* marks a significant point of disillusionment.[88] But there is also an enabling aspect to the withdrawal into the self: it has an intensifying effect. Heaney notes the need for Yeats to find strength within himself, and also his capacity to take the risks involved with confronting the possibility of disillusionment.[89]

It would be possible to characterize Yeats's response to his isolation as making a virtue out of necessity, but the idea of the artist's shaping joy also makes possible an active counterpart to this more passive interpretation. The celebration of oneself as individual, as removed from the necessity imposed by the world, allows that separation, that distinction between self and world, between self and not-self, which makes orientation to the world, and so the achievement of identity, possible. It is the quality in excess of the necessary which the artist's style, the expression of his individuality available to him through his absorption of a tradition of culture, imparts to what he creates in how it is ordered. In life, this idea of a shaping joy frees the individual from fate, in that it enables him to rise above the merely necessary in imposing his own pattern upon it. In the case of the artist, this joy is the active, creative complement to that passive observation which must take in things known to all: it is the individual expression of the universal:

> This joy, because it must be always making and mastering, remains in the hands and in the tongue of the artist, but with his eyes he enters upon a submissive, sorrowful contemplation of the great irremediable things, and he is known from other men by making all he handles like himself, and yet by the unlikeness to himself of all that comes before him in a pure contemplation. (E&I 254–5)

This joy is also what prevents a man being left 'helpless before the contents of his own mind' (E&I 405). Man's perceptions, what realist philosophy might describe as the objective facts, present the universal tragedy of death: not the particular tomb or asp, but 'all men's fate' (E&I 255). The joy associated with the artist's style, a surplus to the merely necessary objective facts, represents an active faculty capable as it completes the world by ordering the perceptions of transforming the contents of the mind in such a way as to free the individual from fate.

There is a complex duality in Yeats's idea of personality. Personality is necessary to personal expression in poetry, to make it 'the absolute speech of a man'; yet it is involved with style, which draws on tradition, suggesting that personality is not radically singular, but, even as absolutely individual expression, is connected with something larger. 'Personality is greater and finer than character ... It is mixed up in style. When a man cultivates a style in literature he is shaping his personality' (YT 38–9). In the poet who achieves personality, tradition achieves expression through its embodiment, a complete rather than an abstracted expression: 'The image of one who has lived passionately and sincerely is always more important than his thought' (YT 39). And this expression is individual, though it relies on the individual's place in tradition. It is a drawing on the past to express a potential present, and a potential present which defines itself against the actual present. Yeats draws strength from his opposition to the contemporary world. The influence of Goethe can be seen in his sense that he benefits from this combativeness:

> For it is in a conflict with natures opposed to his own that a man must collect his strength to fight his way through, and thus all our different sides are brought out and developed, so that we soon feel ourselves a match for every foe.[90]

At the same time it is the contemporary world which has forced him in on himself and compelled his definition of himself. 'Paudeen' (VP 291) indicates the depth and significance of that essential quality within the individual at his most alone and apparently silent to which the work of an artist like Synge, as Yeats sees him, seeks to give expression. The soul's 'sweet crystalline cry' is the one possession most particular to that soul, and the possession of this one absolutely particular cry is the one thing all souls hold in common. Anger at the false commonality represented by the politics of Murphy and the class he appeals to is what has driven the poet far enough into himself for this insight to be achieved.

5
Responsibilities

I

The Cuala volume *Responsibilities: Poems and a Play* (1914) includes the poems of *Poems Written in Discouragement*. The play is a new version of *The Hour Glass*, which fits well thematically, since it concerns the discovery by a wise man that his teaching that only the material exists is wrong. *The Hour Glass* was also included in the Macmillan publication *Responsibilities and Other Poems* (1916), though at the end of the volume, excluded from the frame formed by the introductory 'Pardon, old fathers' and the closing 'While I, from that reed-throated whisperer'. *Responsibilities and Other Poems* also includes the poems from *The Green Helmet and Other Poems*, but not the play. This enhances the sense of the poems of *Responsibilities* as a unit. The newer poems are presented first, followed by those from *The Green Helmet and Other Poems*, and the closing part of the frame is moved inside the volume to contain only the poems of *Responsibilities*. 'Friends', 'The Cold Heaven' and 'That the Night Come', published in *The Green Helmet and Other Poems* and *Responsibilities: Poems and a Play*, are kept within the *Responsibilities* frame. Yeats was following a practice established with *In the Seven Woods* of issuing an expensive limited edition through his sister's press, to be followed by a trade edition.

The Cuala Press was the source of some tension in the Yeats family. Michael Yeats in his preface to Liam Miller's book on Cuala says that his father, grandfather and uncle, as well as his aunts, were all involved. John Butler Yeats seems to have found himself acting as mediator between Willie and Elizabeth. According to Michael:

> Inside the family ... Cuala was looked upon as something of an incubus. One's attitude to it was ambivalent. On the one hand its

very existence presented a constant threat of some financial disaster, on the other hand it was an enterprise of such literary and artistic importance that everyone was willing to endure a good deal of family tension and inconvenience in order to preserve it.[1]

Yeats's anxiety over the Dun Emer venture is evident in his letter to Lady Gregory of 8 February 1904, and similar anxiety must have carried over to Cuala. He was concerned that whatever financial assistance he gave would not be enough, and that if the venture were not run soundly as a business then his money would be wasted anyway.[2] Nevertheless, his enthusiasm for the printing side of Dun Emer was clear from the start.[3] Some of the paradoxical nature of the relationship between art and the commercial world is suggested here. It is undesirable for the artistic venture to appear commercially motivated, but perhaps there is a cachet of professionalism to an art that can support itself financially.

Though there were quarrels between Yeats and his sister Elizabeth over business matters too, great tension arose because of Yeats's position as literary adviser to his sister's press. He caused trouble over George Russell's *The Nuts of Knowledge*, the second book produced by Dun Emer, Cuala's predecessor.[4] He retired from his position temporarily during 1906 because of a quarrel over Russell's *By Still Waters*, Russell's second selection of poems for Dun Emer. Yeats vetoed the book as not up to scratch, but Elizabeth declared she would publish it anyway. John Butler Yeats's attempts to mediate were unsuccessful, as his son continued to insist he must have absolute control over what was published.[5] To help him regain control after he had resigned, he asked Katharine Tynan to demand that he edit her poems for Dun Emer.[6] Yeats would obviously have been concerned over the nature of literary publications with which his name was connected. Of course, his own work was forming part of the same series. He was helping his sister out in providing work for her press – and work which would attract subscribers – but the nature of the series in which his own books would take their place was important to him. He described *In the Seven Woods* in a letter to Lady Gregory as 'a specially beautiful and expensive edition of certain of my best things' (CL3 298, 6 January 1903). The Cuala Press books were aimed at a particular audience. Editions were limited to 200 to 400 copies, with an average price of ten shillings.

Further frank exchanges occurred in 1913 when, without consulting Yeats, Elizabeth agreed with Edward Dowden's widow to publish some of the love-poems he had written to her. 300 copies of *A Woman's*

Reliquary were published in November 1913.⁷ An appalled Yeats had written the previous month to Elizabeth:

> I am sorry to say that the poems are even worse than I feared. There is no chance of my being mistaken for the fault is a general flaccidity of technique. The matter is beyond helping now ... Do not forget what I said about the circular. It is entirely necessary that your circular make it plain that I am not responsible for this book. Remember that my critical reputation is important to me. It is even financially important. I cannot have anyone suppose that I am responsible for the selection of this book.⁸

Miller quotes a note in the 1914 Cuala prospectus stating, 'This book is not a part of the Cuala series arranged by W. B. Yeats.'⁹ Yeats's phrase 'financially important' carries a veiled threat. The implication is that the success of the Cuala series depends on his critical reputation, and to undermine this is for Cuala to foul its own nest. The success of this sort of concern – publishing limited, expensive editions – depends on the quality of its product. Of course, the idea that commercial considerations might be paramount could be fatal; for such a concern to turn out a mere money-spinner would run counter to its perceived *raison d'être*.

But here we come back to Michael Yeats's comments: Cuala was both enormously valuable in artistic terms and the source of a constant threat of financial disaster. Elizabeth had been incapacitated by illness in 1911, leaving her sister virtually to run things. Between December 1910 – 400 copies of Yeats's *The Green Helmet and Other Poems* – and October 1912 – 250 copies of *Selections from the Writings of Lord Dunsany* – only Yeats's *Synge and the Ireland of his Time* (350 copies) was published (July 1911). The press was in debt, and in 1913 needed work. One title is listed in preparation in Cuala's 1913 prospectus: *New Poems by W. B. Yeats*. In spring 1913, Cuala issued a leaflet to say that 'the Volume of New Poems by W. B. Yeats will not be issued until the Autumn, Poems of Love Selected from the Writings of W. B. Yeats will be ready in June.'¹⁰ The literary supplement of the *New Statesman* of 20 September 1913 mentions the announcement of a long-awaited new volume of verse from Yeats to be published by Cuala at half a guinea. The truth was that Yeats did not have enough lyrics written to make up the book his sister had proposed to publish in May. This problem was compounded by the fact that he had been writing the series 'Upon a Dying Lady' about Mabel Beardsley, and these poems could not be published while she was still alive.¹¹ *A Selection from the*

Love Poetry of William Butler Yeats is a slim volume indeed to sell at seven shillings and sixpence: only 30 pages of verse and 10 blank pages to close. But Yeats's letter to the publisher of his *Collected Works* of 1908, A. H. Bullen, asking his permission to publish the Cuala selection from the love poetry, shows his readiness to turn the financial necessity to artistic account. His annoyance at the effect of *Poems* 1895, which continued to be successful, is clear.

> So far as I have any object of my own in it, apart from feeding my sister's hungry press, a task of growing difficulty, I want to draw attention to my later work. Accident has given the work written before I was thirty all the public attention I get. For many years Unwin's volume has brought me in between £30 and £40 a year, and the sale's always slightly increasing. (L 576, 22 February 1913)

Indeed, the 'Early Poems' section of the 1913 Cuala selection takes up only three pages, with eight pages for poems from *The Wind Among the Reeds*, 12 from *In the Seven Woods*, and 6 1/2 for poems from *The Green Helmet*. Yeats's creation of his textual self was important to him, and deliberate. His revision of his earlier work was a part of this. When revising, he was adjusting the textual self on which the later textual self was to be founded, adding a layer to the deliberate nature of his self-construction. The continued success of *Poems* 1895, which Fisher Unwin kept churning out, must have hampered his attempts to shape his oeuvre, affected the reception of his work and distorted the poetic figure he sought to create. There is a sharp example of the conflict of commercial and artistic values here as, though the effect of the book annoyed Yeats, he had to concede that for a long period it paid better than any other of his books.[12]

The significance of Cuala and Yeats's placing of his own books in what could be seen to constitute a series of a special kind is clear in his introduction to *Selections from the Writings of Lord Dunsany*:

> When our age too has passed, when its moments also, that are so common and many, seem scarce and precious, students will perhaps open these books, printed by village girls at Dundrum, as curiously as at twenty years I opened the books of history and ballad verse of the old 'Library of Ireland.' They will notice that this new 'Library,' where I have gathered so much that seems to me representative or beautiful, unlike the old, is intended for few people, and written by men and women with that ideal condemned by 'Mary of the

Nation,' who wished, as she said, to make no elaborate beauty and to write nothing but what a peasant could understand. If they are philosophic or phantastic, it may even amuse them to find some analogy of the old with O'Connell's hearty eloquence, his winged dart shot always into the midst of the people, his mood of comedy; and of the new, with that lonely and haughty person below whose tragic shadow we of modern Ireland began to write.[13]

He perhaps saw some amends for his loss to Charles Gavan Duffy of the battle in the early 1890s over a 'Library of Ireland' series.[14] He finds the opportunity to further the effort taken up with Lionel Johnson to move Ireland on from the literary tastes of *The Nation* and Thomas Davis. He can maintain his pitch for a more exclusive audience. Here too is his promotion of the isolated figure of Parnell as exemplar and inspiration. He projects his and other work published by Cuala as cultural foundation for the future as he imagines that future looking back on his own time. Even in this, there is a projection of himself into the past, and it is a projection which aims at some control over future reception of his work.

II

The dispute over the best arrangement of Yeats's poems for a collected edition to follow is one which has 'died away, as such controversies do',[15] but my study of early-middle Yeats was greatly influenced by the arrangement chosen for A. N. Jeffares's edition, *Yeats's Poems*. It is not my intention to recur to a stale dispute, and I shall refer to it minimally.[16] What interests me is how a response to the arrangement of the poems has informed my view of what Yeats's poems as a body constitute and how the figure of Yeats is constructed within that body, and also what may lie behind other views. I think of it as a reader's interest.

The issue arising from the dispute which is most important to my own study is that of the placing of the longer narrative poems in their own section at the back of the volume, following the format adopted for the *Collected Poems* of 1933. This chapter and my chapter on *In the Seven Woods* argue that a more satisfying reading of *In the Seven Woods* and *Responsibilities* is made possible by the placing of 'The Two Kings' within the context of the *Responsibilities* frame and 'The Old Age of Queen Maeve' and 'Baile and Aillinn' immediately preceding the lyrics of *In the Seven Woods*. Some comment on the divided format of the

Collected Poems of 1933, so influential in the reception of Yeats's poems, is therefore necessary here.

The placing of the longer poems in their own section at the back of the book was suggested by Yeats's publisher, Macmillan. The idea was that the book would then appeal more to potential buyers.[17] Richard Finneran dubs those who oppose the separate narrative division 'quasi-chronologists'.[18] He then points out that Yeats did not favour strictly chronological arrangement of his work. Of course, Yeats did not arrange his poems in order of composition. Hugh Kenner long ago argued convincingly that the context of Yeats's poems enhances a reading of them.[19] The placing of lyrics in relation to each other is important. My contention is that the placing of narrative poems in relation to lyrics can be viewed similarly. One objection to the two-part division of the *Collected Poems* (1933) is that it destroys the relationship between 'The Two Kings' and other poems in the *Responsibilities* volume unit. I have discussed the value of an arrangement which preserves the proximity of 'The Old Age of Queen Maeve' and 'Baile and Aillinn' to the lyrics of *In the Seven Woods* in Chapter 2. The importance of having 'The Wanderings of Oisin' at the beginning of the arrangement is clear from Yeats's comment, 'from the moment when I began *The Wanderings of Oisin* ... my subject matter became Irish' (VP 841).[20]

My other objection to the two-part division is that it has the effect of relegating the longer narrative poems to the back of the book, implying their inferiority to the rest and their relative lack of significance. Finneran comments:

> [the idea of division] allows him to partially de-emphasise a genre which he had abandoned since 1924 and in which significant success had been elusive; it gives rightful emphasis to the essentially lyrical nature of his achievement.[21]

This suggests that Finneran takes a similar view of Yeats's poetry to some turn-of-the-century reviewers, notably Strachey, who considered Yeats to be at his best as a lyric poet, with the implied conclusion that he should stick to this.[22] Louis MacNeice's view is again similar: 'The Old Age of Queen Maeve' and 'Baile and Aillinn' are 'flat, faded, two-dimensional pieces'. He dislikes 'The Wanderings of Oisin' and 'The Two Kings'.[23] What Finneran means by 'significant success' is hard to determine. If he means that the relegated narrative poems are bad poems, then he is simply wrong.

There is a further, partly time-oriented, point to make here, which may leave me open to the charge of being a 'quasi-chronologist'. The point involves how we might approach the book containing the collected poems, what it represents for the reader, and how they might want it to present itself in view of this. Obviously the book of collected poems is more than a resource from which individual poems can be recovered via an index. Chronological arrangement in order of composition might, to some extent, facilitate analysis of changes in the work over time,[24] but leaves no place for the important construction from its constituent parts of the volume unit. Particularly in the case of Yeats, the book containing the collected poems needs to be organized on a principle which accounts for the development of the figure, Yeats the poet, who inhabits the poetry and is related in a rather problematical way to the Yeats who sits down to breakfast. The poems 'The Old Age of Queen Maeve' and 'Baile and Aillinn' are no less a crucial part of the development of this figure than are the lyrics of *In the Seven Woods* with which they are *in terms of this development* contemporary, and to which they are thematically related. Attention to the relationship between the poet's biography and his work shows the importance of the placing of these two poems following *The Wind Among the Reeds*.[25] Yeats's reference to 'The Wanderings of Oisin' as the foundation of his work as Irish poetry places it at the head of this development, not in a section at the back where casual browsers will not be put off by its length, nor critics by its lack of 'significant success'.[26] Yeats did move away from narrative after 1923 (earlier if we see 'The Gift of Harun Al-Rashid' as a one-off), but the narrative he had written is not rendered insignificant by this. The later Yeats is founded on, develops from, the earlier. To this earlier Yeats, narrative poems were essential, part of his construction of the figure who inhabits the poems, and part of the construction of the work within which the figure of Yeats the poet is generated. The figure constructed through the poems is severely distorted by a division which takes no account of the process of construction. The integrity of the 'permanent self' generated by the poems, integrated in their arrangement in the book, is destroyed by such a division.[27]

III

Responsibilities: Poems and a Play distinguishes typographically between two levels of framing. 'Pardon, old fathers' and 'While I, from that reed-throated whisperer', which frame the volume, are printed in rubric and italic; 'The Grey Rock' and 'The Three Beggars' have their framing lines printed in black italic ('The Grey Rock' also has a long italicized interjection). The framing verses help to establish the volume as a performance, to establish the figure who is responsible for the book, and the audience to which the utterance is addressed.

'Pardon, old fathers' addresses as one possible audience for the poems the poet's ancestors. The tragic note is evident, as he imagines these ancestors listening, awaiting the end of the story, the finish of the line of descent which ends with the poet. He distances himself from the lower middle class which he despises, distinguishing between the 'merchant' and '[t]raders' from whom he is descended and the huckster by whose type his blood has not been tainted. He claims that his anti-utilitarianism began in his youth, inspired not by his grandfather but by the spectacle his grandfather was. He asks pardon because his love for Maud Gonne has meant that he has not continued the family line, but produced only a book. The description of his love as a 'barren passion' might lead us to think of 'Against Unworthy Praise', and what the poet can produce from barrenness.[28] Although the poem is an apology to his ancestors, there is a hint of equivocation between life, represented by procreation, and the work, represented by the book. The volume continues to establish an unresolved debate between the virtues of life and those of art, and between life limited by mortality and eternal life.

As well as presenting the volume as dramatized utterance, the introductory rhyme contributes to the creation of the figure of Yeats the poet. The self-consciousness and apparent revelation of character in the volume show the artifice involved in Yeats's idea of personality. Some reviews consider *Responsibilities and Other Poems* alongside the autobiographical *Reveries over Childhood and Youth*.[29] Yeats's preface to *Reveries* warns that the book may not be a factual account.[30] The past on which the present Yeats stands is to be reshaped quite deliberately through the perception of the present Yeats, uncorrected by reference to chronicled record of fact.

In the introductory rhyme he identifies himself by claiming an ancestry defined by its opposition to the values he believes are those of modern Ireland. The 'old Butlers' who 'did not weigh the cost' are a passing breed in an Ireland increasingly dedicated to thoughts of utility and profit.[31] The poet's lack of progeny links him with them. The failure of the line of descent matches the passing of the way of life associated by the poet with his ancestors. His book will establish him as a figure identified with the values he claims for his ancestors here.

'While I, from that reed-throated whisperer' shows a similar tendency to embrace isolation in an age with which the poet has no affinity. The notoriety he feels has come to him is something which can be seized. He links himself with the part of ancient tradition that fame represents, accepting that in a time when this is no longer available, notoriety will be his lot. The implication is that notoriety in such a time is a badge that can be worn with pride. The sentiment of 'To a Friend Whose Work Has Come to Nothing' is similar. Notoriety is a sign of his difference from that which he sees as wrong in contemporary Ireland. His embracing of this separation reflects an inwardness marked by the opening of the poem, where the whisperer is surmised inwardly, rather than, as formerly, '*A clear articulation in the air*' (VP 320). There *is* an ambiguity here: It might be the 'whisperer' or the 'companions' who were once clearly articulated. Articulation is, perhaps, more suggestive of voice.

Ezra Pound's account in the *Cantos* of Yeats composing 'The Peacock' at Stone Cottage illustrates that, for Yeats, poetry was something addressed to the ear rather than to the eye.[32] The syntax of 'While I, from that reed-throated whisperer' is complicated, yet still follows a type of speech pattern. The poem contains fourteen lines in one sentence. The chief complicating factor is parenthesis. The phrases that make up the poem are easily enough understood, but are ordered in such a way that what we might think of as the basic thread is continually interrupted. The best way to grasp the content of the poem seems to be to exclude parenthetical phrases initially, and then to add them back in. Perhaps even the parallel

> *and find when June is come*
> *At Kyle-na-no under that ancient roof*
> *A sterner conscience and a friendlier home* (VP 321),

can be held in abeyance momentarily in this way. This section of the sentence is itself built up in a manner which reflects the whole: '*and find ... / A sterner conscience and a friendlier home*' interrupted by three modifications. This gives to the poem a studied quality. It suggests a care for precision in the process of composition, to have expression just so before closure is made. Linda Dowling suggests that Yeats is caught in the 'fin de siècle hesitation between the two competing ideals of Pater's elaborate written language and the idiomatic speaking voice'.[33] But the complications in the construction of the poem are also part of the oral aspect of Yeats's work commented on in Chapter 3 on

From *'The Green Helmet and Other Poems'*. Though his audience is an imagined one, the quality of orality in the verse strengthens the sense of communication and limits the threat of the solipsism which the willed isolation, often present in *Responsibilities* and necessary to the distinct definition of the poet's personality, courts.

IV

In *Responsibilities: Poems and a Play*, 'Pardon, old fathers' is followed by 'The Grey Rock' and 'The Two Kings'. 'The Grey Rock' dramatizes its poet in italicized passages which are frankly personal. The creation in this way of a second level recalls 'The Old Age of Queen Maeve' and 'Baile and Aillinn', but in addressing the poem to his former companions in the Rhymers' Club, Yeats identifies the dramatized poet more closely, more clearly, with himself. As in 'Pardon, old fathers', the supposed audience is a company which has passed but with which the poet identifies himself. Similarly, he opposes himself to the time in which he lives by this identification. The story he chooses to tell is better suited to a time now passed, but with which the poet claims affinity. He claims his place in the nineties generation of poets and in praising them justifies his own position. The poem gains poignancy from the emphasis on the poet's aloneness as survivor of his poetic generation. The sacrifice of easy friendship for the sake of that association with immortality which contributing to art can confer is heightened for Yeats because the friends who shared his artistic standard are dead. Just as John O'Leary was used to personify a set of political values associated with the past with which Yeats wished to identify himself, so the Rhymers' Club could be used to personify artistic values. Foster quotes a letter to Edwin Ellis, which he dates 'probably' 2 August 1912: 'I have begun to feel that I belong to a romantic age that is passed away. I am becoming mythical even to myself.'[34] Opposition to the present is expressed by the projection of the values the poet holds onto the past, which he then claims to remain part of. Political, artistic and personal all connect here if we reflect on the disappearance from Yeats's life of the Maud Gonne he first knew, or the figure coincident with Gonne whom he imagined into existence. The effect in 'A Woman Homer Sung' of the creation in the past of the figure of Maud Gonne, a creation which takes place within the writing of the poem, is mirrored in the projection of the figure of Yeats himself into a past generation by those parts of 'The Grey Rock' that refer to the Rhymers'

Club. The element of appropriation in Yeats's use of the Rhymers' Club in this poem is highlighted by Ernest Rhys's resentment of the implication that he and all the other Rhymers bar Yeats were dead.[35]

It was perhaps embarrassing for Yeats to have the weight of his purse increased by the *Poetry* prize for 'The Grey Rock'. Eventually most of the money went to Ezra Pound, on Yeats's recommendation. This does smack rather of log-rolling, since Pound had strongly recommended 'The Grey Rock', *Poetry*'s editor Harriet Monroe herself favouring Vachel Lindsay's 'General Booth'.[36] Pound's review of the Cuala *Responsibilities* found a 'curious nobility' in 'The Grey Rock', but disliked this poem's narrative partner at the head of the volume, 'The Two Kings': 'it is impossible to take any interest in a poem like *The Two Kings* – one might as well read the *Idylls* of another.'[37] Although Pound's review claims that the nobility found in 'The Grey Rock' is 'the very core of Mr Yeats' production, the constant element in his writing',[38] the title, 'The Later Yeats', and much else give the sense of Pound's wanting to move Yeats on, to see him making a kind of progress. He feels that some of Yeats's old admirers will be displeased with *Responsibilities*, and that this is a good thing, since admirers tend to want the poet to 'stay put'. This is in sympathy with Yeats's own dissatisfaction at the continuing influence of *Poems* 1895. But I think that at least part of the reason for Pound's finding of nobility in 'The Grey Rock' is its appeal to the values of the nineties generation of poets, a generation Pound admired too. I think that his valuing of this poem and his tendency to see Yeats's work as moving forward in a way especially marked by some of the poems of this volume fit with a particular way of seeing Yeats and also of seeing the period in literature after the turn of the century. One view of literary history sees a movement later called 'literary modernism' emerging from the nineties, incorporating some of its qualities, such as elitism and anti-commercialism, or rather, on looking more closely, an attitude to the commercial which is ambivalent. The ironic winning of money by 'The Grey Rock' even prefigures the winning of the *Dial* award by T. S. Eliot for *The Waste Land*.[39] Pound dismisses 'The Two Kings' with an inept piece of word play. There is a peculiarly apt fit between Pound's tastes and the *Responsibilities* volume unit as it appears in the *Collected Poems* (1933) and subsequent editions which have chosen to follow the divided format. 'The Two Kings' when in place in the *Responsibilities* volume unit carries too much weight to be dismissed because its form does not fit with a particular theory of the development of poetry into modernist poetry.[40]

There is no disputing the assistance that Pound gave to Yeats with some of his poems. Yeats gave him five contributions for *Poetry*, of which he was self-styled 'overseas editor', and he took it upon himself to make small alterations to 'Fallen Majesty', 'To a Child Dancing in the Wind', and 'The Mountain Tomb'. Yeats's initial reaction was that of 'an outraged monarch', but he did come to accept that Pound had a point and to accept further that Pound could be useful in helping to edit his work.[41] But this hardly justifies the claim of influence, especially as Pound was helping Yeats to move his work in a direction decided before they met. Yeats's valuation of Pound's poetry fell short of his valuation of Pound as editorial assistant.[42] The centrality of Pound to the perception of a movement called 'literary modernism' gives a distorting perspective on the development of Yeats's work.

Some difficulty in finding a satisfying reading of the 'The Grey Rock' arises from the obvious appeal of the heroic action of the warrior whom Aoife loves in the story it tells. But the appeal to this form of the heroic is the popular appeal the poet rejects: in allowing his story to do justice to the appeal of physical heroism, the poet stresses the difficulty of this rejection. The poem compares Maud Gonne to Aoife, and so the poet keeps faith with his muse, with art, rather than being seduced by the appeal of the heroic, which would have kept him in better repute with the mass of the people. Maud Gonne herself, of course, sought to involve herself in mass politics. She saw herself, though, as 'the soul of the crowd'. She wrote this in a reply to Yeats's appeal to her not to marry John MacBride and not to become a Catholic. His draft letter to her on this indicates the belief that her power of influence over the people came from a kind of separation from them, and that in marrying one of them and accepting their faith she would lose this separation.[43] Her claim to be the soul of the crowd is not, perhaps, such a contradiction of what Yeats thought. Her claim does, after all, suggest that she thought of herself not just as one of the crowd but rather as something singular, a kind of representative of its essence. In a scenario for *The Player Queen* the Prime Minister tells the Queen that '[s]he must be the people's soul made greater, as they understand greatness.'[44] There is a hint in this idea of the soul of the crowd of the image Yeats had of Maud Gonne as the embodiment of an ideal, and an ideal associated with the poet's past:

> Thinking of her, as I do, as in a sense Ireland, a summing up in one mind of what is best in the romantic political Ireland of my youth and of the youth of others for some years yet. (1910 Journal, Mem 247)

The keeping of faith with art and with his nationalism can be reconciled, in fact are one, provided it is remembered that the mass nationalist cause is something different again. The poem gains nobility from the integrity shown in keeping faith with a love that has been, in a physical sense, 'a barren passion', and with an ideal nationalism, closely tied to art, which means the rejection of popular appeal and the acceptance of ill-fame.

Aoife's complaint of her mortal beloved is that he chose to risk his life in battle, throwing away the charm she had given him to keep him safe; and was killed, forgoing the two hundred years with her that she had promised him, betraying her for the sake of his new friend the king's son. The poem resumes the theme of contact between the temporal and eternal worlds, of the conflict between these worlds, and the need the eternal world has of the temporal, the attraction the temporal world holds for the eternal:[45]

> Why must the lasting love what passes,
> Why are the gods by men betrayed? (VP 275)

'The Two Kings' tells the story of the conflict of King Eochaid and his wife Edain with a figure who had been her husband in her former, supernatural, existence. Eochaid battles this figure in the form of a white stag which vanishes once he has overcome it, before he can kill it. Edain debates the relative merits of love in the temporal and the eternal worlds with her former husband. He disputes the validity of happiness limited by death. She answers that the very limitations her former husband sees in love in the mortal world give it its power. Her reply might also be seen as a rejoinder to the closing lines of 'Baile and Aillinn':

> 'How should I love,' I answered,
> 'Were it not that when the dawn has lit my bed
> And shown my husband sleeping there, I have sighed,
> "Your strength and nobleness will pass away"?
> Or how should love be worth its pains were it not
> That when he has fallen asleep within my arms,
> Being wearied out, I love in man the child?
> What can they know of love that do not know
> She builds her nest upon a narrow ledge
> Above a windy precipice?' (VP 285)

Compare the line 'She will grow old and die, and she has wept' from 'The Old Age of Queen Maeve' with 'Your strength and nobleness will pass away' in their preoccupation with the passing away of the beloved. Edain turns her former husband's question about the ability of mortals to be happy in love back on him, asking how it is possible for love to be built on the security of eternal foundations. Her argument implies that love must be built on the risk of loss, if it is to be love. Love can only be brought into existence if its foundations are insecure; risk must be confronted. Her answer uses a spatial metaphor for time: love must be founded above (in a sense, necessarily in spite of) the void of ultimate nothingness. This is its miraculous quality. Love gains intensity from the limitation of time in the mortal world, from the inevitability of its passing.

Since Edain is a supernatural creature in a mortal incarnation, her argument answers the question Aoife puts in complaining of her dead beloved. There is an attraction in the mortal world for the eternal: the mortal world has something not available to the eternal. It is the wholesomeness of forgetting that it doubles the hunger for, and the intensity of, experience; and the value of the limitation of the temporal that it allows the intensity not possible to the eternal, which is not similarly concentrated. The overcoming of the immortal by the mortal is reflected in the outcome of the battle between Eochaid and the stag. Terence Brown is right to comment on the presence of death in this volume,[46] but 'The Two Kings' offers a perspective on death and what lies each side of it that plays a part in the dynamic of the volume.

'The Grey Rock' and 'The Two Kings' both concern the contact of the mortal and immortal worlds. In the first poem, the poet tells a story of commitment to the mortal world and the value conferred on life by heroic death, by the acceptance of risk and the refusal of the immortal lover. Having told this story, the poet affirms his own commitment to the eternal. 'The Two Kings' similarly tells the story of commitment to the mortal world, this time on the part of Edain, and the value conferred on love in the mortal world by the inevitability of death, by the limit placed on its duration which is the source of its intensity. In the second poem there is no second level in which the poet rejects this commitment to the mortal world. The poem effectively takes the opposite stance to that of 'The Grey Rock' in allowing the claims of the mortal to prevail. It is worth noting that Yeats's source for the story of 'The Two Kings', 'The History of Ailell and Etain' in the *Revue Celtique*, places more emphasis on Etain's wish to stay with Eochaid than does Lady Gregory's 'Midhir and Etain' in her *Gods and Fighting Men*.[47] It is in this difference between the poems that the value of their presence at the head of the *Responsibilities* volume unit lies.

The mortal and the immortal worlds are shown as antithetical in both poems, and this continues a theme begun much earlier. Taken together the poems indicate the ability of the poet to see the attractions of mortal and immortal, to create his work from the tension and conflict generated by these opposite forces of attraction.

Gould suggests that

> it is inside, as it were, the antinomy of the complementary heroic narratives that the poet dwells, and he dwells uncomfortably. His stage is lit by their contrasting spotlights, he is trapped in their double focus. For the minstrel in the ghostly theatre, immortal and mortal responsibilities are antithetical. Yet he is mortal – and torn: the book or children, the wandering foot or the loud host.[48]

The poet's ultimate commitment is to his poetry, and this must contain the antithesis generated between mortal and immortal, and between life and art. To claim an absolute correspondence between the immortal world and art would be to oversimplify, but the association of the two suggests a consequence of the view of the poet as inhabiting the space between opposing worlds. The poet must feel the claims of art and life. Though he cannot allow the values of art to be subject to worldly values, he cannot allow that art is autonomous, completely separated from the life which is the source of its intensity. Yet he must also be aware of the incompatibility of the values of art and those of the world. The reconciliation of these opposing sets of values would deny the power of art to indict the world for its shortcomings. On a personal level, the poems cannot be read as literal autobiography, but this is not to say that they have no connection at all with the poet's biography. The relationship between the poet's art and his biography is problematical: it is not an exact correspondence, nor is it non-existent. The two narratives at the head of the *Responsibilities* volume unit establish a debate which finds no resolution. They cast a light by which other poems in the volume can be read.

V

The titles of 'The Three Beggars' and 'The Three Hermits' invite comparison of the poems. The former's story is of King Guaire's experiment with three beggars, to help him decide between two propositions:

> Do men who least desire get most,
> Or get the most who most desire? (VP 295)

Guaire's response to one beggar's answer in favour of the second proposition suggests that he himself favours the first. His experiment offers a thousand pounds to the first to fall asleep, provided this is before the third noon. The beggars keep each other awake, first in fantasizing over the spending of the prize, and then through rivalry, each seeking to avoid defeat in the competition by preventing the others from winning. Once the time limit is passed, all three fall asleep immediately. The experiment demonstrates that not everything is available through conscious volition, so that strength of will does not always determine success. The choice of sleep as the requirement of the competition seems particularly to favour the first of Guaire's propositions, and almost to contradict in itself the beggar's answer to Guaire's question. The crane in the italicized framing verses seems at first similar to the beggars in that he waits in an uncomfortable situation for meagre sustenance. But in the closing lines he aligns himself with the idea that volition can in some circumstances be a barrier to success. He has ignored trivial rewards in the hope of better:

> *I've stood as I were made of stone*
> *And seen the rubbish run about* ... (VP 297)

These lines distance him from the beggars, who can also be seen as rubbish running about.

'The Three Hermits' follows the agonistic tone established in the debate between Edain and her former husband in 'The Two Kings'. The first two hermits dispute what happens after death. The first is troubled by his own lack of piety when he is so close to death. The second believes that holy men whose will has been weak will fail to escape the wheel of reincarnation until their dislike of crowds generates sufficient will for them to escape. The third is set in opposition to both the others by his cheerful unconcern. The poem takes up the purport of 'The Three Beggars' together with the volume's theme of incarnation.[49] Read in this light, the poem indicates a progression in the ability not to care which might lead to whatever counts as success for a hermit. The first hermit is the most deliberately pious. He is also the most fearful of his fate after death. The second is more relaxed about this, though he still believes that passion is necessary to the escape from reincarnation. The third, whose advanced age is emphasized, merely sings, already partly escaped from the world which he seems not to notice and which does not notice him, withdrawn into secret exultation.

'The Hour before Dawn' again involves debate, this time between a crippled beggar and the sleeping man he stumbles on. Goban's oblivion-inducing beer provides a link with 'The Grey Rock'. The beggar is at first tempted by the idea of sleeping until better weather arrives, but bridles when the sleeper complains of the noises which occasionally disturb him and suggests that to be active in the world is foolish. The sleeper claims to demonstrate the fact that the wishing away of uncomfortable circumstances is the beginning of a slippery slope. His growing preference for sleep demonstrates what the beggar does not know: that his own wish for winter to pass is the trace of a deeper wish, held by all life, for its own ending, for oblivion.[50]

The sleeper's argument can be compared to that of Edain's former husband in that he suggests the futility of suspending the inevitable, in this case oblivion. Indeed, the sleeper meets this end rather more than halfway. The poem differs from 'The Two Kings' in that the beggar is not given the arguments in favour of the mortal world that Edain is given. It is clear from his anger which side he is on, but his flight and fear make this poem rather more unsettling. The beggar's fear stems from a recognition of the attraction of the sleeper's argument, a sense that the desire of oblivion lurks within his own mind. In *Responsibilities: Poems and a Play*, the poem indicates more openly the threat to life in the mortal world represented by the attraction of giving up this deferral of oblivion, of opting for oblivion now. In this version, the beggar cries, 'Oh God if he got loose!' (VP 307v), as he heaps stones on the sleeper's den. In all versions, the beggar does not feel safe from the temptations of oblivion until the sun has risen to make manifest again the world available to the senses and dispel the darkness.

Another revision changes 'From the Hell Mouth at Cruachan' to 'From Maeve and all that juggling plain'.[51] This makes the poem more equivocal. Clearly, 'Hell Mouth' has pejorative overtones and in this context associates with damnation the sleeper's position in his debate with the beggar. The replacement of the reference to Hell by a reference to the plain of the immortals strengthens the link with the conflict between immortal and mortal worlds and weakens the possibility of associating the sleeper's position with more Christian overtones of damnation and immorality. The poem becomes even more clearly a part of the poet's meditation on the conflict between worlds and the possible effects of each on the other.

Terence Brown criticises the beggars of *Responsibilities*:

The several poems in which Yeats celebrates Irish beggary as a metaphor of the spiritual freedom the Irish materially minded moneyed class so signally lacks, are without purchase on much beyond the literary salon's version of mendicancy.[52]

This is fair enough: Yeats's attempt to embody a principle can be seen as leading to a foolish stereotyping that bears no relation to the realities of poverty. The three narrative poems I have considered may offer some criticism of materialism, but they also form a meditation on attitude and philosophy where Yeats rehearses his own anxieties. Should one strive, or is determination counter-productive? Should one accept that life is only a deferral of a much-to-be-desired oblivion, or is this to deny and so destroy the desirability of life and the beauty of the mortal world? 'The Three Beggars' encourages us to laugh at grasping materialism, and 'The Three Hermits' suggests value in a kind of quietism. But 'The Hour before Dawn' gestures to the abyss that yawns beneath the tenuous foothold that our desire for life maintains in the world, pointing to the attractions of accepting futility as a threat to the enjoyments the natural world can offer.

Some of the poems of *Responsibilities* are clearly paired, numbered I and II. 'The Magi' and 'The Dolls' are presented in this way, and Yeats's note on 'The Dolls' couples the two (VP 820). Yeats's first idea for 'The Dolls' may have come from his disgust at the formulaic thinking of nationalists who objected to Synge's *Playboy*, from the insistence of some nationalists on service to a cause which was a political abstraction and their attempt to set this above artistic vision.[53] The dolls represent an age of mechanical thought, resistant to the direct expression of life Yeats saw in Synge. But the poem has further implications. The magi, seeking incarnation, unsatisfied with the Christian incarnation, complement the dolls, who are disgusted by incarnation. The reference to 'generations' of dolls is a complication, perhaps demonstrating that this is a fable and that the dolls are to be likened to people. Phillip Marcus comments on 'The Dolls':

> the poem recalls the enigma of 'The Magi' and points to a perplexing problem inherent in those philosophical systems, such as Neo-Platonism, in which the 'fallen' condition is generally so devalued: what motivates souls to sacrifice their more exalted state in order to enter that condition? (YA1 74)

Marcus's question indicates that this pair of poems contributes a further angle to the meditation on the value of incarnation, on the value of the mortal world. The dolls represent a fixed expression of art which parodies art's relation to human life. Their resentment of the baby marks the opposition between this form of art and genuine life. The magi, though similarly dissatisfied with the 'actuality' of incarnation, continue to seek it.[54] The human form's lack of that perfection which is available to the artificial leads to the show-doll's accusation that the doll-maker's wife disgraces them in bringing the baby into the house. The baby's noise and filth are, of course, manifestations of its vitality. The question arises, then, of whether lack of perfection is a necessary part of incarnation. Setting Marcus's exalted souls on the same side as the immortals in *Responsibilities* suggests an answer to this question. The mortal has the advantage of experience whose intensity derives from its temporal limitation. But the necessary imperfection of the incarnate form means that the magi are doomed to dissatisfaction. There are further implications for art. The seeking of perfection must include a knowledge that, if art is to accept its responsibility to both immortal and mortal sides of the debate, it must continue to strive for a perfection it knows to be unavailable.

VI

'A Memory of Youth' is reminiscent of 'Adam's Curse':

> We sat as silent as a stone,
> We knew, though she'd not said a word,
> That even the best of love must die ... (VP 314)
> We sat grown quiet at the name of love.
> We saw the last embers of daylight die ... (ISW 19)

In 'A Memory of Youth' the poet recalls a scene where the moon was hidden by a cloud, as, in spite of the sincerity of the poet's praise of his beloved, and her pleasure at this praise, their minds were clouded by the thought that love must die. The reappearance of the moon saved them from a complete loss of spirits. The theme of the limitations of love within the mortal world central to 'The Old Age of Queen Maeve', 'Baile and Aillinn' and the lyrics of *In the Seven Woods* is continued in the *Responsibilities* volume unit. The close of 'A Memory of Youth' suggests an intuitive enlightenment, where the power of love to transcend awareness of its limitation is grasped. The poem continues to address the theme of the debate in 'The Two Kings'. In 'A Memory of Youth' the re-emergence of the moon, which is the symbol of love, marks the re-emergence from clouding doubt of love's power to charge life with light. The 'most ridiculous little bird' puts in its place the thoughtful doubt which silenced the pair. The unconcerned happiness of birdsong, no matter how apparently trivial its singer, restores the particular reality of love.

The concern with the past of the group of poems 'A Memory of Youth', 'Fallen Majesty', 'Friends', 'The Cold Heaven' and 'That the Night Come' indicates that what the poet values of his relationship with Maud Gonne lies in the past. 'Fallen Majesty' (VP 314-15) accuses the Ireland of its time of writing of failing to understand the significance of Maud Gonne. The poem opposes to this time a former time when people gathered just to see her. Again, the poet identifies himself as the last of a passing age in setting himself to 'record what's gone'. The pun suggests that how she was in the time of which he writes is the reality of Maud Gonne. It is a reality his recording creates, as much as re-creates, an imagined perfection generated from the actuality of the past and transcending it.[55]

The memory of what Maud Gonne was and the reminders of this that she still brings are also in 'Friends', and are enough to overcome any resentment the poet might feel at the pain of their earlier relationship. The effect of his memories in this poem and in the one that follows are worth comparing. 'Friends' closes:

> While up from my heart's root
> So great a sweetness flows
> I shake from head to foot. (VP 316)

In 'The Cold Heaven', the memories evoked by the winter sky cause a sense of guilt which recalls his self-questioning after Maud Gonne's revelation of her relationship with Millevoye.[56]

> And I took all the blame out of all sense and reason,
> Until I cried and trembled and rocked to and fro,
> Riddled with light. (VP 316)

The positive, accepting state of mind that closes 'Friends' is balanced by the poet's fear in 'The Cold Heaven' that his relationship with Maud Gonne was a failure for which he was to blame. Yeats founds himself on the continuously re-formed earlier self created in his poems, and especially on his love for Maud Gonne. But this is not a stable foundation. The poet follows a poem where love outweighs past pain with one which confronts the possibility that his love was a failure for which he was responsible. Love must continuously re-establish itself above the 'windy precipice', must confront the void which is the impossibility of its existence in the mortal world where circumstance is set against it, and transcend its own awareness of this impossibility by sheer force of assertion.

'Riddled with light' recalls the 'blinding light' which follows death in 'King and No King'. 'The Cold Heaven' opens a different perspective on the relationship of life in the mortal world with what lies beyond. 'Baile and Aillinn' uses the trope of an immortal world that makes the mortal world seem inadequate in order to express dissatisfaction with the mortal world. The poet's anxiety in 'King and No King' is over the possibility that the ecstasy of spiritual marriage attained by the sacrifice of conventional pleasure in the mortal world would not justify the sacrifice. In 'The Cold Heaven', life beyond death brings punishment for life's errors and evasions. The poem's bleak quality suggests a stripping away of justifications in the cold light of death. There is the kind of honesty implied by 'A Coat' here, but in punishment by the 'injustice' of the skies there is a further honesty. The poet's sense of blame, of responsibility, goes beyond human notions of justice or fairness.

The presence of the poems of *Poems Written in Discouragement*, openly dealing with public affairs, within the *Responsibilities* volume unit adds to the sense of the poet's inhabiting the space between the immortal and mortal worlds. Their presence demonstrates the need for the poet to be aware of the claims of both worlds, to feel the attraction of the forces that each generates. To view these poems as merely the emergence into the real world of a poet formerly concerned with a dream world is a mistake. The epigraph 'In dreams begins responsibility', attributed to an 'old play', is probably an invention.[57] This comment by J.B. Yeats is from a letter to his son written after the publication of *Responsibilities: Poems and a Play*, but shows how close the thought of the two men sometimes came:

> a people who do not dream never attain to inner sincerity, for only in his dreams is a man really himself. Only for his dreams is a man responsible – his actions are what he must do.[58]

According to this comment, actions are hopelessly entangled in the web of determinism. In order to achieve responsibility, then, to cut free of this web which leads to the infection of thought by utilitarian concerns of action and fixed, logical consequence, one must have faith in dreams. The poems of *Poems Written in Discouragement* do concern public affairs, and so do show a commitment to the world of action. But this commitment is of a particular type, and maintains at the same time the commitment to dream. The poet stubbornly maintains his vision in spite of the reverses dealt him in the world of action, indeed making such reverses an opportunity to define the more strongly his particular vision and its values. The figure of the poet created within the *Responsibilities* volume unit is engaged with the world and with the immortal, supernatural world, *and* with the relationship between these worlds. His situation is complex and paradoxical and refuses reconciliation or stabilization. The figure, Yeats the poet, mediates between two irreconcilable worlds, the values of both of which are necessary to Yeats's work.

Conclusion

The work is the only place where the attempt – the drive – to unify, which is the only possible mode of existence of unity of personality, can happen. It can only happen here by means of the continual reforging of the personality within and through the work. But while analysis of this process of forging and reforging is necessary, it is not necessary to accept that only process is possible. George Bornstein seeks to use Yeats as a link between textual scholarship and literary theory:

> In remaking his poems Yeats remade himself, as his quatrain on the subject reminds us. In so doing, he offers us today a middle ground between the old fixed, stable author and fixed, stable text on the one hand, and the elimination of the author and substitution of endless textual free-play on the other. For what Yeats finally created was a process rather than a product, in which a successive but finite remaking of texts and selves substitutes for the fixing of them. That process should be distinguished from a permanent order on the one hand and an endless series of referrals and deferrals on the other.[1]

I see the value of the relinking of these two aspects of literary studies, but I think that today's informed reader should be able to read in a way that avoids what seems a compromise between valueless theories. That reading and understanding has a creative element and is not merely the recovery of something encoded in a text and that no language is a self-enclosed system mean that the idea of fixed texts is no longer tenable. Endless textual free-play suggests an infinite play of meaning, and where no meaning is excluded, none can exist.

Bornstein writes of the importance of process in Yeats's work only to go on to imply that he sees such process as without progress or value:

Knowledge of the successive formations of Yeats's early canon already deconstructs whatever final order an editor may have chosen to print, just as knowledge of the successive revisions of any particular poem displaces the privileging of the final version to the exclusion of all others. It also deconstructs the image of an apparently stable early self provided by the canonical poems. And if we turn back to the earlier gatherings we still find not a unified and stable 'author' but rather a series of fictional constructs of one and by one. Nor can we push even further back, to the unorganized early publications in journals or the even more unorganized welter of early manuscripts from which Yeats chose what to publish in the first place, for the point of the subsequent gatherings was to construct a more unified self out of the primeval components.[2]

The suggestion that the 'privileging of the final version' must be 'to the *exclusion* of all others' marks a method of argument often used by 'deconstructors': either the final version is absolute, and consequently other versions have no value (a position no serious student of Yeats could hold), or all versions have equal value and the final version is just another version among versions. The latter alternative denies any value or purpose to the shaping of his work – the development of his personality – by Yeats.[3] Of course the 'stable early self' is an image deliberately created by the later, but the idea that it could be anything else is no longer worthy of consideration. No-one's biographical self is unified; the unified self is an imagined self, a necessity for the creation of the work and possible only within the work.

Bornstein's description of the arrangement of *The Variorum Edition of the Poems of W. B. Yeats* – it 'proceeds through Yeats's canon by interspersing the longer narrative poems chronologically between the various books of lyrics' – shows him clearly out of sympathy with my wish to see the poems as forming volume units.[4] The focus of his essay is the early poems, and the contents lists he quotes go no further than 'To Ireland in the Coming Times'. Nevertheless, he refers here to the book of the collected poems as a whole, and therefore implies that 'The Two Kings' is not part of the *Responsibilities* volume, and that *Responsibilities* is a book of lyrics. This is clearly not the case. Attention to *Responsibilities* as a volume unit, including the paired narratives 'The Grey Rock' and 'The Two Kings', and to the narratives 'The Old Age of Queen Maeve' and 'Baile and Aillinn' in their position following *The Wind Among the Reeds* and preceding the *In the Seven Woods* lyrics, has helped to show the development of Yeats's personality – as it exists and is deliberately created within the poems – during a period of transition in his work and in his life. It is only in the book of the poems that Yeats's particular conception of the personality, of the poet who fulfils responsibilities to irreconcilable worlds, can be brought into being. This book is made up of volume units. To see the longer narrative poems as chronologically shuffled into books of lyrics shows no sense of the integrity of the work, or of the will to integrity which is essential to 'unity of being'.

Bornstein's comments on chronology return us to the problem of the arrangement of any collected edition of the poems:

> *No* extant ordering corresponds in detail to the sequence of composition; *all* derive from fictive constructs of his early career later created by Yeats himself. As critics of either the work or the life, we need to know enough textual scholarship to be our own editors, rather than to have our critical field irrevocably defined by an editor's prior judgments:[5]

I want to move beyond the implication that we can be critics of either the work or the life by an emphasis on the essential and complex relationship between the work and the life, an interactive relationship which makes the arrangement of the poems in any collected edition such an important issue. There is an attractive openness here in Bornstein's view of how Yeats should be read, and his caution concerning Yeats's earlier selves is judicious, but the critical state of mind can carry us to the point where we are in danger of dismissing a crucial part of Yeats's art as some sort of obscuring of the truth. Ultimately, it is in his poems that Yeats projects his life as 'something intended, complete', and a sense of this whole is essential to a satisfactory understanding of the parts that make it up. The significance of context in Yeats's work is more than just the relationship between poems within volume units.

> Why I have been so insistent upon my revisions etc. in this expensive edition [the *Collected Works* (1908)] is that I know I must get my general personality and the total weight of my work into people's minds, as a preliminary to new work.[6]

The revisions are part of a second-order poetic development. They adjust the earlier poetic personality in the light of the development both work and life have brought about in the older poet. Yeats assumed control over the path of his development by absorbing it into the project of the creation of the personality within the work.

The idea of a hypertext edition which would make disputes over arrangement redundant or outdated has distinct attractions. The dis- and reassembly of Yeats's textual self might well be rewarding and fun. But I think back to Yeats's pleasure at the Dun Emer *In the Seven Woods* and to the importance to him of his sister's Cuala Press. It seems to me not too fanciful to make the link between the book and the idea of incarnation discussed in relation to 'The Dolls' and 'The Magi'. Even if no edition can be perfect, its physicality as a book stands as a symbol for the attempt to achieve completion and embodiment and forms a link between the infinite potential for rearticulation into new contexts of the poems and the physical nature of the different worlds (times, societies) which are those contexts. But perhaps I am merely justifying my own prejudice as I compare the pleasure of holding and reading a book with that of sitting in front of a screen.

Yeats's last published letter indicates the link between the theory of the hermeneutic circle and the necessity of a sense of closure, completeness, to expression; '"Man can embody truth but he cannot know it." I must embody it in the completion of my life' (L 922, 4 January 1939). He expresses his resistance to the falsification of intellectual thought abstracted from its context of emotion and lived experience here as earlier; but also, in the sense that art is an incarnation, then the poet's life is itself art, and demands the completion of death that will give it form. The letter indicates the significance of the life to the work by suggesting that the poet considered his life itself to be a 'work'.

The idea of embodiment is crucial. Embodiment necessitates containment within limits, within form. This limitation distinguishes what is embodied, allows it to be recognized, and so completes its expression. In envisioning his life in this way, projecting himself beyond its end in seeing the gathering of his final thoughts as a completion, Yeats sought to give form to his life, deliberately, to give his life a shape consciously chosen and worked for, and so to confer a significance on it in saving it from mere contingency.

The sense of a deathly perspective present in *Responsibilities*, in its addressing of dead audiences and its contemplation of what lies beyond death, no doubt owes something to Yeats's increasing interest in spiritualism. But the engagement with the theme of the relationship between the temporal and the intemporal through the trope of two worlds, mortal and eternal, is picked up from the earlier narratives 'The Old Age of Queen Maeve' and 'Baile and Aillinn'. Frank Kermode's response to Joseph Frank's theory of spatial form points to the centrality to literature of this engagement: 'Literature, or the reading of literature, seems always to be concerned with the immanence of the intemporal in the temporal'.[7] The closure performed by spatial form removes the work from the temporal aspect necessary to its understanding and to its closeness to lived experience.

The interpreter's own historical conditioning is involved in his understanding of the work and builds on previous similarly conditioned understandings intervening between his time and that of the author. The understanding of meaning as process allows the seemingly closed renewed access to the temporal, continuing and open. Meaning is something produced between the work and its audience, not something contained within the work itself. The placing of Yeats's work in its historical context attaches it to history, history viewed as a process to which we too are attached. Respect for the particularity of the historical moment does not close the work off from us:

> Time is no longer primarily a gulf to be bridged because it separates; it is actually the supportive ground of the course of events in which the present is rooted ... In fact the important thing is to recognize temporal distance as a positive and productive condition enabling understanding.[8]

The historical understanding of the work is not merely the repetition of contemporary understanding, but it does involve some examination of the critical air in which the work has breathed between its time and our own.

The apparent closure conferred by form is never a true closure, since the form exists within the open system of language. The printed word is actually less closed than the spoken, since it is preserved to be realized in a potentially infinite number of contexts.[9] The figure of the poet existing within and created by the work offers a paradigm for the necessary coexistence of openness and closure. The life of this figure is complete, yet it is not fixed but rather rearticulated into new contexts by new readers. The poetic figure resists both absolute identification with and absolute detachment from the biographical figure and so maintains the link between art and life; refuses to allow the work to become a self-enclosed text, and accepts the poetic responsibility to both mortal and immortal worlds.

Jerome McGann's view sees hope in, and so I suppose *for*, poetry:

> [p]oetry is a discourse deploying a form of total coherence – and thereby a hope of coherence – within the quotidian world, which is

dominated by various forms of relative incoherence. No other form of human discourse manages to do this, which is paradoxical since poetic forms are in another important respect fundamentally unstable and incommensurate.[10]

Poetry provides the hope of an escape from the fragmentation threatened by reality by offering a form of closure. Yet its existence in time lends it the interpretability that means it remains unstable, or open. Only in his poetic personality can Yeats hope to achieve 'Unity of Being', and then only by constant remaking. It is always an image of aspiration; no-one's biographical self is or could be so unified.

Though it is a mistake to read the book of the poems as a 'Mallarméan sacred book', detached from its writer and the versions of poems and poet on which it stands,[11] we miss the full achievement of Yeats's poetry if we disregard the integrity of the work which is created by the deliberate and self-conscious shaping of the whole, including the personality it embodies, by the poet himself. The reality of this poetic personality is that it is an evolved self, consciously developed by Yeats through his work and through the interactions and reciprocal exchanges between the work and the life, between the achieved self and the accidents of circumstance. Our understanding of this process constantly feeds into our understanding of the personality which it forms, but an idea of the achieved personality is essential to an adequate understanding of a process which would otherwise be directionless and itself accidental and incoherent.

Notes

Introduction

1. Thomas Parkinson, 'Yeats and Pound: The Illusion of Influence', *Comparative Literature*, 6:3 (Summer 1954), 256–64.
2. See John Harwood, *Eliot to Derrida: The Poverty of Interpretation* (London: Macmillan, 1995).

1 Problems with Modernism

1. The Spanish term is *el modernismo*. See Matei Calinescu, *Five Faces of Modernity: Modernism, Avant-Garde, Decadence, Kitsch, Postmodernism* (Durham, N.C.: Duke University Press, 1987), 68.
2. Ibid., 81.
3. Ransom's article appears in *The Fugitive*, 3:1 (Feb. 1924), 2–4. Laura Riding began contributing poems in this issue and is noted as one of the Fugitives in the March 1925 number. The group included Ransom, Allen Tate and Robert Penn Warren.
4. See Harwood, *Eliot to Derrida*, 32–3.
5. R. A. Scott-James, *Modernism and Romance* (London and New York: John Lane, 1908), ix.
6. Laura Riding and Robert Graves, *A Survey of Modernist Poetry* (London: William Heinemann, 1927).
7. Calinescu, *Five Faces of Modernity*, 83.
8. Ibid., 85.
9. See also Harwood, *Eliot to Derrida*, 33.
10. Riding and Graves, *A Survey of Modernist Poetry*, 9.
11. See Kermode, *Romantic Image* (London: Routledge & Kegan Paul, 1957), 5–6. Arthur Symons is a vector of the influence of French Symbolism for both Yeats and Eliot. Blake and Pater are more obvious influences on Yeats.
12. Davie, 'Common and Uncommon Muses', *Twentieth Century*, Vol. 162 (November 1957), 458–68. Kermode's reply in the December number, 582–5, claims that 'the grip of the Symbolist aesthetic, in its nature unreceptive to the spoken word, on modern theory' is 'formidable'.
13. Edmund Wilson, *Axel's Castle: A Study in the Imaginative Literature of 1870–1930* (New York and London: Charles Scribner's Sons, 1931), 1.
14. Ibid., 19–20.
15. Riding and Graves, *A Survey of Modernist Poetry*, 124.
16. Davie, 'Common and Uncommon Muses', 467.
17. See also Wilson, *Axel's Castle*, 120–3.
18. Said, 'Opponents, Audiences, Constituencies and Community', in Hal Foster, ed., *Postmodern Culture* (London and Sydney: Pluto Press, 1985) (first published as *The Anti-Aesthetic*, Port Townsend: Bay Press, 1983), 135–59, 140. Said is pessimistic about literary biography in this piece, claiming that it elevates individuals beyond their society. It seems to me that good

literary biography can explore how individuals fitted into the society of their time, and so can connect literature with life and society rather than driving it further into a world of its own.
19. J. G. Merquior, *From Prague to Paris: A Critique of Structuralist and Post-structuralist Thought* (London: Verso, 1986). See especially 177–82.
20. Ibid., 181.
21. Donald Davie, 'Impersonal and Emblematic' (1960), *The Poet in the Imaginary Museum*, ed. Barry Alpert (Manchester: Carcanet New Press, 1997), 76–80, 78. Davie's use of the words 'seem' and 'illusion' suggest that this impersonality is purely a matter of technique.
22. Charles Feidelson, *Symbolism and American Literature* (University of Chicago Press, 1960, first published 1953), 45.
23. Ibid., 51.
24. See Ruth Finnegan, *Oral Poetry: Its Nature, Significance and Social Context*, 2nd edn. (Bloomington and Indianapolis: Indiana University Press, 1992), 216.
25. See also Hans-Georg Gadamer, *Truth and Method*, 2nd edn, revised translation revised from that of W. Glen-Doepel by Joel C. Weinsheimer and Donald G. Marshall (London: Sheed and Ward, 1989), 108–10, on the 'directedness' of representation and the necessity of an audience.
26. See Roger Shattuck, 'The Prince, the Actor, and I: The Histrionic Sensibility', *The Innocent Eye: On Modern Literature and the Arts* (New York: Farrar, Straus, Giroux, 1984), 107–24. Shattuck also expresses a wish to restore the place of the voice in literature. See 'How to Rescue Literature', 311–28.
27. Stephen Spender, *The Struggle of the Modern* (London: Hamish Hamilton, 1963), 133–4.
28. Ibid., 140.
29. Ibid., 141. Spender comments that over the course of Yeats's career, his ' "I" was transferred from "Mask" into acted upon consciousness' (139).
30. Quoted in Sven Loevgren, *The Genesis of Modernism: Seurat, Gaugin, Van Gogh, and French Symbolism in the 1880s*, 2nd edn (Bloomington and London: Indiana University Press, 1971), 83.
31. Quoted in Davie, *The Poet in the Imaginary Museum*, 285.
32. This view is evident in Davie's essay on *Briggflats* in *The Poet in the Imaginary Museum*.
33. Erik Svarny, *'The Men of 1914': T. S. Eliot and Early Modernism* (Milton Keynes and Philadelphia: Open University Press, 1988), 85.
34. E. H. Gombrich cautions against believing that the plastic arts can literally be taken in in an instant. See *The Image and the Eye: Further Studies in the Psychology of Pictorial Representation* (Oxford: Phaidon Press, 1982), 50.
35. See W. K. Wimsatt and Monroe C. Beardsley, 'The Intentional Fallacy', *Sewanee Review*, LIV (Summer 1946), 468–88.
36. See also Hayden White, 'The Absurdist Moment in Contemporary Literary Theory' (1976), in *Tropics of Discourse: Essays in Cultural Criticism* (Baltimore and London: The Johns Hopkins University Press, 1978), 261–82.
37. Jonathan Culler, 'Commentary', *New Literary History*, 6:1 (Autumn 1974), 219–29, 219.
38. David Robey, 'Modern Linguistics and the Language of Literature', in Ann Jefferson and David Robey, eds, *Modern Literary Theory: A Comparative Introduction* (London: Batsford Academic and Educational, 1982), 38–64, 43.

39. Such a detachment of language from the world is not actually justified by Saussure or anyone else.
40. See Walter Ong, *Orality and Literacy: The Technologizing of the Word* (London and New York: Methuen, 1982), 133. Ruth Finnegan criticizes Ong's tendency to over-generalize, to imply that too much is determined by the medium of communication while eliding other social and historical factors. Nevertheless, she seems to accept that such broad theories can be stimulating and suggestive. See her *Literacy and Orality: Studies in the Technology of Communication* (Oxford: Basil Blackwell, 1988), 154–61.
41. Gadamer, *Truth and Method*, 166–7.
42. Walter Pater, *Plato and Platonism* (London and New York: Macmillan, 1893), 137.
43. Ibid., 64.
44. See also Chapter 4 on how the artist's expression of his individuality depends on his place in a tradition, giving a sort of reciprocal idea to this one, in that the collective mind, through tradition, offers the artist the opportunity to become truly individual. Yeats's metaphysical beliefs add a conviction and coherence that seem lacking in Eliot's 'Tradition and the Individual Talent'.
45. See also Peter Allan Dale, *The Victorian Critic and the Idea of History: Carlyle, Arnold, Pater* (Cambridge, Mass. and London: Harvard University Press, 1977), 193–5. Hayden White suggests the difference between understanding, which mediates between different periods, and mere reconstruction when he claims that Burkhardt's use of 'a metaphor constructed out of his own immediate experience' gave a new clarity to his view of fifteenth-century life. White, *Tropics of Discourse*, 44.
46. See also Gadamer, *Truth and Method*, 473.
47. See also John Harwood, '"Secret Communion": Yeats's Sexual Destiny', YA9 (1992), 3–30, especially 10–13.
48. See George Bornstein, *Transformations of Romanticism in Yeats, Eliot, and Stevens* (Chicago and London: University of Chicago Press, 1976), 15–16 for a discussion.
49. See, for instance, Bornstein, *Transformations*, 106.
50. Carol T. Christ, *Victorian and Modern Poetics* (Chicago and London: University of Chicago Press, 1984), 3.
51. See also R. G. Hampson, '"Experiments in Modernity": Ford and Pound', in Andrew Gibson, ed., *Pound in Multiple Perspective: A Collection of Critical Essays* (London: Macmillan, 1993), 93–125. Richard Aldington thought Ford's influence on Pound 'disastrous', since Yeatsian romanticism, to which he thought Pound naturally suited, and Fordian realism were incompatible. See Aldington, 'The Poetry of Ezra Pound', *The Egoist* (1 May 1915), 71–2.
52. See Arthur Mizener, *The Saddest Story A Biography of Ford Madox Ford* (New York and Cleveland: World Publishing, 1971), xx.
53. See Michael Levenson, *A Genealogy of Modernism: A Study of English Literary Doctrine 1908–1922* (Cambridge University Press, 1984), 61.
54. For Nietzsche, it is the transformation of vivid impressions into concepts which allows the construction of a hierarchically ordered world. The shared world is the instrument of man's self-subjection. See Nietzsche, 'On Truth

and Lies in a Nonmoral Sense', *Philosophy and Truth: Selections from Nietzsche's Notebooks of the Early 1870s*, ed. and trans. Daniel Breazeale (Atlantic Highlands, N. J.: Humanities Press; Hassocks, Sussex: Harvester Press, 1979), 84.
55. Pater, *Studies in the History of the Renaissance* (London: Macmillan, 1873), viii.
56. Levenson, *Genealogy*, 132.
57. Ibid., 132.
58. *The Letters of Ezra Pound 1907–1941*, ed. D. D. Paige (London: Faber & Faber, 1951), 91.
59. See also Louis Menand, *Discovering Modernism: T. S. Eliot and His Context* (New York: Oxford University Press, 1987), 5.
60. Thomas Jackson, *The Early Poetry of Ezra Pound* (Cambridge University Press, Mass.: Harvard University Press, 1968), 241.
61. L. S. Dembo, *Conceptions of Reality in Modern American Poetry* (Berkeley and Los Angeles: University of California Press, 1966), 6. See also Christ, *Victorian and Modern Poetics*, 99.
62. Joel C. Weinsheimer, *Philosophical Hermeneutics and Literary Theory* (New Haven and London: Yale University Press, 1991), 13.
63. Pound, 'Status Rerum', *Poetry*, 1:4 (January 1913), 123–7, 125.
64. Pound, *Gaudier-Brzeska: A Memoir* (London: John Lane, The Bodley Head; New York: John Lane, 1916), 99.
65. Ibid., 103–4.
66. Ibid., 123.
67. Ronald Schuchard, 'Yeats, Titian and the New French Painting', in A. Norman Jeffares, ed., *Yeats the European* (Gerrards Cross: Colin Smythe, 1989), 142–59, 148.
68. See also Monroe K. Spears, *Dionysus and the City: Modernism in Twentieth-Century Poetry* (New York: Oxford University Press, 1970), 55.
69. Joyce, *A Portrait of the Artist as a Young Man* (London: Paladin, 1988, first published 1916), 219. See also Flaubert's letter to Mademoiselle Leroyer de Chantepie (18 March 1857), *Correspondance*, Vol. 2, ed. Jean Bruneau (Bibliothèque de la Pléiade) (Paris: Gallimard, 1980), 691.
70. Jonathan Culler, *Flaubert: The Uses of Uncertainty* (London: Paul Elek, 1974), 15.
71. Ibid., 17.
72. Menand, *Discovering Modernism*, 143. Note also Eliot's comparison of Yeats with Pater in an unfavourable review of *The Cutting of an Agate*: 'A Foreign Mind', *Athenaeum* (4 July 1919), 552–3.
73. Pound, *Selected Prose 1909–1965*, ed. William Cookson (London: Faber & Faber, 1978), 346. See also Menand, *Discovering Modernism*, 143–4.
74. See also Menand, *Discovering Modernism*, 36–41.
75. See Edward Lobb, *T. S. Eliot and the Romantic Critical Tradition* (London: Routledge & Kegan Paul, 1981), 6.
76. On the difficulty of defining modernism, see Christopher Butler, 'The Concept of Modernism', in Susan Dick, Declan Kiberd, Dougald McMillan, Joseph Ronsley, eds., *Omnium Gatherum: Essays for Richard Ellmann* (Gerrards Cross: Colin Smythe, 1989), 49–59. The term 'postmodernism' also suffers from the problem (postmodernists might deny that it is a

problem) of a multiplicity of definitions. See Koelb's introduction to Clayton Koelb, ed., *Nietzsche as Postmodernist: Essays Pro and Contra* (Albany: The State University of New York Press, 1990), 4.
77. George Bornstein, *Transformations*, 19.
78. George Bornstein, 'Romancing the Native Stone', in Gene W. Ruoff, ed., *The Romantics and Us* (New Brunswick and London: Rutgers University Press, 1990), 108-29, 116.
79. Pater, *Plato and Platonism*, 63-4.
80. See Hugh Kenner, *A Colder Eye: The Modern Irish Writers* (London: Allen Lane, 1983), 13-14.
81. Pound, *Literary Essays*, ed. T. S. Eliot (London: Faber & Faber, 1985, reprinted from the 1954 edition), 205 (from 'Hell', *The Criterion*, April 1934), quoted by Bornstein on 117 of his essay. See also Pound, *Literary Essays*, 34. See also Kenner, 'The Making of the Modern Canon', in Robert von Hallberg, ed., *Canons* (Chicago and London: University of Chicago Press, 1984), 363-75, where Kenner's determination to exclude English writers from 'international modernism' leads to his describing Virginia Woolf as 'an English novelist of manners, writing village gossip from a village called Bloomsbury for her English readers...' (371). See further Kenner, *A Colder Eye*, 16.
82. In connection with the internationalism of anglophone modernism, see Bruce Robbins, 'Modernism in History, Modernism in Power', in Robert Kiely, ed. (assisted by John Hildebidle), *Modernism Reconsidered* (Cambridge, Mass. and London: Harvard University Press, 1983), 229-45. See also Calinescu, *Five Faces of Modernity*, 69-70.
83. Sean Golden, 'Post-Traditional English Literature: A Polemic', *Crane Bag*, 3:2 (1979), 7-18, 16.
84. Again, see also Pater, *Plato and Platonism*, 63-4.
85. See Levenson, *Genealogy*, 63-79 and 218-20.
86. T. S. Eliot, *Selected Essays* (London: Faber & Faber, 1951), p.21.
87. See also Levenson, *Genealogy*, 211-13.
88. See Mem 142.
89. Joseph Frank, *The Widening Gyre: Crisis and Mastery in Modern Literature* (New Brunswick: Rutgers University Press, 1963), 60.
90. Ibid., 59.
91. Pound's 'ego scriptor' (*Canto LXXVI*), seems to me a *similar* self-projection, but his 'rag-bag' approach makes *his* mythologized figure particularly uncommunicative, except at odd moments occurring especially in the *Pisan Cantos* and *Drafts and Fragments*.
92. See YT 38-9.

2 *In the Seven Woods*

1. See especially E&I 240.
2. Arthur Schopenhauer, *The World as Will and Idea*, trans. R. B. Haldane and J. Kemp (London: Trübner, 1883-6), vol. 3, 210-11.
3. Arthur Symons, 'Fact in Literature', *Saturday Review* (24 August 1901), 232.
4. Symons, *Fortnightly Review*, vol. 65 (May 1899), 745-57, 745.

5. Symons, *London Nights*, 2nd edn (London: Leonard Smithers, 1897), xiv. This preface is collected in *Studies in Prose and Verse* (London: J. M. Dent, 1904), and is dated 2 September, 1896, Rosses Point, Sligo.
6. See E&I 271–2.
7. 'Ireland ... a country which in every region preserves massive residual orality.' Walter Ong, *Orality and Literacy*, 69.
8. See, for instance, 'Literature and the Living Voice' (1906), Ex 202–221, especially 206.
9. See Mem 131–4, CL2 314–15, and R. F. Foster, *W. B. Yeats: A Life, Volume One: The Apprentice Mage* (Oxford and New York: Oxford University Press, 1997), 201–3. The break in his writing of new poetry lasted from this revelation, on 8 December 1898, until he wrote 'The Withering of the Boughs' in July 1900. See Deirdre Toomey, 'Labyrinths: Yeats and Maud Gonne', YA9 (1992), 95–131, 96, 103.
10. Harwood, '"Secret Communion", Yeats's Sexual Destiny', YA9 (1992), 3–30, 15–16. Elizabeth Butler Cullingford, 'At the Feet of the Goddess: Yeats's Love Poetry and the Feminist Occult', YA9 (1992), 31–59, 34.
11. See Anon., 'Mr Yeats' New Book', *The Academy* (6 May 1911), 547; Darrell Figgis, 'Mr. W. B. Yeats's Poetry', *Studies and Appreciations* (London: J. M. Dent, 1912), 119–37, 127–8 (reprinted from the *New Age*, 4 August 1910, 325–8); and Ernest Boyd, *Ireland's Literary Renaissance* (Dublin and London: Maunsel, 1916), 140.
12. Foster, *Yeats*, 284.
13. Terence Brown, *The Life of W. B. Yeats: A Critical Biography* (Oxford: Blackwell, 1999), 103.
14. Ibid., 148.
15. Ibid., 150.
16. W. B. Yeats, *The Secret Rose* (Dublin: Maunsel, 1905), 260.
17. See also Frank Kermode, 'Poet and Dancer Before Diaghilev', in *Modern Essays* (Glasgow: Fontana Press, 1990), 11–38; and Stéphane Mallarmé, 'Ballets', *Oeuvres Complétes*, ed. Henri Mondor and G. Jean-Aubry (Bibliothèque de la Pléiade) (Paris: Gallimard, 1945), 303–7.
18. Ex 214–15.
19. See 'The Literary Movement in Ireland' (1899), in Lady Gregory, ed., *Ideals in Ireland* (London: Unicorn Press, 1901), 87–102. See Frank Kermode, *Romantic Image*, 138–61, on the unreliability of the idea of 'dissociation of sensibility'. There is a similarity here with an aspect of Eliot's thought.
20. See 'First Principles', *Samhain* (1904), Ex 145–6.
21. See Nancy Cardozo, *Maud Gonne: Lucky Eyes and a High Heart* (London: Victor Gollancz, 1979), 262–3.
22. See GYL 158.
23. See Elizabeth Butler Cullingford, '"Thinking of Her ... as ... Ireland": Yeats, Pearse and Heaney', *Textual Practice*, 4: 1 (Spring 1990), 1–21, 7.
24. Ibid., 8.
25. 'Red Hanrahan', VSR 83–95; 'The Book of the Great Dhoul and Hanrahan the Red' and 'The Devil's Book', VSR 183–97.
26. Toomey, 'Labyrinths', YA9 102.
27. See Mem 133.

28. See Toomey 'Labyrinths', YA9 130, and Cullingford, 'Thinking of Her ... as ... Ireland', 8.
29. Toomey, 'Labyrinths', YA9 102.
30. *Is the Order of R. R. & A. C. to remain a Magical Order?* Written in March 1901 and given to the adepti of the Order of R. R. & A. C. in April 1901, 21. Quoted in George Mills Harper, *Yeats's Golden Dawn* (London: Macmillan, 1974), 265. See also Terence Brown, *The Life of W. B. Yeats*, 116–17. Brown sees an indication of Yeats's acceptance of hierarchy contrary to the democratic spirit of the age.
31. H. W. Boynton, 'Books New and Old', *Atlantic Monthly*, 93: 555 (January 1904), 119–27, 120.
32. 'Audience' is appropriate, bearing in mind Yeats's project for spoken verse. See Ex 220–1. See also Ronald Schuchard, 'The Minstrel in the Theatre: Arnold, Chaucer, and Yeats's New Spiritual Democracy', YA2 (1983), 3–24, especially 16–21.
33. The sound of the reeds evokes thoughts of the timeless in an early version of the poem 'Ephemera': 'The innumerable reeds / I know the word they cry, "Eternity!"' (VP 81v).
34. Preface to Lady Gregory, *Cuchulain of Muirthemne: The Story of the Men of the Red Branch of Ulster* (London: John Murray, 1902), xii–xiii. The similarity of thought of Yeats and his father is often remarkable. Note this comment by John Butler Yeats from an argument conducted in the *Leader*: 'he becomes an artist when he learns to use the eyes of desire, and he paints great pictures when he can make appearances so plastic to his hand that ... he can create a world of desire ... '(CL3 349n7).
35. See also Eliot's review of *The Cutting of an Agate*, 'A Foreign Mind', *Athenaeum* (4 July 1919), 552–3. 'Mr. Yeats's dream is identical with Mr. Yeats's reality. *His* dream is a qualification or continuation of himself ... ' (553).
36. Charles Tennyson, 'Irish Plays and Playwrights', *Quarterly Review*, 215: 428 (July 1911), 219–43, 220.
37. Robert Browning, 'Essay on Shelley', in Shelley, *Letters* (London: Edward Moxon, 1852), 7. See also CL3 451 for a comment by Yeats on 'that experimental digging in the deep pit of themselves' by cultivated men, 'which can alone produce great literature'.
38. Browning, 'Essay on Shelley', 7.
39. See Eliot, *Selected Prose*, ed. Frank Kermode (London: Faber & Faber, 1975), 177.
40. Yeats, 'The Literary Movement in Ireland', in Lady Gregory, ed., *Ideals in Ireland*, 90–1.
41. See Ex 199.
42. Francis Bickley, 'The Development of William Butler Yeats', *Thrush*, 1: 2 (January 1910), 147–51.
43. [Lytton Strachey], 'Mr. Yeats's Poetry', *Spectator* (17 October 1908), 588–9.
44. Anon., 'Poetry and Neo-Kelticism', *Saturday Review* (7 November 1908), 577–8.
45. Hardness is also a key term for Hulme and Pound in their attempts to point a new direction for poetry. See, for instance, Hulme, *Speculations*, 126–7. and Pound, *Literary Essays*, 285–9.

46. F. M. Hueffer, 'Mr. W. B. Yeats and His New Poems', *Outlook* (6 June 1914), 783–4.
47. Yeats, Preface to Lady Gregory, *Cuchulain of Muirthemne*, xiv.
48. Yeats, 'A Canonical Book', *The Bookman* (May 1903), UP2 300 (reviewing Lady Gregory's *Poets and Dreamers*). Note especially the idea that passion should be beautifully *spoken*. See also YT 28.
49. Strachey, 'Mr. Yeats's Poetry', 588.
50. See Hulme, *Further Speculations*, ed. Sam Hynes (Minneapolis: University of Minnesota Press, 1955), 10.
51. Ibid., 77.
52. Alun Jones, *The Life and Opinions of T. E. Hulme* (London: Victor Gollancz, 1960), 52.
53. See Kermode's reply to Donald Davie, *Twentieth-Century*, vol. 162 (December 1957), 584, and Ong, *Orality and Literacy*, 72–7.
54. Ex 145. See also E&I 107–8 on Shakespeare's Richard II and Henry V as expressing his own particular myth. Yeats's idea of Richard II shows the influence of Pater. See his 'Shakspere's English Kings', *Appreciations* (London: Macmillan, 1889).
55. P. B. Shelley, 'A Defence of Poetry', *Essays and Letters*, ed. Ernest Rhys (London: Walter Scott, 1886), 1–41, 33.
56. Mem 178. Though note also Foster's idea of a conflation of Maud Gonne and Ireland in the image. See Foster, *Yeats*, 420.
57. See also Warwick Gould, 'An Empty Theatre? Yeats as Minstrel in *Responsibilities*', *Studies on W. B. Yeats* (1989), ed. Jacqueline Genet, 79–118, 93–5.
58. See also Mem 40 for the association of Maud Gonne with apple blossom.
59. See Terence Brown, *The Life of W. B. Yeats*, 148.
60. Helen Vendler, 'Technique in the Earlier Poems of Yeats', YA8 (1991) 3–20, 19. On the magical power of spoken verse, see Ronald Schuchard, 'The Minstrel in the Theatre: Arnold, Chaucer and Yeats's New Spiritual Democracy', YA2 (1984) 3–24, 20–1.
61. Joseph Hone, *William Butler Yeats: The Poet in Contemporary Ireland* (Dublin and London: Maunsel, 1916), 74.
62. See Ronald Schuchard, '"An Attendant Lord": H. W. Nevinson's Friendship with W. B. Yeats', YA7 (1990) 90–130, 110–11; and Foster, *Yeats*, 301.
63. Eliot, *Selected Prose*, 251.
64. William Wordsworth, *Poetical Works*, ed. Edward Dowden (London: George, 1893), vol. 5, 227.
65. Eliot, *Selected Prose*, 177 (*Ulysses*, Order, and Myth, 1923).
66. Michael J. Sidnell, *Yeats's Poetry and Poetics*, 69–70.
67. See Gould, 'An Empty Theatre?', 96–7, 115.
68. See also Ong, *Orality and Literacy*, 73–7. But note Kermode's dislike of the term 'spatial' in relation to literature. See, for instance, *The Sense of an Ending* (New York: Oxford University Press, 1967), 52.
69. Eliot's introduction to Paul Valéry, *The Art of Poetry* (vol. 7 of the *Collected Works*), trans. Denise Folliot (London: Routledge & Kegan Paul, 1958), xiv. Eliot's comment suggests a sophisticated response to music.
70. Yeats, 'The Literary Movement in Ireland', in Gregory, ed., *Ideals in Ireland*, 99.

71. Ibid., 100.
72. For an interesting discussion of this area, see Daniel Albright, *Quantum Poetics: Yeats, Pound, Eliot, and the Science of Modernism* (Cambridge University Press, 1997).
73. See also Frank Lentricchia, *Modernist Quartet* (Cambridge University Press, 1994) on 'modernist' moves to counter the 'feminizing' of poetry.
74. H. C. Beeching, 'Mr. Yeats's New Poems', *Bookman*, 31: 182 (November 1906), 74–5, 74.
75. Menand, *Discovering Modernism*, 117.
76. F. M. Hueffer, 'Mr. W. B. Yeats and His New Poems', *Outlook* (6 June 1914), 783–4, 783.
77. Yeats, 'Literature and the Living Voice', Ex 205.
78. Ong, *Orality and Literacy*, 74.
79. Richard Londraville, ed., 'Four Lectures by W. B. Yeats, 1902–4', YA8 78–122, 97.
80. YT 74. Compare Browning: 'Both for love's and for understanding's sake we desire to know him, and as readers of his poetry must be readers of his biography also.' 'Essay on Shelley', P. B. Shelley, *Letters*, 8.
81. See Deirdre Toomey, 'Bards of the Gael and Gall: an Uncollected Review by Yeats in *The Illustrated Evening News*', YA5 203–11.
82. Londraville, 'Four Lectures', 90.
83. Wordsworth, *Poetical Works*, vol. 5, 227.
84. Lionel Johnson, 'The Man Who Would Be King' (a review of R.Barry O'Brien's biography of Parnell), *Academy* (19 November 1898), 293–4, 294. Barton R. Friedman suggests that Johnson had the idea of Parnell which it took Yeats much longer to develop. See his 'Yeats, Johnson, and Ireland's Heroic Dead', *Eire–Ireland*, 7: 4 (Winter 1972), 32–47, 39–40. But note this from Johnson's *Academy* piece: 'Probably no one ever knew all that was in his unique nature: his, as an Irish writer has said, was an "ice–clear, ice–cold intellect, working as if in the midst of fire"' (294).
85. Foster, *Yeats*, 314.
86. Ibid., 315–16.
87. See the letter to John Quinn, 24 January 1904, CL3 533–4. Yeats *had* thought of 'going on the stage in small parts' but did not actually do so. See CL3 161.
88. Arthur Symons, 'Dowson', *Fortnightly Review*, vol. 67 (June 1900), 947–57, 950.
89. Eliot, *Selected Prose*, 235.
90. Yeats, 'The Literary Movement in Ireland', in Gregory, ed., *Ideals in Ireland*, 94.
91. Ong, *Orality and Literacy*, 71.
92. Ibid., 81. See also Schuchard, 'The Minstrel in the Theatre', 11.
93. Yeats's preface to Lady Gregory, *Gods and Fighting Men: The Story of the Tuatha de Danaan and of the Fianna of Ireland* (London: John Murray, 1904), xix, xx–xxi.
94. Mem 88. See also VSR 159.
95. See CL1 411.
96. See Toomey, 'Labyrinths', 108. Toomey's idea that 'Under the Moon' is 'covertly confessional' makes one think of the 1902 lecture.

97. Yeats, *The Celtic Twilight* (London: A. H. Bullen, 1902), 193–4. See also the dedication to AE, VSR 233.
98. Yeats, *The Secret Rose*, 226.
99. ISW 24. See also VSR 147–8. See further James Pethica, 'Contextualising the Lyric Moment: Yeats's "The Happy Townland" and the Abandoned Play *The Country of the Young*', YA 10 (1993) 65–91, on the way this poem takes on a different significance, and a rather ominous note, in being separated from the play which was its original context. See especially 80–82.
100. See CL3 147.
101. Yeats's preface to Lady Gregory, *Gods and Fighting Men*, xxi. 'Supreme art' and 'supreme life' refer to alchemy. See also Au 371 on sun and moon symbolism learned from Macgregor Mathers.
102. See also CL3 498 n2 and 3. Kelly and Schuchard refer to criticism of Yeats by Paul Elmer More, who saw in his work a decadence which he likened to Arthur Symons. Kelly and Schuchard point out that Yeats thought of himself as moving away from such a style.
103. John Eglinton, 'The Philosophy of the Celtic Movement', collected in Eglinton, *Anglo–Irish Essays* (Dublin: Talbot Press; London: T. Fisher Unwin, 1917), 41–6, 42.
104. See, for instance, Otto Bohlmann, *Yeats and Nietzsche* (London: Macmillan, 1982); Joyce Carol Oates, *The Edge of Impossibility: Tragic Forms in Literature* (New York: Vanguard, 1972); Conor Cruise O'Brien, *The Suspecting Glance* (London: Faber & Faber, 1972); Frances Nesbitt Oppel, *Mask and Tragedy: Yeats and Nietzsche* (Charlottesville: University Press of Virginia, 1987).
105. See *Letters to W. B. Yeats*, ed. Richard J. Finneran, George Mills Harper, and William M. Murphy, with the assistance of Alan B. Himber (London: Macmillan; New York: Columbia University Press, 1977), vol. 1, 106, and George Mills Harper, 'The Creator as Destroyer: Nietzschean Morality in Yeats's *Where there is Nothing*', *Colby Library Quarterly*, 15: 2 (June 1979), 114–25, 115.
106. John Quinn, 'Lady Gregory and the Abbey Theatre', in E. H. Mikhail, ed., *Lady Gregory: Interviews and Recollections* (London: Macmillan, 1977), 77–84, 80.
107. See CL3 238–40 (Letter to Quinn 22 October 1902).
108. Henry Havelock Ellis, 'Friedrich Nietzsche', *Savoy*, 2 (April 1896), 79–94, 3 (July 1896), 68–81, 4 (August 1896), 57–63. See also Marjorie Reeves and Warwick Gould, *Joachim of Fiore and the Myth of the Eternal Evangel in the Nineteenth Century* (Oxford: Clarendon Press, 1987), 238–40.
109. Symons, 'A Censor of Critics', *Fortnightly Review*, vol. 69 (June 1901), 1003–12, 1012.
110. See Ex 139–40 and 82n.
111. I found David S. Thatcher, *Nietzsche in England, 1890–1914* (Toronto: University of Toronto Press, 1970) very helpful on Nietzsche's influence, not just on Yeats but more pervasive, at this time.
112. For Nietzsche as Yahoo, see J. B. Yeats, *Letters to his Son W. B. Yeats and Others*, ed. Joseph Hone (London: Secker and Warburg, 1983, first published 1944), 97.

113. Ernest Rhys, introduction to Nietzsche, *Thus Spake Zarathustra*, trans. A. Tille, revised by M. M. Bozman (London and Toronto: J. M. Dent; New York: E. P. Dutton, 1933), xvi.

3 From 'The Green Helmet and Other Poems'

1. See GYL 294.
2. See A. E. Waite, *Lives of Alchemystical Philosophers* (London: George Redway, 1888), 107, 117–18.
3. See Mem 141 and Maud Gonne, *A Servant of the Queen: Reminiscences* (London: Victor Gollancz, 1938), 257–60, 345.
4. At this time Yeats thought the death was of a child she had adopted. See Mem 47.
5. The poem is reproduced in Warwick Gould and Deirdre Toomey, '"Take Down This Book": *The Flame of the Spirit*, Text and Context' YA 11 (1994) 133, in Foster, *Yeats*, 116, and in W. B. Yeats, *The Early Poetry*, vol. II: '*The Wanderings of Oisin and Other Early Poems to 1895, Manuscript Materials*, ed. George Bornstein (Ithaca and London: Cornell University Press, 1994), 487. See also Gould and Toomey, '"Cycles Ago", Maud Gonne and the Lyrics of 1891', YA7 (1990) 184–93. On *the Flame of the Spirit*, see George Bornstein and Warwick Gould, '"To a Sister of the Cross & the Rose": An Unpublished Early Poem', YA 7 179–83.
6. Toomey, 'Labyrinths', YA9 95–131.
7. Brown, *The Life of W. B. Yeats*, 174. See also Foster, *Yeats*, 383–5.
8. Brown, *The Life of W. B. Yeats*, 174.
9. See GYL 34 and Toomey, 'Labyrinths', YA9 110.
10. Mem 165. See Elizabeth Heine, 'Yeats's and Maud Gonne: Marriage and the Astrological Record, 1908–09', YA13 (1998) 3–33, 10, for the 'pairing of opposites' in Yeats's and Maud Gonne's horoscopes.
11. See also Wayne Chapman, *Yeats and English Renaissance Literature* (London: Macmillan, 1991), 121. Chapman links the use of Helen in these poems with Marlowe.
12. Mark Freeman, *Rewriting the Self: History, Memory, Narrative* (London and New York: Routledge, 1993), 89.
13. Ibid., 29.
14. Maud Gonne MacBride, *A Servant of the Queen*, 329–30.
15. GYL 302. Lady Gregory thought of his plays as his and her children. See Foster, *Yeats*, 357.
16. See also Yeats's letter to Arthur Griffith of 16 July 1901, where he claims to write for his own people though knowing that they may not accept his work immediately, CL3 88.
17. See also Brown, *The Life of W. B. Yeats*, 184–5.
18. Foster, *Yeats*, 388 and 393. See also Heine, 'Yeats and Maud Gonne', YA13 20–1.
19. See note 5 above.
20. Yeats's quotation from Spenser in *Per Amica Silentia Lunae* suggests that there is a period of a thousand years between incarnations. See Myth 363. See also Chapman, *Yeats and English Renaissance Literature*, 195.
21. See the draft of his letter to her, GYL 164–6 and CL3 315–17.

22. See Foster, *Yeats*, 330–1. See 331 also for details of the behaviour of MacBride which led to the final breakdown of the marriage.
23. Nevinson quoted in Schuchard, 'An Attendant Lord', YA7 113.
24. Ibid., 114.
25. Foster, *Yeats*, 391.
26. Quoted in Freeman, *Rewriting the Self*, 88.
27. James Olney, 'Some Versions of Memory' in Olney, ed., *Autobiography: Essays Theoretical and Critical* (Princeton University Press, 1980), 236–67, 241.
28. GYL 35. This is not the journal reproduced in *Memoirs*.
29. See Hueffer, 'Mr. W. B. Yeats and His New Poems', 783–4.
30. John Harwood, '"Secret Communion"', YA9 15.
31. See Mem 159. The idea of passivity in Pater here is similar to later comments which link Pater with Pound: 'did Pater foreshadow a poetry, a philosophy, where the individual is nothing, the flux of *The Cantos* of Ezra Pound, objects without contour as in *Le Chef-d'oeuvre Inconnu* … ?' *The Oxford Book of Modern Verse*, chosen and with an introduction by W. B. Yeats (Oxford: Clarendon Press, 1936), xxx.
32. Olney, 'Autobiography and the Cultural Moment', in Olney ed., *Autobiography*, 3–27, 22.
33. James Pethica's view is rather more critical than mine, suggesting that the development of Yeats's ideas on the relationship between artist and patron displaces an original material indebtedness. He also brings out a subtly agonistic quality in the relationship between Yeats and Lady Gregory. See his 'Patronage and Creative Exchange: Yeats, Lady Gregory and the Economy of Indebtedness', YA 9 (1992) 60–94.
34. See also Pethica, 'Patronage and Creative Exchange', 79–80.
35. Michael North, *The Political Aesthetic of Yeats, Eliot, and Pound* (Cambridge University Press, 1991), 41.
36. E&I 364. The thought comes from Pater: 'Forms of intellectual and spiritual culture sometimes exercise their subtlest and most artful charm when life is already passing from them.' *Appreciations*, 64.
37. It was finished at the end of 1902. See CL3 291.
38. See Chapman, *Yeats and English Renaissance Literature*, 46, for the possibility of an age being represented by a person. The idea of a country being represented by one person is part of the extreme nationalism of fascism. The fascist leader is seen as an 'emanation' of a people, much more directly its expression than democratically elected leaders could be. See Eugen Weber, *Varieties of Fascism: Doctrines of Revolution in the Twentieth Century* (Princeton: Van Nostrand, 1964), 35. I find Elizabeth Cullingford's counter to the charge that Yeats's association with fascism was more than a flirtation, in her *Yeats, Ireland and Fascism* (London: Macmillan, 1981), the most convincing argument I have read on the subject.
39. See also Chapman, *Yeats and English Renaissance Literature*, 36.
40. Foster notes, 'several Coole tenants applied to the Land Court to have their rents reduced'. Foster, *Yeats*, 411.
41. Henry Havelock Ellis, 'Friedrich Nietzsche', *Savoy*, nos. 2–4. *The Birth of Tragedy* is dealt with in the first article. *The Twilight of the Idols* is included in a volume Yeats received from John Quinn in 1902. Yeats had clearly assimilated Nietzsche's Dionysian and Apollonian principle to his own

thoughts by the time he gave the lecture which Henry Nevinson reports in the *Daily Chronicle* (13 May 1903), 3. See Ronald Schuchard, 'An Attendant Lord', YA7 105–6.
42. See, just as possible instances, Pater, *Greek Studies: A Series of Essays* (London and New York: Macmillan, 1895), 28–9, or G. R. S. Mead, *Orpheus: The Theosophy of The Greeks* (London: Theosophical Publishing Society, 1896), 180–1.
43. Edward Thomas, 'An Irish Poet', *Daily Chronicle* (6 March 1909), 3.
44. Mem 187–9. Yeats here relates form and proportion to Greek gymnastics as does Pater in his *Greek Studies*, 267–8.
45. Mem 179–80. Yeats also comments on the degeneration of the classical standard of form in the lecture 'Friends of My Youth'. See YT 27.
46. See Mem 203. He was later informed that Synge had been ill for some time, and that his death was not related to the trouble over *Playboy*. See YT 52.
47. L 501. In the letter he refused to assign plays to a theatrical venture backed by Horniman in Manchester. Wade dates the letter (tentatively) early 1908. Foster corrects to 18 June 1907. See Foster, *Yeats*, 369–70.
48. *Discoveries: A Volume of Essays by W. B. Yeats* (Dundrum: Dun Emer, 1907), 14.
49. Jerome J. McGann, 'Which Yeats Edition?', *TLS* (11–17 May 1990), 493–4, 493.
50. *Discoveries*, 13–14.
51. On the verse-speaking project, see Ronald Schuchard, 'The Minstrel in the Theatre', 3–24.
52. T. E. Hulme, *Further Speculations*, ed. Sam Hynes (Minneapolis: University of Minnesota Press, 1955), 79.
53. See Ong, *Orality and Literacy*, 76.
54. Walter Ong, *Interfaces of the Word: Studies in the Evolution of Consciousness and Culture* (Ithaca and London: Cornell University Press, 1977), 125.
55. Balz Engler, 'Textualization', in Roger D. Sell, ed., *Literary Pragmatics* (London and New York: Routledge, 1991), 179–89, 185.
56. Finnegan, *Oral Poetry*, 24.
57. Ong, *Interfaces of the Word*, 297. See also Eric A. Havelock, *The Muse Learns to Write : Reflections on Orality and Literacy fron Antiquity to the Present* (New Haven and London: Yale University Press, 1986), 112.
58. Ong, *Interfaces of the Word*, 314–15. See also ibid., 302, and Roger Shattuck, *The Innocent Eye*, 107–24.
59. Eric Havelock, *The Muse Learns to Write*, 68–78. R. B. Kershner claims that '[r]eading Yeats is like listening to an oral informant', and points to the 'linear, sequential, additive nature of oral communication ... ' Kershner, 'Yeats / Bakhtin / Orality / Dyslexia', in Leonard Orr, ed., *Yeats and Postmodernism* (Syracuse, N. Y.: Syracuse University Press, 1991), 167–88, 185–6.
60. See Kershner, 'Yeats / Bakhtin', 181–2.
61. Walter de la Mare, 'The Works of Mr. Yeats', *Bookman* 35: 208 (January 1909), 191–2. In the dedication de la Mare detects, we might see an instance of the submarine influence of Lionel Johnson, and the example of his idea of Parnell: 'we might almost say that Parnell irresistibly predestined his own free will, and went forward by inevitable compulsion of his own creating. By the side of most other Irishmen, in whom versatility is a charm and instability a danger, he appears the incarnation of set and sworn

endeavour.' 'The Man Who Would Be King', *Academy* (19 November 1898), 193–4, 194

4 Poems Written in Discouragement

1. See Yeats's notes on these poems, VP 818–19. See also Jeanne Sheehy, *The Rediscovery of Ireland's Past* (London: Thames & Hudson, 1980), 116. On Dublin attitudes to Hugh Lane see Lady Gregory, *Hugh Lane's Life and Achievement, With Some Account of the Dublin Galleries* (London: John Murray, 1921), 42–4. Maud Gonne thought that Lane behaved like 'a jew picture dealer'. See GYL 324–5.
2. See Richard Kearney, 'Beyond Art and Politics', *Crane Bag*, 1:1 (Spring 1977), 8–16, especially 9–11. See also Denis Donoghue, *We Irish: Essays on Irish Literature and Society* (Brighton: Harvester Press, 1986), 63–6.
3. Kearney, 'Beyond Art and Politics', 9.
4. See Terry Eagleton, *Criticism and Ideology: A Study in Marxist Literary Theory* (London: NLB, 1976), 151–4.
5. Seamus Deane, *Celtic Revivals: Essays in Modern Irish Literature 1880–1980* (London: Faber & Faber, 1985), 33. Elsewhere Deane describes Yeats's authoritarianism as 'that of a symbolist rather than that of a Fascist or even of a Nietzschean. Mussolini and General O'Duffy were briefly admitted to his esoteric band, but they were quickly dismissed precisely because they were exponents of the idolatry of the State, not heroic individuals in themselves.' 'National Character and National Audience: Races, Crowds and Readers', in Michael Allen and Angela Wilcox, eds, *Critical Approaches to Anglo-Irish Literature* (Gerrards Cross: Colin Smythe, 1989), 40–52, 47.
6. Luke Gibbons in the *Field Day Anthology*, general editor Seamus Deane (Derry: Field Day Publications, 1991), vol. 3, 612.
7. Kearney, 'Beyond Art and Politics', 9.
8. See James Longenbach, *Stone Cottage: Pound, Yeats, and Modernism* (New York and Oxford: Oxford University Press, 1988), 263–9.
9. Jerome McGann, *Towards a Literature of Knowledge* (Oxford: Clarendon Press, 1989), 99.
10. See also Frank Kermode, 'Modernisms', *London Review of Books* (22 May 1986), 3–6.
11. On Moran, see Brian Inglis, 'Moran of The *Leader* and Ryan of The *Irish Peasant*' in Conor Cruise O'Brien, ed., *The Shaping of Modern Ireland* (London: Routledge and Kegan Paul, 1960), 108–23; and R. F. Foster, *Modern Ireland, 1600–1972* (London: Penguin, 1989), 454–6.
12. See Thomas Kilroy, 'The Irish Writer: Self and Society, 1950–80', in Peter Connolly, ed., *Literature and the Changing Ireland* (Gerrards Cross: Colin Smythe; Totowa, New Jersey: Barnes and Noble Books, 1982), 175–87, 179–80.
13. See Raymond Williams, *Problems in Materialism and Culture* (London: Verso Editions and NLB, 1980), 45–7.
14. Donald Davie, *Ezra Pound: Poet as Sculptor* (New York: Oxford University Press, 1964), 242.
15. Kilroy, 'The Irish Writer', 182.

16. For an example of the exaggeration of Pound's influence, see C. K. Stead, *Pound, Yeats, Eliot and the Modernist Movement* (New Brunswick, N. J: Rutgers University Press, 1986). See Chapter 2, note 104, for a list of examples of the exaggeration of Nietzsche's influence.
17. See VP 841.
18. Seamus Heaney, 'A tale of two islands: reflections on the Irish Literary Revival', *Irish Studies* I (1980), ed. P. J. Drudy, 1–20, 4. See also Richard Kearney, 'The Transitional Crisis of Modern Irish Culture', in *Irishness in a Changing Society* (The Princess Grace Irish Library, 2) (Gerrards Cross: Colin Smythe, 1988), 78–94. 'It was Yeats and Lady Gregory, however, who brought this revivalist tendency in Irish literature into sharpest relief by founding a National Theatre, the Abbey, where ideals of the Anglo-Irish Ascendancy and of the Gaelic peasantry could find common cause in a shared reliving of the ancient Celtic heritage', 80–1.
19. Samuel Ferguson, 'Hardiman's Irish Minstrelsy I', *Dublin University Magazine*, 3:16 (April 1834), 456–78, 457. See also Oliver MacDonagh, *States of Mind: A Study of Anglo-Irish Conflict 1780–1980* (London: George Allen & Unwin, 1983), 109.
20. But see also R. F. Foster, 'Protestant Magic: W. B. Yeats and the Spell of Irish History' in *Paddy and Mr Punch*. Foster challenges the received opinion that 'the self-consciously Protestant Yeats emerges only in the 1920s, pointing out that '[t]hat strain in Yeats and its inheritance had always been powerful factors.' *Paddy and Mr Punch: Connections in Irish and English History* (London: Allen Lane, 1993), 212–32, 213.
21. See Au 199. See for a similar, recent view Tom Garvin, *Nationalist Revolutionaries in Ireland 1858–1928* (Oxford: Clarendon Press, 1987), 81.
22. John S. Kelly, 'The Fall of Parnell and the Rise of Anglo-Irish Literature: An Investigation', *Anglo-Irish Studies*, II (1976), ed. P. J. Drudy, 1–23, 21. R. F. Foster finds Yeats's version of events from 1891–1916 'unconvincing and ahistorical'. See 'Protestant Magic', 229.
23. See Mem 184.
24. 'The Poetry of Rabindrinath Tagore', *Irish Times* (24 March 1913), 11.
25. 'Mr. Yeats's Ideals', *Freeman's Journal* (24 March 1913), 2. This article also reports the lecture on Tagore. The reporter quotes this phrase from Yeats.
26. See John Hutchinson, *The Dynamics of Cultural Nationalism: The Gaelic Revival and the Creation of the Irish Nation State* (London: Allen & Unwin, 1987), 283–4.
27. See F. S. L. Lyons, *Culture and Anarchy in Ireland 1890–1939* (Oxford: Clarendon Press, 1979), 82.
28. John Murphy takes this identification of Catholicism and Irishness back as far as the 1880s. See his 'Religion and Irish Identity', in *Irishness in a Changing Society* (The Princess Grace Irish Library, 2), 132–51, 133.
29. [D. P. Moran], 'At the Abbey Theatre', *Leader* (7 January 1905), 330–1, 330.
30. D. P. Moran, *The Philosophy of Irish Ireland* (Dublin: James Duffy & Co., 1905), 22.
31. See Tom Garvin, *The Evolution of Irish Nationalist Politics* (Dublin: Gill and Macmillan, 1981), 102.
32. See R. F. Foster, *Modern Ireland*, 459, and Oliver MacDonagh, *States of Mind*, 116.

33. See Foster, *Modern Ireland*, 452.
34. Augustine Martin, 'What Stalked through the Post Office', *Crane Bag*, 2 (1978), 164–77, 165.
35. *Leader* (25 November 1911), 348.
36. 'A Pensioner on Paudeen', *Sinn Fein* (18 January 1913), 1.
37. *Irish Times* (25 January 1913), 9. For the Senate speech see *The Senate Speeches of W. B. Yeats*, ed. Donald R. Pearce (Bloomington: Indiana University Press, 1960; London: Faber & Faber, 1961), 99.
38. Thomas Kinsella, 'The Irish Writer', in Yeats and Kinsella, *Davis, Mangan, Ferguson? Tradition and the Irish Writer* (Dublin: The Dolmen Press, 1970), 57–70, 62.
39. 'An Irish National Theatre', *Irish Daily Independent and Daily Nation* (8 October 1903), 4.
40. Standish O'Grady's editorial comment following Yeats's 'A Postscript to a Forthcoming Book of Essays by Various Writers', *All Ireland Review* (1 December 1900), 6.
41. 'Imaal'[J. J. O'Toole], 'A Rather Complex Personality', *Leader* (26 September 1903), 71–2, 72.
42. Eugenia Brooks Frothingham, 'An Irish Poet and His Work', *The Critic* (New York), 44:1 (January 1904), 26–31, 27.
43. John S. Kelly, 'Books and Numberless Dreams: Yeats's Relations with his Early Publishers', in A. Norman Jeffares, ed., *Yeats, Sligo and Ireland* (Gerrards Cross: Colin Smythe, 1980), 232–53, 241.
44. See also Francis Shaw S. J. , 'The Celtic Twilight' and 'The Celtic Element in the Poetry of W. B. Yeats', *Studies*, 23 (1934), 25–41 and 260–78 for a later attack on the literature of the Celtic Revival as based on something non-Irish.
45. Pierre Bourdieu, 'The Field of Cultural Production, or: The Economic World Reversed', trans. Richard Nice, *Poetics*, 12 (1983), 311–56, 321.
46. Note also Yeats's wish to keep his distance from George Bryan's 'proposed Irish Anthology', because Bryan 'is a more enthusiastic advertiser than I think becomes my dignity' (CL3 493).
47. See James W. Flannery, *W. B. Yeats and the Idea of a Theatre: The Early Abbey Theatre in Theory and Practice* (New Haven and London: Yale University Press, 1976), 344–5.
48. F. M. Atkinson, 'A Literary Causerie', *Dana*, 10 (February 1905), 314–17, 315–16. Compare Deane's criticism of Yeats for his flight from modernity quoted earlier in this chapter. I don't know if F. M. is the F. M'Curdy Atkinson who turns up in Joyce's parody of 'Baile and Aillinn' in *Ulysses*.
49. On the tension between a commitment to political and social modernity and the aspect of literary modernism which appeals to a sense of tradition, see Calinescu, *Five Faces of Modernity*, 41–6.
50. Edward Garnett, 'The Work of W. B. Yeats', *The English Review*, 2: 1 (April 1909), 148–52, 149–50. Garnett was Yeats's editor at T. Fisher Unwin, commissioning *John Sherman*. See CL1 230 and 245, and Kelly, 'Books and Numberless Dreams', 232–3. Yeats described him as a 'personal friend' (Au 200). Henry Nevinson's unsigned 'By the Waters of Babylon', *Nation* (17 October 1908), 122, is similarly a partisan statement from within the Yeats camp. See also Ronald Schuchard, 'An Attendant Lord', YA7 90–130.

51. Lionel Johnson's lecture 'Poetry and Patriotism', given in Dublin on 26 April 1894 and published with Yeats's 'Poetry and Tradition' in 1907 by the Cuala Press (*Poetry and Ireland*), makes many of the same points as Garnett makes. The lecture reflects Johnson's (and Yeats's) efforts to move Irish literature on from Thomas Davis.
52. Antony Coleman, 'The Big House, Yeats, and the Irish Context', YA3 (1985) 33–52, 34.
53. Foster, *Modern Ireland*, 195.
54. North, *The Political Aesthetic of Yeats, Eliot, and Pound*, 41. See also Chapter 3.
55. Theodore Maynard, 'The Metamorphosis of Mr. Yeats', *The Poetry Review*, 10: 3 (May–June 1919), 169–75, 172, 174. The article considers *Responsibilities and Other Poems, Per Amica Silentia Lunae, The Wild Swans at Coole, The Cutting of an Agate*, and *Two Plays for Dancers*. That Maynard was staunchly Catholic may not be without significance.
56. Daniel Corkery, *Synge and Anglo-Irish Literature: A Study* (Dublin and Cork: Cork University Press; London: Longmans, Green, 1931), ix. But note also that Corkery distinguished between the English mind and the Ascendancy mind. See *The Hidden Ireland: A Study of Gaelic Munster in the Eighteenth Century* (Dublin: M. H. Gill , 1925), x.
57. See also Joel C. Weinsheimer, *Gadamer's Hermeneutics: A Reading of* Truth and Method (New Haven and London: Yale University Press, 1985), 228.
58. Corkery, 'The Nation That Was Not a Nation', *Studies*, 23 (1934), 611–22, 612.
59. Corkery, 'Ourselves and Dean Swift', *Studies*, 23 (1934), 203–18, 209. Foster suggests a less exclusive view of nationality: '*Pace* recent commentators like Edward Said, the Irish traditions which Yeats was conditioned by and reclaimed were not automatically those supposed "nationalist" (at least in the sense of Anglophobic, Gaelic Revivalist and puritanically Catholic-Republican). But they constituted no less an Irish subculture for that.' Foster, *Paddy and Mr Punch*, 232.
60. Quoted in Foster, *Yeats*, 458.
61. Seamus Heaney, *Preoccupations: Selected Prose 1968–1978* (London: Faber & Faber, 1980), 108. The fur coat refers to George Moore's attack on Yeats's scorn of the middle class, to which, Moore points out, Yeats belongs. See Moore, *Hail and Farewell: Ave, Salve, Vale*, ed. Richard Cave (Gerrards Cross: Colin Smythe, 1976), 540–1.
62. Joseph Hone, 'Art and Aristocracy', *Irish Times* (11 January 1913), 6. Yeats indicated in a letter to Lady Gregory dated 14 January 1913 that he had 'suggested … the lines of' the article. See 'Some New Letters from W. B.Yeats to Lady Gregory', ed. Donald T.Torchiana and Glenn O'Malley, *A Review of English Literature*, 4: 3 (July 1963), 9–47, 16.
63. Synge, 'Good Pictures in Dublin', *Manchester Guardian* (24 January 1908), collected in Synge, *Collected Works*, ed. Alan Price, Vol. 2 (London: Oxford University Press, 1966), 390–2, 390.
64. Foster, *Yeats*, 461.
65. See Flannery, *W. B. Yeats and the Idea of a Theatre*, 337. In 1912 Yeats asked Edward Martyn if a rapprochement with the Roman Catholic Church was possible. Martyn thought not. See Joseph Hone, *W. B. Yeats 1865–1939* (London: Macmillan, 1943), 257.

66. George Russell in a letter to George Moore dated 6 April 1916, in *Letters from AE*, ed. Alan Denson (London, New York, Toronto: Abelard-Schuman, 1961), 109–10.
67. Quoted by Ronald Schuchard, from a conversation with Richard Ellmann filmed by Radio Telefís Eireann for their programme 'Joyce, Yeats and Wilde' (1982), in his introduction to Heaney, *The Place of Writing* (Atlanta: Scholars Press, 1989), 11.
68. *Irish Times* (25 January1913), 9.
69. D. G. Boyce, ed., *The Revolution in Ireland 1879–1923* (London: Macmillan, 1988), 11 and 12. See also Patrick Buckland, *Irish Unionism: One: The Anglo-Irish and the New Ireland 1885–1922* (Dublin: Gill & Macmillan; New York: Barnes and Noble Books, 1972), xx-xxii, on the Anglo-Irish Ascendancy attitude.
70. Yeats quoted from Hugh Lunn, 'An Interview with Mr. W. B. Yeats', *Hearth and Home* (28 November 1912), 229.
71. Lyons, *Culture and Anarchy in Ireland*, 82–3. See also Lyons, 'The Parnell Theme in Literature', in Andrew Carpenter, ed., *Place, Personality and the Irish Writer* (Gerrards Cross: Colin Smythe, 1977), 69–95.
72. Lionel Johnson commented on Parnell's aloofness, '"*Secretum meum mihi*" he seems always to have said ...'; see Johnson, 'The Man Who Would Be King', 293. Yeats picks up the phrase in his preface to *Poems 1899–1905* (VP 849). Concentration within the self is a source of intensity which Yeats, too, seeks to tap.
73. See Mem 163 and Au 316.
74. See CL3 688.
75. See David Miller, *Church, State and Nation in Ireland 1898–1921* (Dublin: Gill & Macmillan, 1973), 2.
76. See Chapter 3. The usual caveats about the idea of unified or dissociated sensibilities apply.
77. R. V. Comerford in 'Political Myths in Modern Ireland', *Irishness in a Changing Society* (The Princess Grace Irish Library, 2, 1998), 1–17, indicates the extent to which ideas of nationality can neglect actualities in the attempt to establish identity. See especially 9–11.
78. *Irish Times* (19 March1913), 5.
79. See Flannery, *W. B. Yeats and the Idea of a Theatre*, 348.
80. Quoted in Foster, *Yeats*, 494.
81. John O'Leary, *Recollections of Fenians and Fenianism* (London: Downey 1896), vol.1, 31. O'Leary points out that the concern of the middle class with the short term works against their usefulness as rebels, since the rebel's aims are set further in the future. Yeats's review (UP2 35–7) concentrates on O'Leary himself as he found the book 'unreadable'. See Au 212.
82. Malcolm Brown, *The Politics of Irish Literature from Thomas Davis to W. B. Yeats* (London: George Allen & Unwin, 1972), 253. Schuchard and Kelly indicate in a note to a Yeats letter of 1903 that his temper and drinking left him isolated later too (CL3 456n1).
83. Foster, *Yeats*, 43.
84. Lunn, 'An Interview with Mr. W.B. Yeats', 229. See Yeats's letter to Thomas MacDonagh of 9 November 1902 for an instance of this advice (CL3 247).

85. Note also J. B. Yeats's comment on dream and responsibility. See Chapter 5.
86. See Mem 155–6.
87. See Seamus Heaney, *The Place of Writing*, 18–35. See also Foster, *Yeats*, 369, for a connection of the image of the poet in his tower with Yeats's visit to Italy.
88. Donald Davie, 'The Young Yeats', in O'Brien, ed., *The Shaping of Modern Ireland*, 140–51.
89. The idea that love is similarly founded on the void of potential nothingness is raised in 'The Two Kings'. See Chapter 5.
90. Goethe, in J. P. Eckermann, *Conversations of Goethe with Eckermann and Soret*, trans. John Oxenford, vol.1 (London: Smith, Elder, 1850),159. See also Marjorie Perloff, 'Yeats and Goethe', *Comparative Literature*, 23: 2 (Spring 1971), 125–40.

5 *Responsibilities*

1. Michael B. Yeats, Preface to Liam Miller, *The Dun Emer Press, Later the Cuala Press* (Dublin: Dolmen, 1973), 8.
2. See CL3 547–8. William M. Murphy points out Yeats's annoyance with family responsibilities, though allowing that 'he ultimately always fulfilled' these. Murphy, *Family Secrets: William Butler Yeats and His Relatives* (Dublin: Gill & Macmillan, 1995), 120. I have to say that Murphy seems hard on Yeats's sister Elizabeth.
3. See Foster, *Yeats*, 274–5.
4. See Murphy, *Family Secrets*, 117.
5. Ibid., 127–8.
6. Ibid., 128–30.
7. Ibid., 191–2.
8. William M. Murphy, *Prodigal Father: The Life of John Butler Yeats (1839–1922)* (Ithaca, N.Y., and London: Cornell University Press, 1978), 408.
9. Miller, *The Dun Emer Press*, 67.
10. See Miller, *The Dun Emer Press*, 66. See Miller 107–18 and Allan Wade, *A Bibliography of the Writings of W. B. Yeats* (London: Rupert Hart-Davis, 1968), 400–4 for a list of Cuala books.
11. See Foster, *Yeats*, 486.
12. See Wade, *A Bibliography of the Writings of W. B. Yeats*, 154–5.
13. Yeats's introduction to *Selections from the Writings of Lord Dunsany* (Dundrum: Cuala, 1912), ii.
14. See Foster, *Yeats*, 118–24.
15. Warwick Gould, '"Witch" or "Bitch" – Which? Yeats, Archives, and the Profession of Authorship', in Gould and Thomas F. Staley, eds, *Writing the Lives of Writers* (London: Macmillan, 1998),173–90, 175.
16. Those interested may wish to consult Richard J. Finneran, *Editing Yeats's Poems: A Reconsideration* (London: Macmillan, 1990), and Warwick Gould, 'The Definitive Edition: a History of the Final Arrangements of Yeats's Work', in *Yeats's Poems*, 706–49.
17. See Finneran, *Reconsideration*, 153–5, and Gould, YP 714–16.
18. Finneran, *Reconsideration*, 155. See also Finneran, 'Editing Yeats', *TLS* (31 August 1984), 969.

19. Hugh Kenner, 'The Sacred Book of the Arts', *Sewannee Review*, 64: 4 (Oct. – Dec. 1956), 574–90, 578.
20. VP 841. I acknowledge that Yeats did experiment with earlier arrangements in response to readers' reactions. Foster notes how in a letter to Bullen of 30 September 1907 Yeats recalled putting *The Wanderings of Oisin* at the end of a collection 'to stop people saying "it was such a pity Mr Yeats had fallen off so after writing it".' Foster, *Yeats*, 372.
21. Finneran, *Reconsideration*, 171.
22. See Chapter 2.
23. MacNeice, *The Poetry of W. B. Yeats* (London: Oxford University Press, 1941), 99, 62–3, 110–11.
24. Yeats's tendency to revise his work would cause problems with this approach, unless we accept that the early Yeats is subject to adjustment by the later Yeats. See also Gould, 'The Definitive Edition', YP 717.
25. See Chapter 2.
26. See also Michael Sidnell, 'Unacceptable Hypotheses: the New Edition of Yeats's Poems and its Making', YA3 (1985) 225–43, 231.
27. See also Gould, 'The Definitive Edition', YP 713, and L 576.
28. See Chapter 3.
29. Anon., 'An English Parnassian – and Some Others', *Athenaeum*, 4611 (Nov. 1916), 527–9; Anon., 'Mr. Yeats on Himself', *Nation* (28 October 1916), 150–2; Anon., 'Looking Backward', *New Statesman* (11 November 1916), 139–40; and [Harold Child], 'Mr. Yeats in Middle Age', *TLS* (19 October 1916), 499.
30. See Au 3. According to William M. Murphy, Yeats 'could remember only the impressions of his boyhood in Sligo' and relied on his sister Lily's memory for the facts. Murphy, *Family Secrets*, 195.
31. Yeats originally placed the Butlers on the wrong side at the Battle of the Boyne. See VP 270.
32. Pound, the *Cantos*, 4th collected edn (London: Faber & Faber, 1987), 533–4 (Canto LXXXIII).
33. Linda Dowling, *Language and Decadence in the Victorian Fin de Siècle* (Princeton University Press, 1986), 249. See also William E. Baker, *Syntax in English Poetry 1870–1930* (Berkeley and Los Angeles: University of California Press, 1967), 85.
34. Foster, *Yeats*, 453.
35. Ibid., 476.
36. See Humphrey Carpenter, *A Serious Character: The Life of Ezra Pound* (London: Faber & Faber, 1988), 214; L 584–5; Pound, *Letters*, 64.
37. Pound, 'The Later Yeats', *Literary Essays*, 378 – 81, 379.
38. Ibid., 379.
39. See Lawrence Rainey, 'The Price of Modernism: Publishing *The Waste Land*', in Ronald Bush, ed., *T. S. Eliot: The Modernist in History* (Cambridge University Press, 1991), 91–133.
40. Though Yeats did include 'The Grey Rock' without its narrative partner in *Selected Poems* (1929), a selection is clearly not the same thing. He also included 'The Magi' without its partner 'The Dolls'.
41. Carpenter, *Pound*, 191–2. On Pound's appointment at *Poetry*, see ibid., 184–5.
42. Ibid., 192.

43. See GYL 164–6.
44. *The Writing of the Player Queen*, ed. Curtis Bradford (DeKalb: Northern Illinois University Press, 1977), 23. See also Chapter 3.
45. See also Chapter 2. *The Hour Glass* also touches on this theme. See VPl 583.
46. See Brown, *The Life of W. B. Yeats*, 207–8.
47. 'The History of Ailell and Etain', ed. and trans. Eduard Müller, *Revue Celtique*, III (1876–8), 355–60. Lady Gregory, *Gods and Fighting Men* (London: John Murray, 1904), 88–100.
48. Gould, 'An Empty Theatre', 89.
49. See also Phillip L. Marcus, 'Incarnation in "Middle Yeats"', YA1 (1982) 68–81.
50. See also Mem 88.
51. VP 307. Hell remains in the poem in line 25. VP 303.
52. Brown, *The Life of W. B. Yeats*, 209.
53. See Marcus, 'Incarnation', YA1 74.
54. Ibid.
55. Poems in the 'Flamel and Pernella' sequence also do this. See Chapter 3.
56. See Mem 133.
57. See Gould, 'An Empty Theatre', 82.
58. J. B. Yeats, *Letters to His Son*, 189 (30 August1914).

Conclusion

1. Bornstein, 'Remaking Himself: Yeats's Revisions of His Early Canon', *Text: Transactions of the Society for Textual Scholarship*, v (1991), ed. D. C. Greetham and W. Speed Hill, 339–58, 356. For Yeats's quatrain, see VP 778.
2. Bornstein, 'Remaking Himself', 356.
3. See also Warwick Gould, 'Yeats Deregulated', YA9 (1992) 356–72, 371. On the deconstructors' method of argument, see John R. Searle's review of Jonathan Culler's *On Deconstruction: Theory and Criticism After Structuralism*. Searle claims that in English departments, 'there is the assumption that unless a distinction can be made rigorous and precise it isn't really a distinction at all', and that '[p]eople who try to hold the assumption that genuine distinctions must be made rigid are ripe for Derrida's attempt to undermine all such distinctions.' 'The World Turned Upside Down', *New York Review of Books* (27 October 1983), 74–9, 78.
4. Bornstein, 'Remaking Himself', 352.
5. Ibid., 356.
6. L 498. See also Gould, 'The Definitive Edition', YP 717.
7. Frank Kermode, 'A Reply to Joseph Frank', *Critical Inquiry*, vol. 4 (1978), 579–88, 588.
8. Gadamer, *Truth and Method*, 297.
9. See Ong, *Interfaces*, 311.
10. Jerome McGann, *Social Values and Poetic Acts: The Historical Judgment of Literary Work* (Cambridge, Mass.: Harvard University Press, 1988), 9.
11. See Gould, 'Yeats Deregulated', YA9 369–71.

Selected Bibliography

Works by W. B. Yeats

Autobiographies (London: Macmillan, 1955).
The Celtic Twilight (London: A. H. Bullen, 1902).
Discoveries: A Volume of Essays by W. B. Yeats (Dundrum: Dun Emer, 1907).
The Early Poetry: Volume II: 'The Wanderings of Oisin' and Other Early Poems to 1895: Manuscript Materials, ed. George Bornstein (Ithaca N.Y., and London: Cornell University Press, 1994).
Essays and Introductions (London and New York: Macmillan, 1961).
Explorations, sel. Mrs W. B. Yeats (London: Macmillan, 1962; New York: Macmillan, 1963).
The Green Helmet and Other Poems (Dundrum: Cuala Press, 1910).
In the Seven Woods: Being Poems Chiefly of the Irish Heroic Age (Dundrum: Dun Emer Press, 1903).
Is the Order of R. R. & A. C. to remain a Magical Order? (privately published, 1901).
Memoirs: Autobiography – First Draft: Journal, transcribed and edited by Denis Donoghue (London: Macmillan, 1972; New York: Macmillan, 1973).
Mythologies (London and New York: Macmillan, 1959).
The Oxford Book of Modern Verse, chosen and with an introduction by W. B. Yeats (Oxford: Clarendon Press, 1936).
The Poems: A New Edition, ed. Richard J. Finneran (New York: Macmillan, 1983; London: Macmillan, 1984).
Responsibilities: Poems and a Play (Dundrum: Cuala Press, 1914).
The Secret Rose (Dublin: Maunsel, 1905).
The Secret Rose, Stories by W. B. Yeats: A Variorum Edition, ed. Warwick Gould, Phillip L. Marcus, and Michael Sidnell (London: Macmillan Academic and Professional, 1992).
The Senate Speeches of W. B. Yeats, ed. Donald R. Pearce (Bloomington: Indiana University Press, 1960; London: Faber & Faber, 1961).
Uncollected Prose by W. B. Yeats, vol. 1, ed. John P. Frayne (London: Macmillan; New York: Columbia University Press, 1970).
Uncollected Prose by W. B. Yeats, vol. 2, ed. John P. Frayne and Colton Johnson (London: Macmillan, 1975; New York: Columbia University Press, 1976).
The Variorum Edition of the Plays of W. B. Yeats, ed. Russell K. Alspach assisted by Catherine C.Alspach (London and New York: Macmillan, 1966).
The Variorum Edition of the Poems of W. B. Yeats, ed. Peter Allt and Russell K. Alspach (New York: Macmillan, 1957).
Yeats's Poems, ed. and annotated by A. Norman Jeffares with an appendix by Warwick Gould (London: Macmillan, 1989).
The Writing of the Player Queen, ed. Curtis Bradford (DeKalb: Northern Illinois University Press, 1977).

Letters by Yeats

The Collected Letters of W. B. Yeats: Volume One, 1865–1895, ed. John Kelly and Eric Domville (Oxford: Clarendon Press, 1986).
The Collected Letters of W. B. Yeats: Volume Two, 1896–1900, ed. Warwick Gould, John Kelly, and Deirdre Toomey (Oxford: Clarendon Press, 1997).
The Collected Letters of W. B. Yeats: Volume Three, 1901–1904, ed. John Kelly and Ronald Schuchard (Oxford: Clarendon Press, 1994).
The Correspondence of Robert Bridges and W. B. Yeats, ed. Richard J. Finneran (London: Macmillan, 1977; Toronto: Macmillan of Canada, 1978).
The Letters of W. B. Yeats, ed. Allan Wade (London: Rupert Hart-Davis, 1954; New York: Macmillan, 1955).
'Some New Letters from W. B. Yeats to Lady Gregory', ed. Donald T. Torchiana and Glenn O'Malley, *A Review of English Literature* 4: 3 (July 1963), 9–47.

Reports of Lectures by Yeats

Anon., 'Central Branch Sgoruigheacht: Address by Mr. W. B. Yeats', *An Claidheamh Soluis* (27 October 1900), 516–17.
Nevinson, Henry, untitled, *Daily Chronicle* (13 May 1903), 7.
Anon., 'Mr. Yeats Unbosoms Himself on Literature and the Stage', *Evening Telegraph* (Dublin) (14 February 1907), 2.
Anon., 'Mr. W. B. Yeats on Art', *Irish Times* (11 February 1908), 7.
Anon., 'Feis Ceoil Association: Address by Mr. W. B. Yeats', *Irish Times* (10 February 1909), 5.
Anon., 'Views of Mr. W. B. Yeats', *Evening Telegraph* (Dublin) (4 March 1910), 2.
Anon., 'The Theatre and Ireland: Lecture by Mr. W. B. Yeats', *Irish Times* (4 March 1910), 9.
Anon., 'Mr. Yeats and Persecution', *Irish Times* (25 January 1913), 9.
Anon., 'The Theatre and Beauty', *Irish Times* (19 March 1913), 5.
Anon., 'Mr. Yeats's Ideals', *Freeman's Journal* (24 March 1913), 2.
Anon., 'The Poetry of Rabindrinath Tagore', *Irish Times* (24 March 1913), 11.
'Four Lectures by W. B. Yeats, 1902–4', ed. Richard Londraville, YA8 (1991), 78–122.
Yeats and the Theatre, ed. Robert O'Driscoll and Lorna Reynolds (Toronto: Macmillan of Canada; Niagara Falls, New York: Maclean-Hunter Press, 1975).

Interviews with Yeats

Anon., 'Mr. W. B. Yeats: Interesting Interview', *Freeman's Journal* (4 January 1913), 8.
Lunn, Hugh, 'An Interview with Mr. W. B. Yeats', *Hearth and Home* (28 November 1912), 229.
W. B. Yeats Interviews and Recollections, ed. E. H. Mikhail (London: Macmillan, 1977), 2 vols.

Reviews of Yeats's Work and Contemporary Articles About Him

Reviews of 'In the Seven Woods'

Boynton, H. W., 'Books New and Old', *Atlantic Monthly*, 93: 555 (January 1904), 120–21.
Nevinson, Henry, 'Across the Irish Sea', *Daily Chronicle* (1 September 1903), 3.

Reviews of Poems 1899–1905

Anon., 'Verse and Its Public', *Saturday Review* (16 February 1907), 206–7.
Beeching, H. C., 'Mr. Yeats's New Poems', *Bookman*, 31: 182 (November 1906), 74–5.
[Buchan, John], 'Recent Verse', *Spectator* (8 December 1906), 930–1.
[Clutton–Brock, A.], 'The Celtic Movement', *Times Literary Supplement* (14 December 1906), 414.
[Pickthall, R. G.], untitled, *Athenaeum* (15 December 1906), 770.
[Thomas], [Edward], 'Mr. Yeats Revises', *Daily Chronicle* (1 January 1907), 3.

Reviews of 'The Poetical Works of William B. Yeats'

Anon., 'Mr. Yeats and the Celtic Quest', *Putnam's Monthly*, 2: 1 (April 1907), 118.
Anon., 'Revised Yeats Plays', *New York Times Book Review* (6 April 1913), 196.
Carman, Bliss, 'William Yeats and Alfred Noyes', *New York Times Saturday Review* (2 February 1907), 68.
Greenslet, Ferris, 'The Year on Parnassus', *Atlantic Monthly*, 100: 6 (December 1907), 843–51.
Johnston, Charles, 'The Poems of W. B. Yeats', *North American Review*, 187: 629 (April 1908), 614–18.
[Towse, John Ranken], untitled, *Nation* (New York) (17 October 1912), 365.
Wilcox, Louise Collier, 'The Poetic Drama', *North-American Review*, 186: 622 (September 1907), 91–7.

Reviews of the 'Collected Works' (1908)

Anon., 'Poetry and Neo-Kelticism', *Saturday Review* (7 November 1908), 577–8.
Baring, Maurice, 'Mr Yeats's Poems', in *Punch and Judy and Other Essays* (London: Heinemann, 1924), 228–32.
de la Mare, Walter, 'The Works of Mr. Yeats', *Bookman*, 35: 208 (January 1909), 191–2.
Garnett, Edward, 'The Work of W. B. Yeats', *The English Review*, 2: 1 (April 1909), 148–52.
[Nevinson, Henry], 'By the Waters of Babylon', *Nation* (17 October 1908), 122.
[Strachey, Lytton], 'Mr. Yeats's Poetry', *Spectator* (17 October 1908), 588–9.
Tennyson, Charles, 'Irish Plays and Playwrights', *Quarterly Review*, 215: 428 (July 1911), 219–43.
Thomas, Edward, 'An Irish Poet', *Daily Chronicle* (6 March 1909), 3.

Reviews of 'The Green Helmet and Other Poems'

Anon., 'Mr. Yeats's New Play', *Nation* (31 December 1910), 578 and 580.
Anon., 'The Later Yeats', *Irish Review*, 1: 2 (April 1911), 100–1.
Anon., 'Mr. Yeats' New Book', *Academy* (6 May 1911), 547.
[Pickthall, R. G.], 'Verse', *Athenaeum* (18 February 1911), 186.

Reviews of 'Responsibilities'

Anon., 'Mr. Yeats on Himself', *Nation* (28 October 1916), 150 and 152.
Anon., 'Looking Backward', *New Statesman* (11 November 1916), 139–40.
Anon., 'The Poetry of Mr. Yeats', *Saturday Review* (11 November 1916), 460–1.
Anon., 'Verse and Verse–Makers', *American Review of Reviews*, 54: 6 (December 1916), 674–6.
B., W. S., 'The Fragile Poetic Art of Mr. Yeats', *Boston Evening Transcript* (6 December 1916), part 3, 4.
[Child, Harold], 'Mr. Yeats in Middle Age', *Times Literary Supplement* (19 October 1916), 499.
Ford, Ford Madox (Hueffer), 'Mr. W. B. Yeats and His New Poems', *Outlook* (6 June 1914), 783–4.
Maynard, Theodore, 'The Metamorphosis of Mr. Yeats', *Poetry Review*, 10: 4 (July–August 1919), 169–75.
P[ound], E[zra], 'Mr. Yeats' New Book', *Poetry*, 9: 3 (December 1916), 150–1.
Robinson, Lennox, 'Beauty Like a Tightened Bow', *New Ireland* (16 December 1916), 90–91.
[Wright, F. H.], 'An English Parnassian – and Some Others', *Athenaeum* (November 1916), 527–9.

Other Contemporary Articles

Anon., 'An Irish National Theatre', *Irish Daily Independent and Daily Nation* (8 October 1903), 4.
Anon., 'The Gael in Trinity', *An Claidheamh Soluis* (28 November 1908), 9.
Anon. (editorial comment), *Leader* (25 November 1911), 348.
Anon., 'A Pensioner on Paudeen', *Sinn Fein* (18 January 1913), 1.
Anon., 'Mr. Yeats's Poetry', *Nation* (23 October 1915), 154, 6.
Atkinson, F. M., 'A Literary Causerie', *Dana*, 10 (February 1905), 314–17.
[Bailey, John Cann], 'Spenser', *Times Literary Supplement* (2 November 1906), 365–6.
Bickley, Francis, 'The Development of William Butler Yeats', *Thrush*, 1: 2 (January 1910), 147–51.
Boyd, Ernest A., 'The Drift of Anglo-Irish Literature', *The Irish Commonwealth*, 1: 1 (March 1919), 19–28.
Brooks, Van Wyck, 'Ireland, 1916', *The Dial* (30 November 1916), 458–60.
Colum, Mary M., 'The Later Yeats', *Poetry*, 7: 5 (February 1916), 258–60.
Cox, Aedan, 'A Weaver of Symbols', *Hermes*, 1: 1 (February 1907), 7–11.
Downes, Robert P., 'William Butler Yeats', *Great Thoughts* (30 January 1915), 214–16.

D[uncan], E[llen] M., 'The Writings of Mr. W. B. Yeats', *Fortnightly Review*, 85 (February 1909), 253–70.
Frothingham, Eugenia Brooks, 'An Irish Poet and His Work', *The Critic*, 44: 1 (January 1904), 26–31.
Gilman, Lawrence, 'The Last of the Poets', *North-American Review*, 202: 719 (October 1915), 592–7.
Herts, B. Russell, 'The Shadowy Mr. Yeats', *Forum*, 52: 6 (December 1914), 911–14.
[Hone, Joseph], 'Art and Aristocracy', *Irish Times* (11 January 1913), 6.
Hone, Joseph, 'W. B. Yeats: A Character Sketch', *Everyman* (27 June 1913), 328–9.
[Hone, Joseph], 'The Art Gallery', *Irish Times* (8 September 1913), 6.
'I', 'Mr. W. B. Yeats', *To–day* (27 April 1904), 366.
'Imaal', 'A Rather Complex Personality', *Leader* (26 September 1903), 71–2.
K[eller], T. G., 'The Poet at the Abbey Theatre', *Northern Whig* (3 November 1908), 5.
Lynd, Robert, 'Poets as Patriots', *British Review*, 6: 2 (May 1914), 264–80.
Marshall, J., 'The Poetry of W. B. Yeats', *Queens Quarterly*, 13: 3 (January–March 1906), 241–5.
Masterman, C. F. G., 'After the Reaction', *Contemporary Review*, 86: 468 (December 1904), 815–34.
Montgomery, K. L., 'Some Writers of the Celtic Renaissance', *Fortnightly Review*, 90 (September 1911), 545–61.
Moore, Isabel, 'William Butler Yeats', *Bookman* (New York), 18: 4 (December 1903), 360–3.
Mör, Ian, 'W. B. Yeats and A. E. ', *Theosophical Review*, 37: 218 (October 1905), 105–17.
[Moran, D. P.], 'At the Abbey Theatre', *Leader* (7 January 1905), 330–31.
O'Grady, Standish (editorial comment), *All Ireland Review* (1 December 1900), 6.
O'Neill, Eamonn, 'An Interesting Meeting' *An Claidheamh Soluis* (9 November 1901), 555.
Orkney, Michael, 'William B.Yeats: A Character Sketch', *Irish Independent* (21 March 1908), 4.
Pearse, Patrick, 'About Literature', *An Claidheamh Soluis* (22 April 1905), 7.
Rifler, Percy Stent, 'Men of the Times, VII: Mr. W. B. Yeats', *Irish Truth* (14 November 1903), 3658.
Roberts, R. Ellis, 'W. B. Yeats', *Bookman*, 50: 299 (August 1916), 139–40.
Sidgwick, F., 'William Butler Yeats: Our Birthday Portraits – IX', *English Illustrated Magazine*, 29: 3 (June 1903), 286–8.
Thomas, Edward, 'An Irish Poet', *Daily Chronicle* (18 May 1908), 3.
Thomas, Edward, untitled review of *Poems* (1912), *Poetry and Drama*, 1: 1 (March 1913), 53–6.
[Thompson, Francis], 'Fiona Macleod on Mr. W. B.Yeats', *Academy and Literature* (25 October 1902), 444–5.
Weygandt, Cornelius, 'The Irish Literary Revival', *Sewanee Review*, 12: 4 (October 1904), 420–31.

Other Sources

Albright, Daniel, *Quantum Poetics: Yeats, Pound, Eliot, and the Science of Modernism* (Cambridge University Press, 1997).

Aldington, Richard, 'The Poetry of Ezra Pound', *The Egoist* (1 May 1915), 71–2.
Anderson, Benedict, *Imagined Communities* (London: Verso, 1983).
Anon., 'The History of Ailell and Etain', ed. and trans. Eduard Müller, *Revue Celtique*, III (1876–8), 355–60.
Arac, Jonathan, ed., *Postmodernism and Politics* (Manchester University Press, 1986).
Baker, William E., *Syntax in English Poetry 1870–1930* (Berkeley and Los Angeles: University of California Press, 1967).
Balliett, Conrad A., 'The Lives – and Lies – of Maud Gonne', *Eire-Ireland*, XIV (1979), 17–44.
Beaumont, Francis, and John Fletcher, *The Works of Francis Beaumont and John Fletcher*, ed. Arnold Glover (Cambridge: Cambridge University Press, 1905–12), vol. 1.
Beckett, J. C., *The Anglo–Irish Tradition* (London: Faber & Faber, 1976).
Bergonzi, Bernard, *The Myth of Modernism and Twentieth-Century Literature* (Brighton: Harvester Press, 1986).
Blacam, Aodh de, 'The Other Hidden Ireland', *Studies*, XXIII (1934), 439–54.
Blackmur, R. P., *Anni Mirabiles 1921–25: Reason in the Madness of Letters* (Washington: Library of Congress, 1956).
Blake, William, *The Works of William Blake*, ed. Edwin John Ellis and W. B. Yeats (London: Bernard Quaritch, 1893), 3 vols.
Bohlmann, Otto, *Yeats and Nietzsche* (London: Macmillan, 1982).
Bornstein, George, 'Last Romantic or Last Victorian: Yeats, Tennyson, and Browning', YA1 (1983), 114–32.
Bornstein, George, *Poetic Remaking: The Art of Browning, Yeats, and Pound* (University Park and London: Pennsylvania State University Press, 1988).
Bornstein, George, 'Remaking Himself: Yeats's Revisions of His Early Canon', *Text: Transactions of the Society for Textual Scholarship*, V (1991), 339–58.
Bornstein, George, 'Romancing the Native Stone', in Gene W. Ruoff, ed.,*The Romantics and Us* (New Brunswick and London: Rutgers University Press, 1990), 108–29.
Bornstein, George, *Transformations of Romanticism in Yeats, Eliot, and Stevens* (Chicago and London: University of Chicago Press, 1976).
Bornstein, George,'What is the Text of a Poem by Yeats?', in George Bornstein and Ralph G. Williams, eds, *Palimpsest: Editorial Theory in the Humanities* (Ann Arbor: The University of Michigan Press, 1993).
Bornstein, George, and Warwick Gould, ' "To a Sister of the Cross & the Rose": An Unpublished Early Poem', YA7 (1990) 179–83.
Bourdieu, Pierre, 'The Field of Cultural production, or: The Economic World Reversed', trans. Richard Nice, *Poetics*, XII (1983), 311–56.
Bourdieu, Pierre, *Language and Symbolic Power*, trans. Gino Raymond and Matthew Adamson, ed. John B. Thompson (Cambridge: Polity Press, in association with Basil Blackwell, Oxford, 1991).
Boyce, D. G., *The Revolution in Ireland 1879–1923* (London: Macmillan, 1988).
Boyd, Ernest A., *Ireland's Literary Renaissance* (Dublin and London: Maunsel and Co., 1916).
Bridgwater, Patrick, *Nietzsche in Anglo-Saxony* (Leicester University Press, 1972).
Brown, Malcolm, *The Politics of Irish Literature from Thomas Davis to W. B. Yeats* (London: George Allen & Unwin, 1972).

Brown, Terence, *The Life of W. B. Yeats: A Critical Biography* (Oxford: Blackwell, 1999).
Browning, Robert, 'Essay on Shelley', in Percy Bysshe Shelley, *Letters* (London: Edward Moxon, 1852).
Buckland, Patrick, *Irish Unionism: One: The Anglo–Irish and the New Ireland 1885–1922* (Dublin: Gill & Macmillan; New York: Barnes and Noble Books, 1972).
Calinescu, Matei, *Five Faces of Modernity: Modernism, Avant–Garde, Decadence, Kitsch, Postmodernism* (Durham, N.C. : Duke University Press, 1987).
Cardozo, Nancy, *Lucky Eyes and a High Heart: The Life of Maud Gonne* (London: Victor Gollancz, 1979).
Carpenter, Andrew, ed., *Place, Personality and the Irish Writer* (Gerrards Cross: Colin Smythe, 1977).
Carpenter, Humphrey, *A Serious Character: The Life of Ezra Pound* (London: Faber & Faber, 1988).
Castiglione, Baldessare, *The Book of the Courtier*, trans. Thomas Hoby (London: David Nutt, 1900).
Chapman, Wayne K., *Yeats and English Renaissance Literature* (London: Macmillan, 1991).
Christ, Carol T., *Victorian and Modern Poetics* (Chicago and London: University of Chicago Press, 1984).
Coleman, Antony, 'The Big House, Yeats, and the Irish Context', YA3 (1985), 33–52.
Comerford, R. V., 'Political Myths in Modern Ireland', *Irishness in a Changing Society* (The Princess Grace Irish Library, 2) (Gerrards Cross: Colin Smythe, 1988), 1–17.
Connolly, Peter, ed., *Literature and the Changing Ireland* (Gerrards Cross: Colin Smythe; Totowa, New Jersey: Barnes and Noble Books, 1982).
Corkery, Daniel, *The Hidden Ireland: A Study of Gaelic Munster in the Eighteenth Century* (Dublin: M. H. Gill & Son, 1925).
Corkery, Daniel, 'The Nation That Was Not a Nation', *Studies*, XXIII (1934), 611–22.
Corkery, Daniel, 'Ourselves and Dean Swift', *Studies*, XXIII (1934), 203–18.
Corkery, Daniel, *Synge and Anglo–Irish Literature: A Study* (Dublin and Cork: Cork University Press; London: Longmans, Green,1931).
Culler, Jonathan, 'Commentary', *New Literary History*, VI (1974), 219–29, 219.
Culler, Jonathan, *Flaubert: The Uses of Uncertainty* (London: Paul Elek, 1974).
Culler, Jonathan, *On Deconstruction: Theory and Criticism after Structuralism* (London: Routledge & Kegan Paul, 1983).
Cullingford, Elizabeth Butler, 'At the Feet of the Goddess: Yeats's Love Poetry and the Feminist Occult', YA9 (1992), 31–59.
Cullingford, Elizabeth Butler, *Gender and History in Yeats's Love Poetry* (Cambridge University Press, 1993).
Cullingford, Elizabeth Butler, 'Thinking of Her ... as ... Ireland": Yeats, Pearse and Heaney', *Textual Practice*, IV (1990), 1–21.
Cullingford, Elizabeth Butler, *Yeats, Ireland and Fascism* (London: Macmillan, 1981).
Dale, Peter Allan, *The Victorian Critic and the Idea of History: Carlyle, Arnold, Pater* (Cambridge, Mass. and London: Harvard University Press, 1977).

Davidson, Donald, *Inquiries into Truth and Interpretation* (Oxford: Clarendon Press, 1984).

Davie, Donald, 'Common and Uncommon Muses', *Twentieth Century*, CLXII (1957), 458–68.

Davie, Donald, *Ezra Pound: Poet as Sculptor* (New York: Oxford University Press, 1964).

Davie, Donald, *The Poet in the Imaginary Museum* (Manchester: Carcanet Press, 1977).

Deane, Seamus, *Celtic Revivals: Essays in Modern Irish Literature 1880–1980* (London: Faber & Faber, 1985).

Deane, Seamus, 'Yeats, Ireland and Revolution', *Crane Bag*, I (1977), 56–64.

Deane, Seamus, ed., *Field Day Anthology* (Derry: Field Day Publications, 1991) 3 vols.

Dembo, L. S., *Conceptions of Reality in Modern American Poetry* (Berkeley and Los Angeles: University of California Press, 1966).

Dick, Susan, Declan Kiberd, Dougald McMillan, Joseph Ronsley, eds, *Omnium Gatherum: Essays for Richard Ellmann* (Gerrards Cross: Colin Smythe, 1989).

Diggory, Terence, *Yeats and American Poetry: The Tradition of the Self* (Princeton University Press, 1983).

Donoghue, Denis, *We Irish: Essays on Irish Literature and Society* (Brighton: Harvester Press, 1986).

Donoghue, Denis, *Yeats* (Fontana Modern Masters) (London: Fontana/Collins, 1971).

Dowling, Linda, *Language and Decadence in the Victorian Fin de Siècle* (Princeton: Princeton University Press, 1986).

Dunsany, Lord Edward, *Selections from the Writings of Lord Dunsany* (Dundrum: Cuala, 1912).

Eagleton, Terry, *Criticism and Ideology: A Study in Marxist Literary Theory* (London: New Left Books, 1976).

Eckermann, J. P., *Conversations of Goethe with Eckermann and Soret*, trans. John Oxenford (London: Smith, Elder and Co., 1850), 2 vols.

Eglinton, John (W. K. Magee), *Anglo–Irish Essays* (Dublin: The Talbot Press; London: T. Fisher Unwin, 1917).

Eliot, T. S., *After Strange Gods* (London: Faber & Faber, 1934).

Eliot, T. S., 'A Foreign Mind', *Athenaeum* (4 July 1919), 552–3.

Eliot, T. S., *Selected Essays* (London: Faber & Faber, 1951).

Eliot, T. S., *Selected Prose*, ed. Frank Kermode (London: Faber & Faber, 1975).

Eliot, T. S., *The Use of Poetry and the Use of Criticism* (London: Faber & Faber, 1933).

Eliot, T. S., Introduction to Paul Valéry, *The Art of Poetry* (*Works* vol. 7), trans. Denise Folliot (London: Routledge & Kegan Paul, 1958).

Ellis, Henry Havelock, 'Friedrich Nietzsche', *Savoy*, 2, 3, 4 (April, July, August 1896), 79–84, 68–81, 57–63 respectively.

Ellmann, Richard, *Golden Codgers: Biographical Speculations* (New York and London: Oxford University Press, 1973).

Ellmann, Richard, and Charles Feidelson Jr, eds, *The Modern Tradition: Backgrounds of Modern Literature* (New York: Oxford University Press, 1965).

Feidelson, Charles, *Symbolism and American Literature* (University of Chicago Press, 1960, first published 1953).

Ferguson, Samuel, 'Hardiman's Irish Minstrelsy', *Dublin University Magazine*, 3 & 4 (April, August, October, November, 1834), 456–78, 152–67, 447–67, 514–42 respectively.
Figgis, Darrell, *Studies and Appreciations* (London: J. M. Dent, 1912).
Finnegan, Ruth, *Literacy and Orality: Studies in the Technology of Communication* (Oxford: Basil Blackwell, 1988).
Finnegan, Ruth, *Oral Poetry: Its Nature, Significance and Social Context*, 2nd edn (Bloomington and Indianapolis: Indiana University Press, 1992).
Finneran, Richard J., *Editing Yeats's Poems: A Reconsideration* (London: Macmillan, 1990).
Finneran, Richard J., George Mills Harper and William M.Murphy, with the assistance of Alan B. Himber, eds, *Letters to W. B. Yeats* (London: Macmillan; New York: Columbia University Press, 1977), 2 vols.
Flanagan, Thomas, 'Yeats, Joyce, and the Matter of Ireland', *Critical Inquiry*, II (1975–6), 43–67.
Flannery, James W., *W. B. Yeats and the Idea of a Theatre: The Early Abbey Theatre in Theory and Practice* (New Haven and London: Yale University Press, 1976).
Flaubert, Gustave, *Correspondance*, ed. Jean Bruneau (Bibliothèque de la Pléiade) (Paris: Gallimard, 1980), vol. II.
Fletcher, Ian, 'Some Anticipations of Imagism', in *A Catalogue of The Imagist Poets* (New York: J. Howard Woolmer, 1966).
Fletcher, Ian, *W. B. Yeats and his Contemporaries* (Brighton: Harvester, 1987).
Flint, F. S., 'The History of Imagism', *Egoist* (May 1915), 70–1.
Fokkema, Douwe, and Elrud Ibsch, *Modernist Conjectures: A Mainstream in European Literature 1910–1940* (London: C. Hurst 1987).
Ford, Ford Madox (Hueffer), *Collected Poems* (London: Max Goschen, 1914).
Ford, Ford Madox (Hueffer), *The Critical Attitude* (London: Duckworth, 1911).
Ford, Ford Madox (Hueffer), *Thus to Revisit: Some Reminiscences* (London: Chapman & Hall, 1921).
Foster, Hal, ed., *Postmodern Culture* (London and Sydney: Pluto Press, 1985 [first published as *The Anti-Aesthetic*; Port Townsend: Bay Press, 1983]).
Foster, R. F., *Modern Ireland 1600–1972* (London: Penguin, 1989, reprinted from the 1988 edn).
Foster, R. F. *Paddy and Mr Punch: Connections in Irish and English History* (London: Allen Lane, 1993).
Foster, R. F., *W. B. Yeats: A Life: Volume One: The Apprentice Mage* (Oxford and New York: Oxford University Press, 1997).
Frank, Joseph, *The Idea of Spatial Form* (New Brunswick, N.J. and London: Rutgers University Press, 1991).
Frank, Joseph, *The Widening Gyre: Crisis and Mastery in Modern Literature* (New Brunswick, N.J.: Rutgers University Press, 1963).
Freeman, Mark, *Rewriting the Self: History, Memory, Narrative* (London and New York: Routledge, 1993).
Freyer, Grattan, *W. B. Yeats and the Anti–Democratic Tradition* (Dublin: Gill & Macmillan, 1981).
Friedman, Barton R., 'Yeats, Johnson, and Ireland's Heroic Dead', *Eire-Ireland*, VII (1972), 32–47.

Fugitive: A Journal of Poetry, The (New York and London: Johnson Reprint Corporation, 1966).
Gadamer, Hans-Georg, *Philosophical Hermeneutics*, trans. and ed. David E.Linge (Berkeley, Los Angeles, London: University of California Press, 1976).
Gadamer, Hans-Georg, *Truth and Method* (2nd edn, revised), translation revised from that of W. Glen-Doepel by Joel C. Weinsheimer and Donald G. Marshall (London: Sheed & Ward, 1989).
Garvin, Tom, *The Evolution of Irish Nationalist Politics* (Dublin: Gill & Macmillan, 1981).
Garvin, Tom, *Nationalist Revolutionaries in Ireland 1858–1928* (Oxford: Clarendon Press, 1987).
Gellner, Ernest, *Nations and Nationalism* (Oxford: Basil Blackwell, 1983).
Gilbert, R. A., *The Golden Dawn Companion: A Guide to the History, Structure, and Workings of the Hermetic Order of the Golden Dawn* (Wellingborough: Aquarian Press, 1986).
Golden, Sean, 'Post-Traditional English Literature: A Polemic', *Crane Bag*, III (1979), 7–18.
Gombrich, E. H., *The Image and the Eye: Further Studies in the Psychology of Pictorial Representation* (Oxford: Phaidon Press, 1982).
Gonne, Maud (Maud Gonne MacBride), *A Servant of the Queen: Reminiscences* (London: Victor Gollancz, 1938).
Gonne, Maud (Maud Gonne MacBride), *The Gonne–Yeats Letters 1893–1938: Always Your Friend*, ed. Anna MacBride White and A. Norman Jeffares (London: Hutchinson, 1992).
Gould, Warwick, 'The Definitive Edition: a History of the Final Arrangements of Yeats's Work', YP 706–49.
Gould, Warwick, 'The Editor Takes Possession', *Times Literary Supplement* (29 June 1984), 731–3.
Gould, Warwick, 'An Empty Theatre? Yeats as Minstrel in *Responsibilities*', *Studies on W. B. Yeats*, ed. Jaqueline Genet (1989), 79–118.
Gould, Warwick, '"Witch" or "Bitch" – Which? Yeats, Archives, and the Profession of Authorship', in Warwick Gould and Thomas F. Staley, eds, *Writing the Lives of Writers* (London: Macmillan, 1998), 173–190.
Gould, Warwick, 'Yeats Deregulated', YA9 (1992), 356–72.
Gould, Warwick, and Deirdre Toomey, '"Cycles Ago", Maud Gonne and the Lyrics of 1891', YA7 (1990), 184–93.
Gould, Warwick, and Deindre Toomey '"Take Down This Book": *The Flame of the Spirit*, Text and Context', YA11 (1995) 124–37.
Gregory, Lady Isabella Augusta, *A Book of Saints and Wonders Put Down Here by Lady Gregory According to the Old Writings and the Memory of the People of Ireland* (London: John Murray, 1907).
Gregory, Lady Isabella Augusta, *Cuchulain of Muirthemne: The Story of the Men of the Red Branch of Ulster* (London: John Murray, 1902).
Gregory, Lady Isabella Augusta, *Gods and Fighting Men: The Story of the Tuatha de Danaan and of the Fianna of Ireland* (London: John Murray, 1904).
Gregory, Lady Isabella Augusta, *Hugh Lane's Life and Achievement, With Some Account of the Dublin Galleries* (London: John Murray, 1921).
Gregory, Lady Isabella Augusta, ed., *Ideals in Ireland* (London: Unicorn Press, 1901).

Gregory, Lady Isabella Augusta, *Our Irish Theatre* (New York and London: G. P. Putnam's Sons, 1914).
Hallberg, Robert von, ed., *Canons* (Chicago and London: University of Chicago Press, 1984).
Hampson, R. G., '"Experiments in Modernity": Ford and Pound', in Andrew Gibson, ed., *Pound in Multiple Perspective: A Collection of Critical Essays* (London: Macmillan, 1993), 93–125.
Harper, George Mills, 'The Creator as Destroyer: Nietzschean Morality in Yeats's *Where there is Nothing*', *Colby Library Quarterly*, XV (1979), 114–25.
Harper, George Mills, *Yeats's Golden Dawn* (London: Macmillan, 1974).
Harwood, John, *Olivia Shakespear and W. B. Yeats: After Long Silence* (London: Macmillan, 1989).
Harwood, John, '"Secret Communion": Yeats's Sexual Destiny', YA9 (1992), 3–30.
Harwood, John, *Eliot to Derrida: The Poverty of Interpretation* (London: Macmillan, 1995).
Havelock, Eric A., *The Muse Learns to Write: Reflections on Orality and Literacy from Antiquity to the Present* (New Haven and London: Yale University Press, 1986).
Heaney, Seamus, *The Place of Writing*, with an introduction by Ronald Schuchard (Atlanta: Scholars Press, 1989).
Heaney, Seamus, *Preoccupations: Selected Prose 1968–78* (London: Faber & Faber, 1980).
Heaney, Seamus, 'A Tale of Two Islands: Reflections on the Irish Literary Revival', *Irish Studies*, ed. P. J. Drudy, I (1980), 1–20.
Heine, Elizabeth, 'Yeats and Maud Gonne: Marriage and the Astrological Record, 1908–09', YA13 (1998), 3–33.
Hermans, Theo, *The Structure of Modernist Poetry* (London: Croom Helm, 1982).
Hirsch, E. D. Jr, *The Aims of Interpretation* (Chicago and London: University of Chicago Press, 1976).
Hone, Joseph, *W. B. Yeats 1865–1939* (London: Macmillan, 1943).
Hone, Joseph, *William Butler Yeats: The Poet in Contemporary Ireland* (Dublin and London: Maunsel, 1916).
Hoy, David Couzens, *The Critical Circle: Literature and History in Contemporary Hermeneutics* (Berkeley, Los Angeles, London: University of California Press, 1978).
Hough, Graham, *Image and Experience: Studies in a Literary Revolution* (London: Gerald Duckworth, 1960).
Howe, Ellic, *The Magicians of the Golden Dawn: A Documentary History of a Magical Order*, 2nd edn (London: Routledge & Kegan Paul, 1985).
Hughes, Glenn, *Imagism and the Imagists: A Study in Modern Poetry* (Palo Alto: Stanford University Press; London: Humphrey Milford, Oxford University Press, 1931).
Hulme, T. E., *Further Speculations*, ed. Sam Hynes (Minneapolis: University of Minnesota Press, 1955).
Hulme, T. E., *Speculations*, ed. Herbert Read (London: Kegan Paul, Trench, Trubner; New York: Harcourt, Brace, 1924).
Hutchinson, John, *The Dynamics of Cultural Nationalism: The Gaelic Revival and the Creation of the Irish Nation State* (London: Allen & Unwin, 1987).

186 Selected Bibliography

Jackson, Thomas H., *The Early Poetry of Ezra Pound* (Cambridge, Mass.: Harvard University Press, 1968).
James, R. A. Scott, *Modernism and Romance* (London and New York: John Lane, 1908).
Jeffares, A. Norman, *W. B. Yeats: A New Biography* (London: Arena, 1990; first edn London: Hutchinson, 1988).
Jefferson, Ann, & David Robey, eds, *Modern Literary Theory: A Comparative Introduction* (London: Batsford, 1982).
Jefferson, George, *Edward Garnett: A Life in Literature* (London: Jonathan Cape, 1982).
Jochum, K. P. S., *W. B. Yeats: A Classified Bibliography of Criticism*, 2nd edn revised & enlarged (Urbana and Chicago: University of Illinois Press, 1990).
Johnson, Lionel, 'The Man Who Would Be King', *The Academy* (19 November 1898), 293–4.
Johnson, Lionel, and W. B. Yeats, *Poetry and Ireland: Essays by W. B. Yeats and Lionel Johnson* (Dundrum: Cuala Press, 1908).
Jones, Alun R., *The Life & Opinions of T. E. Hulme* (London: Victor Gollancz, 1960).
Kearney, Richard, 'Beyond Art and Politics', *Crane Bag*, I (1977), 8–16.
Kearney, Richard, 'The Transitional Crisis of Modern Irish Culture', *Irishness in a Changing Society* (The Princess Grace Irish Library, 2) (Gerrards Cross: Colin Smythe, 1988), 78–94.
Kelly, John S., 'Books & Numberless Dreams: Yeats's Relations with his Early Publishers', in A. Norman Jeffares, ed., *Yeats, Sligo and Ireland* (Gerrards Cross: Colin Smythe, 1980), 232–53.
Kelly, John S., 'The Fall of Parnell & the Rise of Irish Literature: An Investigation', *Anglo-Irish Studies*, ed. P. J. Drudy, II (1976), 1–23.
Kenner, Hugh, *A Colder Eye: The Modern Irish Writers* (London: Allen Lane, 1983).
Kenner, Hugh, *The Pound Era* (Berkeley and Los Angeles: University of California Press, 1971).
Kenner, Hugh, 'The Sacred Book of the Arts', *Sewannee Review*, LXIV (1956), 574–90.
Kermode, Frank, *Forms of Attention* (Chicago and London: University of Chicago Press, 1985).
Kermode, Frank, *Modern Essays* (Glasgow: Fontana Press, 1990).
Kermode, Frank, 'Modernisms', *London Review of Books* (22 May 1986), 3–6.
Kermode, Frank, 'A Reply to Joseph Frank', *Critical Inquiry*, IV (1978), 579–88.
Kermode, Frank, *Romantic Image* (London: Routledge & Kegan Paul, 1957).
Kermode, Frank, *The Sense of an Ending: Studies in the Theory of Fiction* (New York: Oxford University Press, 1967).
Kiely, Robert, ed. (assisted by John Hildebidle), *Modernism Reconsidered* (Cambridge, Mass. and London: Harvard University Press, 1983).
Kinsella, Thomas, *Davis, Mangan, Ferguson? Tradition and the Irish Writer* (Dublin: Dolmen Press, 1970).
Koelb, Clayton, ed., *Nietzsche as Postmodernist: Essays Pro and Contra* (Albany: The State University of New York Press, 1990).
Kuch, Peter, *Yeats and A. E.: 'The Antagonism that Unites Dear Friends'* (Gerrards Cross: Colin Smythe, 1986).
Lentricchia, Frank, *Modernist Quartet* (Cambridge: Cambridge University Press, 1994).
Levenson, Michael, *A Genealogy of Modernism: A Study of English Literary Doctrine 1908–1922* (Cambridge University Press, 1984).

Lobb, Edward, *T. S. Eliot and the Romantic Critical Tradition* (London: Routledge & Kegan Paul, 1981).
Loevgren, Sven, *The Genesis of Modernism: Seurat, Gauguin, Van Gogh, and French Symbolism in the 1880s*, 2nd edn (Bloomington and London: Indiana University Press, 1971; first published Stockholm: Almquist & Wiksell, 1959).
Longenbach, James, *Stone Cottage: Pound, Yeats, and Modernism* (New York and Oxford: Oxford University Press, 1988).
Lyons, F. S. L., *Culture and Anarchy in Ireland 1890–1939* (Oxford: Clarendon Press, 1979).
McAlindon, T., 'Yeats and the English Renaissance', *PMLA*, LXXXII (1967), 157–69.
MacDonagh, Oliver, *States of Mind: A Study of Anglo-Irish Conflict 1780–1980* (London: George Allen & Unwin, 1983).
MacDonald, Gail, *Learning to be Modern: Pound, Eliot, and the American University* (Oxford: Clarendon Press, 1993).
McGann, Jerome J., *A Critique of Modern Textual Criticism* (Chicago and London: University of Chicago Press, 1983).
McGann, Jerome J., *Social Values and Poetic Acts: The Historical Judgment of Literary Work* (Cambridge, Mass. and London: Harvard University Press, 1988).
McGann, Jerome J., 'Theory of Texts', *London Review of Books* (18 February 1988), 20–1.
McGann, Jerome J., *Towards a Literature of Knowledge* (Oxford: Clarendon Press, 1989).
McGann, Jerome J., 'Which Yeats Edition?', *Times Literary Supplement* (11–17 May 1990), 493–4.
McKenzie, D. F., *Bibliography and the Sociology of Texts: The Panizzi Lectures 1985* (London: British Library, 1986).
MacNeice, Louis, *The Poetry of W. B. Yeats* (London: Oxford University Press, 1941).
Mallarmé, Stéphane, *Oeuvres Complètes*, ed. Henri Mondor and G. Jean Aubry (Bibliothèque de la Pléiade) (Paris: Gallimard, 1945).
Marcus, Phillip L., 'Incarnation in "Middle Yeats"', YA1 (1982), 68–81.
Marcus, Phillip L., *Yeats and Artistic Power* (London: Macmillan, 1992).
Martin, Augustine, 'What Stalked through the Post Office', *Crane Bag*, II (1978), 164–77.
Mead, G. R. S., *Orpheus: The Theosophy of the Greeks* (London: Theosophical Publishing Society, 1896).
Meir, Colin, *The Ballads and Songs of W. B. Yeats: The Anglo-Irish Heritage in Subject and Style* (London: Macmillan, 1974).
Menand, Louis, *Discovering Modernism: T. S. Eliot and His Context* (New York: Oxford University Press, 1987).
Merquior, J. G., *From Prague to Paris: A Critique of Structuralist and Post-structuralist Thought* (London: Verso, 1986).
Mikhail, E. H., ed., *Lady Gregory: Interviews and Recollections* (London: Macmillan, 1977).
Miller, David W., *Church, State and Nation in Ireland 1898–1921* (Dublin: Gill & Macmillan, 1973).
Miller, Liam, *The Dun Emer Press, Later the Cuala Press* (Dublin: Dolmen, 1973).
Mizener, Arthur, *The Saddest Story: A Biography of Ford Madox Ford* (New York and Cleveland: World Publishing, 1971).

Moore, George, *Hail and Farewell: Ave, Salve, Vale*, ed. Richard Cave (Gerrards Cross: Colin Smythe, 1976).
Moran, D. P., *The Philosophy of Irish Ireland* (Dublin: James Duffy, 1905).
Murphy, John, 'Religion and Irish Identity', *Irishness in a Changing Society* (The Princess Grace Irish Library, 2) (Gerrards Cross: Colin Smythe, 1988), 132–51.
Murphy, William M., *Family Secrets: William Butler Yeats and His Relatives* (Dublin: Gill & Macmillan, 1995).
Murphy, William M., *Prodigal Father: The Life of John Butler Yeats (1839–1922)* (Ithaca and London: Cornell University Press, 1978).
Nicholls, Peter, *Modernisms: A Literary Guide* (London: Macmillan, 1995).
Nietzsche, Friedrich, *The Birth of Tragedy*, trans. William A. Haussmann (Edinburgh and London: T. N. Foulis, 1909).
Nietzsche, Friedrich, *The Case of Wagner, Nietzsche Contra Wagner, The Twilight of the Idols, The Anti-Christ*, trans. Thomas Common (London: H. Henry, 1896).
Nietzsche, Friedrich, *The Dawn of Day*, trans. Johanna Volz (London: T. Fisher Unwin, 1903).
Nietzsche, Friedrich, *Nietzsche as Critic, Philosopher, Poet and Prophet*, ed. Thomas Common (London: Grant Richards, 1901).
Nietzsche, Friedrich, *Philosophy and Truth: Selections from Nietzsche's Notebooks of the Early 1870s*, ed. and trans. Daniel Breazeale (Atlantic Highlands, N. J.: Humanities Press; Hassocks, Sussex: Harvester Press, 1979).
Nietzsche, Friedrich, *Thus Spake Zarathustra: A Book for All and None*, trans. A. Tille, revised by M. M. Bozman, with an introduction by Ernest Rhys (London and Toronto: J. M. Dent; New York: E. P. Dutton, 1933).
North, Michael, *The Political Aesthetic of Yeats, Eliot, and Pound* (Cambridge University Press, 1991).
Oates, Joyce Carol, *The Edge of Impossibility: Tragic Forms in Literature* (New York: Vanguard, 1972).
O'Brien, Conor Cruise, 'Politics and the Poet', *Irish Times* (21 August 1975), 10.
O'Brien, Conor Cruise, ed., *The Shaping of Modern Ireland* (London: Routledge & Kegan Paul, 1960).
O'Brien, Conor Cruise, *The Suspecting Glance* (London: Faber & Faber, 1972).
O'Leary, John, *Recollections of Fenians and Fenianism* (London: Downey, 1896), 2 vols.
Olney, James, ed., *Autobiography: Essays Theoretical and Critical* (Princeton: Princeton University Press, 1980).
Ong, Walter J., *Interfaces of the Word: Studies in the Evolution of Consciousness and Culture* (Ithaca and London: Cornell University Press, 1977).
Ong, Walter J., *Orality and Literacy: The Technologizing of the Word* (London and New York: Methuen, 1982).
Oppel, Francis Nesbitt, *Mask and Tragedy: Yeats and Nietzsche 1902–1910* (Charlottesville: University Press of Virginia, 1987).
Orr, Leonard, ed., *Yeats and Postmodernism* (Syracuse University Press, 1991).
Parkinson, Thomas, 'Yeats and the Limits of Modernity', *Yeats An Annual of Critical and Textual Studies*, III (1985), 60–71.
Parkinson, Thomas, 'Yeats and Pound: The Illusion of Influence', *Comparative Literature*, VI (1954), 256–64.
Pater, Walter, *Appreciations* (London: Macmillan, 1889).

Pater, Walter, *Greek Studies* (London: Macmillan, 1895).
Pater, Walter, *Plato and Platonism* (London: Macmillan, 1893).
Pater, Walter, *Studies in the History of the Renaissance* (London: Macmillan, 1873).
Perloff, Marjorie, 'Yeats and Goethe', *Comparative Literature*, XXIII (1971), 125–40.
Pethica, James, 'Contextualising the Lyric Moment: Yeats's "The Happy Townland" and the Abandoned Play *The Country of the Young*', YA10 (1993), 65–91.
Pethica, James, 'Patronage and Creative Exchange: Yeats, Lady Gregory, and the Economy of Indebtedness', YA9 (1992), 60–94.
Pound, Ezra, *The Cantos*, 4th collected edn (London: Faber & Faber, 1987).
Pound, Ezra, *Gaudier-Brzeska: A Memoir* (London: John Lane, The Bodley Head; New York: John Lane, 1916).
Pound, Ezra, 'In Metre', *The New Freewoman*, VI (1913), 113.
Pound, Ezra, *The Letters of Ezra Pound 1907–1941*, ed. D. D. Paige (London: Faber & Faber, 1951).
Pound, Ezra, *Literary Essays*, ed. T. S. Eliot (London: Faber & Faber, 1985, reprinted from the 1954 edition).
Pound, Ezra, *Selected Prose 1909–1965*, ed. William Cookson (London: Faber & Faber, 1978, reprinted from the 1973 edition).
Pound, Ezra, 'Status Rerum', *Poetry*, 1: 4 (January 1913), 123–7.
Quinn, John, *The Letters of John Quinn to William Butler Yeats*, ed. Alan Himber (Epping: Bowker, 1983).
Rainey, Lawrence, 'The Price of Modernism: Publishing *The Waste Land*', in Ronald Bush, ed., *T. S. Eliot: The Modernist in History* (Cambridge: Cambridge University Press, 1991).
Ransom, John Crowe, 'The Future of Poetry', *The Fugitive: A Journal of Poetry*, III (1924), 2–4 (New York and London: Johnson Reprint Corporation, 1966).
Reeves, Marjorie, and Warwick Gould, *Joachim of Fiore and the Myth of the Eternal Evangel in the Nineteenth Century* (Oxford: Clarendon Press, 1987).
Reid, B. L., *The Man from New York: John Quinn and His Friends* (New York: Oxford University Press, 1968).
Reid, Forrest, *W. B. Yeats: A Critical Study* (London: Martin Secker, 1915).
Riding, Laura, and Robert Graves, *A Survey of Modernist Poetry* (London: William Heinemann, 1927).
Russell, George W., *Letters from A. E.*, ed. Alan Denson (London, New York, Toronto: Abelard-Schuman, 1961).
Saddlemyer, Ann, ed., *Theatre Business: The Correspondence of the First Abbey Theatre Directors: William Butler Yeats, Lady Gregory and J. M. Synge* (Gerrards Cross: Colin Smythe; University Park,Penn., Pennsylvania State University Press, 1982).
Saddlemyer, Ann, and Colin Smythe, eds, *Lady Gregory Fifty Years After* (Gerrards Cross: Colin Smythe, 1987).
Schopenhauer, Arthur, *The World as Will and Idea*, trans. R. B. Haldane and J.Kemp (London: Trübner, 1883–6), 3 vols.
Schuchard, Ronald, '"An Attendant Lord": H. W. Nevinson's Friendship with W. B. Yeats', YA7 (1990), 90–130.
Schuchard, Ronald, 'The Minstrel in the Theatre: Arnold, Chaucer and Yeats's New Spiritual Democracy', YA2 (1984), 3–24.
Schuchard, Ronald, 'Yeats, Titian and the New French Painting', in A. Norman Jeffares, ed., *Yeats the European* (Gerrards Cross: Colin Smythe, 1989), 142–59.

Schwarz, Sanford, *The Matrix of Modernism: Pound, Eliot, and Early Twentieth-Century Thought* (Princeton: Princeton University Press, 1985).
Searle, John R., 'The World Turned Upside Down', *New York Review of Books* (27 October 1983), 74–9.
Sell, Roger D., ed., *Literary Pragmatics* (London and New York: Routledge, 1991).
Shattuck, Roger, *The Innocent Eye: On Modern Literature and the Arts* (New York: Farrar, Straus, Giroux, 1984).
Shaw, Francis S. J., 'The Celtic Element in the Poetry of W. B. Yeats', *Studies*, XXIII (1934), 260–78.
Shaw, Francis S. J., 'The Celtic Twilight', *Studies*, XXIII (1934), 25–41.
Sheehy, Jeanne, *The Rediscovery of Ireland's Past* (London: Thames & Hudson, 1980).
Shelley, Percy Bysshe, *Essays and Letters*, ed. Ernest Rhys (London: Walter Scott, 1886).
Sidnell, Michael J., *Yeats's Poetry and Poetics* (London: Macmillan, 1996).
Sidnell, Michael J., 'Unacceptable Hypotheses: the New Edition of Yeats's Poems and its Making', YA3 (1985), 225–43.
Spears, Monroe K., *Dionysus and the City: Modernism in Twentieth-Century Poetry* (New York: Oxford University Press, 1970).
Spender, Stephen, *The Struggle of the Modern* (London: Hamish Hamilton, 1963).
Stead, C. K., *Pound, Yeats, Eliot and the Modernist Movement* (New Brunswick, N. J.: Rutgers University Press, 1986).
Svarny, Erik, *'The Men of 1914': T. S. Eliot and Early Modernism* (Milton Keynes and Philadelphia: Open University Press, 1988).
Symons, Arthur, 'An Anonymous Review of W. B. Yeats's *Ideas of Good and Evil*' *Athenaeum* (27 June 1903), ed. Bruce Morris (Edinburgh: Tragara Press, 1988).
Symons, Arthur, 'Balzac', *Fortnightly Review* (May 1899), 745–57.
Symons, Arthur, 'A Censor of Critics', *Fortnightly Review*, LXIX (June 1901), 1003–12.
Symons, Arthur, 'Dowson', *Fortnightly Review*, LXVII (June 1900), 947–57.
Symons, Arthur, 'Fact in Literature', *Saturday Review* (24 August 1901), 232.
Symons, Arthur, *London Nights*, 2nd edn (London: Leonard Smithers, 1897).
Symons, Arthur, 'Nietzsche on Tragedy', *Academy* (30 August 1902), 220.
Symons, Arthur, *Studies in Prose and Verse* (London: J. M. Dent, 1904).
Symons, Arthur, *The Symbolist Movement in Literature* (New York: E. P. Dutton, 1958, first published 1899).
Synge, John Millington, *Collected Works*, vol. 2, ed. Alan Price (London: Oxford University Press, 1966).
Thatcher, David S., *Nietzsche in England, 1890–1914* (Toronto: University of Toronto Press, 1970).
Toomey, Deirdre, 'Bards of the Gael and Gall: An Uncollected Review by Yeats in *The Illustrated Evening News*', YA5, 203–11.
Toomey, Deirdre,'Labyrinths: Yeats and Maud Gonne', YA9 (1992), 95–131.
Vendler, Helen, 'Technique in the Earlier Poems of Yeats', YA8 (1991), 3–20.
Wade, Allan, *A Bibliography of the Writings of W. B. Yeats*, 3rd edn revised (London: Rupert Hart-Davis, 1968).
Waite, A. E., *Lives of Alchemystical Philosophers* (London: George Redway, 1888).
Ward, Margaret, *Maud Gonne: Ireland's Joan of Arc* (London: Pandora Press, 1990).
Weber, Eugen, *Varieties of Fascism: Doctrines of Revolution in the Twentieth Century* (Princeton: D. Van Nostrand, 1964).

Weinsheimer, Joel C., *Gadamer's Hermeneutics: A Reading of Truth and Method* (New Haven and London: Yale University Press, 1985).

Weinsheimer, Joel C., *Philosophical Hermeneutics and Literary Theory* (New Haven and London: Yale University Press, 1991).

Weygandt, Cornelius, *Irish Plays and Playwrights* (London: Constable; Boston and New York: Houghton Mifflin, 1913).

Weygandt, Cornelius, *The Time of Yeats: English Poetry of To-day Against an American Background* (New York and London: Appleton-Century, 1937).

Weygandt, Cornelius, *Tuesdays at Ten* (Philadelphia: University of Pennsylvania Press, 1928).

White, Hayden, *Tropics of Discourse: Essays in Cultural Criticism* (Baltimore and London: Johns Hopkins University Press, 1978).

Williams, Raymond, *Problems in Materialism and Culture* (London: Verso Editions and NLB, 1980).

Wilson, Edmund, *Axel's Castle: A Study in the Imaginative Literature of 1870–1930* (New York: Charles Scribner's Sons, 1931).

Wimsatt, W. K., and Monroe C. Beardsley, 'The Intentional Fallacy', *Sewanee Review*, LIV (Summer 1946), 468–88.

Wordsworth, William, *Poetical Works*, ed. Edward Dowden (London: George Bell, 1893), vol. 5.

Yeats, John Butler, *Letters to His Son W. B. Yeats and Others*, ed. Joseph Hone (London: Secker & Warburg, 1983, first published 1944).

Index

Abbey Theatre   82, 119, 168
Alexander the Great   83
Aldington, Richard   156
Archilogus   52
Arnold, Matthew   15, 89, 106
Atkinson, F. M.   107, 110

Beaumont, Francis   76
Beeching, H. C.   50
Bennett, Arnold   8
Bickley, Francis   39
Blackmur, R. P.   98
Blake, William   4, 21, 61, 65–6, 154
Bloom, Harold   22
Bornstein, George   19–22, 148–50
Bourdieu, Pierre   106
Boyce, D. G.   116
Boynton, H. W.   35
Brett, George   54
Bridges, Robert   43, 45
Brown, Terence   29, 46, 70, 139, 142–3, 160
Browning, Robert   37–8, 52
Bryan, George   169
Bryn Mawr College   54
Bullen, A. H.   85, 129
Burke, Edmund   104, 117
Burke, Kenneth   98
Burns, Robert   74
Byron, George Gordon   84

Calinescu, Matei   3–4
Carman, Bliss   40
Castiglione, Baldassare   85, 112, 120, 122
Christ, Carol T.   14
Chapman, Wayne K.   164
Coleman, Antony   108–10
Common, Thomas   65
Coole   65, 72, 85–7, 89, 94–5, 109, 112, 165
Corkery, Daniel   109–11

Crashaw, Richard   43
Cromwell, Oliver   87
Crosby, Ernest   55
Cuala Press   126–30, 151
Culler, Jonathan   17–18
Cullingford, Elizabeth Butler   29–30, 34

Dari, Ruben   3
Davie, Donald   4–7, 9, 100, 124
Da Vinci, Leonardo   58
Davis, Thomas   90, 130
Deane, Seamus   98, 167
De la Mare, Walter   96
Dial   136
Dickinson, Mabel   70
Dillard, Annie   80
Donne, John   122–3
Donoghue, Denis   98
Dowden, Edward   127–8
Dowling, Linda   134
Dowson, Ernest   53–6
Duffy, Charles Gavan   130
Dun Emer Press   29, 58, 62, 127, 151

Eagleton, Terry   98
Eglinton, John *see* W. K. Magee
Eliot, T. S.   5, 7–8, 13–14, 18–19, 23–4, 48–50, 53, 55–6, 99–100, 136, 154, 156, 160
Ellis, Edwin   135
Ellis, Havelock   65, 88
Emmet, Robert   104, 117
Ercole de l'Este, Duke of Ferrara   113

Farr, Florence   43, 77–8
Feidelson, Charles   7
Ferguson, Samuel   101–2
Finnegan, Ruth   93–4, 155
Finneran, Richard   131
Fitzgerald, Lord Edward   104, 117
Flamel, Nicolas   46, 68–9, 79–80

Index

Flaubert, Gustave 17
Fletcher, John 76
Ford, Ford Madox (F.M.Hueffer) 14–17, 23, 41, 50, 81–3
Foster, R. F. 29, 54, 75, 77–8, 109, 113, 121, 135, 161, 168, 170, 173
Frank, Joseph 10, 24, 49, 152
Freeman, Mark 73
Friedman, Barton R. 162
Frothingham, Eugenia Brooks 106
Fugitive, The: A Journal of Poetry 3

Gadamer, Hans-Georg 11–12
Galsworthy, John 8, 44
Garnett, Edward 107–8
Georgian poets 8
Gibbons, Luke 98
Gladstone, William Ewart 117
Goethe, Johann Wolfgang von 125
Golden Dawn 35, 68–9
Golden, Sean 22–3
Gonne, Iseult 77
Gonne, Maud 2, 28–30, 32–34, 36, 41, 46–8, 58–9, 66–7, 68–81, 86, 133, 135, 137, 145, 161, 167
Gould, Warwick 48, 140
Grattan, Henry 104, 117, 120–1
Graves, Robert 4–5, 8
Gregory, Lady Isabella Augusta 28, 37, 45, 47, 54, 60–1, 63, 72, 75, 77, 85, 123, 127, 139, 165
Gregory, Robert 109
Grierson, H. J. C. 123
Griffith, Arthur 118

Hardy, Thomas 3
Harwood, John 1, 3, 29–30
Heaney, Seamus 101, 111, 114–15, 124
Heine, Elizabeth S. 164
Hillis-Miller, J. 19
Homer 51, 121
Hone, Joseph 46, 112
Horniman, Annie 91
Hugo, Victor 51
Hulme, T. E. 18–19, 43, 93, 160
Hyde, Douglas 104, 116

Ibsen, Henrik 67
Irish Times 104, 112

Jackson, Thomas 15–16
James, Henry 8
Jeffares, A. Norman 61–2, 71, 76, 130
John, Augustus 89
Johnson, Lionel 54, 56, 90, 117, 123, 130, 166–7, 170, 171
Jones, Alun 43
Jonson, Ben 85–6, 109
Joyce, James 17, 48

Kahn, Gustave 9
Kearney, Richard 98, 168
Keats, John 22, 43, 51, 59, 122
Kelly, John S. 102, 106
Kenner, Hugh 15–16, 22, 131, 158
Kermode, Frank 4–7, 43, 151–2, 154, 161
Kershner, R. B. 166
Kilroy, Thomas 100
Kinsella, Thomas 104–5

Lane, Hugh 97, 112–13, 117–20, 167
Leader 104–5, 160
Leavis, F. R. 6
Levenson, Michael 23
Lewis, Wyndham 18
Lindsay, Vachel 136
Longenbach, James 99
Lully, Raymond 46, 68
Lunn, Hugh 121–2
Lyons, F. S. L. 116

MacBride, John 75–7, 137, 165
McGann, Jerome J. 91, 99, 152–3
Macleod, Fiona (William Sharp) 70
Macmillan (publisher) 131
MacNeice, Louis 131
MacNeill, Eoin 108
Magee, W. K. (John Eglinton) 64–5, 111
Mallarmé, Stéphane 4–5
Manchester Guardian 119
Manet, Edouard 17
Marcus, Phillip 143–4
Marlowe, Christopher 164

194 *Index*

Martin, Augustine   104
Martyn, Edward   170
Marx, Karl   89
Maynard, Theodore   110
Medici, Cosimo de   113
Menand, Louis   18, 50
Merquior, J. G.   6
Michelozzi, Michelozzo de Bartolommeo   113
Miller, David   118
Miller, Liam   126, 128
Millevoye, Lucien   28–30, 46, 58, 69, 76–7, 145
Milton, John   89
Modernist, The: A Monthly Magazine of Modern Arts and Letters   3
Monroe, Harriet   15, 136
Montefeltro, Guidobaldo di, Duke of Urbino   113
Moore, George   170
More, Paul Elmer   163
Moran, D. P.   99, 103–5, 107, 110
Morris, William   67, 89
Murphy, William Martin   118, 125

Napoleon   83
Nation, The   130
Nevinson, Henry Woodd   77–8
New Criticism   1–2, 5–6, 10–11, 13, 94, 97, 100
New Statesman   128
New York Times   40
Nietzsche, Friedrich   51, 62–3, 65–7, 80, 88, 101, 121, 123, 156–7
North, Michael   109

'Objectivists' Anthology, An   9
O'Brien, Conor Cruise   98
O'Connell, Daniel   130
O'Donnell, Manus   109
O'Grady, Standish James   63, 105, 116
O'Leary, John   21, 104, 119–21, 135
O'Toole, J. J. ('Imaal')   105–6
Olney, James   80, 84
Ong, Walter J.   43, 57, 93–4
Oppen, George   9

Outlook   41

Paracelsus   46
Parnell, Charles Stewart   54, 102–3, 113, 116–18, 120, 123, 130, 166–7, 170
Parkinson, Thomas   1
Pater, Walter   4, 12–13, 15, 18–19, 21, 24, 66, 84, 134, 154, 161, 165
Pethica, James   165
Poe, Edgar Alan   43
Poetry   136–7
Poirier, Richard   98
Pound, Ezra   1, 5, 7, 9, 14–20, 22, 49–50, 99–101, 134, 136–7, 158, 160, 165

Quinn, John   51, 54, 62, 65–6, 81

Ransom, John Crowe   3, 98
Raphael (Raffaello Sanzio)   90
Revue Celtique   139
Rhymers' Club   53, 67, 135–6
Rhys, Ernest   67, 136
Riding, Laura   4–5, 8, 154
Rimbaud, Arthur   8
Russell, George ('A. E.')   27, 36, 62–4, 114, 127

Said, Edward   6, 154
Saturday Review   40, 106
Saussure, Ferdinand de   10
Savoy   65–6, 88
Schopenhauer, Arthur   26–7, 39
Schuchard, Ronald   17
Scott-James, R. A.   3–4
Searle, John R.   174
Shakespeare, William   21, 44, 87
Shaw, George Bernard   8
Shelley, Percy Bysshe   20, 44, 84, 122
Sidnell, Michael J.   48
Sinn Fein   104
Spender, Stephen   8
Spenser, Edmund   21, 85–9
Strachey, Lytton   39
Svarny, Erik   9–10
Swift, Jonathan   117
Swinburne, Algernon Charles   46

Symbolism 4–6, 8–10, 28, 30–1, 43, 47, 154
Symons, Arthur 27–8, 30, 55–6, 65, 154, 163
Synge, John Millington 74, 90, 102, 104, 108, 113, 116, 125, 143

Tagore, Rabindrinath 102
Tennyson, Charles 37, 39
Thomas, Edward 88–9
Titian 17
Tolstoi, Count Lev Nikolayevich 67
Tone, Theobald Wolfe 104
Toomey, Deirdre 34, 58, 70–1
Tynan, Katharine 127

United Irishman 64, 118
Unwin, T. Fisher 129

Vendler, Helen 46

Wagner, Richard 67
Watts, George Frederic 48
Wells, H.G. 8
Whim 55
White, Hayden 156
Whitman, Walt 67
Wilde, Oscar 114
Williams, William Carlos 9
Wilson, Edmund 5, 7
Wordsworth, William 22, 48, 52–3, 84, 89, 122

Yeats, Elizabeth Corbet ('Lollie', WBY's sister) 126–9
Yeats, John Butler (WBY's father) 53–4, 99, 126–7, 146, 160
Yeats, Michael Butler (WBY's son) 126–8
Yeats, Susan Mary ('Lily', WBY's sister) 54, 128, 173
'Adam's Curse' 48, 50, 55–6, 144
'Against Unworthy Praise' 72, 79–81, 83, 133
'The Arrow' 45–7, 78–9
'At Galway Races' 94
Autobiographies 56, 62, 117–18

'Baile and Aillinn' 28, 33, 35–37, 45, 47, 57, 59, 130–2, 135, 144, 146, 149, 151
'Bishop Berkeley' 17, 124
'The Book of the Great Dhoul and Hanrahan the Red' 34
'A Canonical Book' (review of Lady Gregory's *Poets and Dreamers*) 42
Cathleen ni Houlihan 104
The Celtic Twilight 59
'Closing Rhymes', *see* 'While I, from that reed-throated whisperer'
'A Coat' 63, 146
'The Cold Heaven' 126, 145–6
Collected Poems (1933) 32, 130–1, 136
Collected Works (1908) 38–40, 45, 88, 96, 129, 150
Collected Works of William B. Yeats 40
'Coole Park 1929' 109–10
The Countess Cathleen 103
'Cycles Ago' 69, 76–7, 80
'The Devil's Book' 34
Discoveries 2, 64–5, 91–2, 94
'Discoveries: Second Series' 17
'The Dolls' 143–4, 151
'Edmund Spenser' 85–9, 118
'Ephemera' 160
'Fallen Majesty' 137, 145
'The Fascination of What's Difficult' 81–2
'The Folly of Being Comforted' 47–8
'Friends' 126, 145
'Friends of My Youth' (1910 lecture) 52, 83–4, 92, 125
From 'The Green Helmet and Other Poems' 55, 68–96, 97, 126, 135
'A General Introduction for my Work' 8, 12, 21, 24, 91
'The Gift of Harun Al-Rashid' 132
The Green Helmet and Other Poems (Cuala) 126, 128
'The Grey Rock' 33, 102, 132–3, 135–40, 142, 149

Yeats, works by *cont.*

'The Happy Townland' ('The Rider from the North')   60–1
'The Hour before Dawn'   142–3
The Hour Glass   126
Ideas of Good and Evil   27, 62, 64, 105–6
'In the Seven Woods'   45, 61–2, 65
In the Seven Woods   3, 20, 26–67, 75–6, 78, 80, 126–7, 129, 130–2, 144, 149, 151
'An Introduction for my Plays'   95
Is the Order of R. R. & A. C. to Remain a Magical Order?   35
'King and No King'   76–8, 95, 146
The King's Threshold   97
'The Lake Isle of Innisfree'   39
'The Literary Movement in Ireland'   38, 49, 56
'Literature and the Living Voice'   31–2, 51
'The Magi'   143–4, 151
'Meditations in Time of Civil War'   109–10
Memoirs   8, 43, 58, 69, 71–2, 74–5, 79, 81–3, 89–90, 123, 137
'A Memory of Youth'   144–5
'Momentary Thoughts'   68, 72, 79, 82
'Mortal Help'   30
'The Mountain Tomb'   137
'Nicolas Flamel and His Wife Pernella' ('Raymond Lully and His Wife Pernella')   68–9, 71
'No Second Troy'   74–5
'The Old Age of Queen Maeve'   28, 30–4, 36, 45, 47, 78, 130–2, 135, 138–9, 144, 149, 151
'Old Memory'   80
On Baile's Strand   62
'Paudeen'   125
'Pardon, old fathers'   126, 132–3, 135
'Peace'   78–9
'The Peacock'   134
Per Amica Silentia Lunae   13, 92
The Player Queen   137

Poems Written in Discouragement   97–125, 126, 146–7
Poems 1895   58, 129, 136
Poems 1899–1905   50
'Poetry and Tradition'   120–5
'The Poetry of Rabindrinath Tagore' (1913 lecture)   102–3
Preface to Lady Gregory's *Cuchulain of Muirthemne*   37, 41
Preface to Lady Gregory's *Gods and Fighting Men*   57–8, 63
'The Queen and the Fool'   59
'Reconciliation'   74–6
'Red Hanrahan'   34
Responsibilities   3, 55, 63, 67, 76, 86, 123, 126–47, 149, 151
Responsibilities and Other Poems (Macmillan)   126, 133
Responsibilities: Poems and a Play (Cuala)   126, 132, 135–6, 142, 146
Reveries over Childhood and Youth, 133
'Rosa Alchemica'   30–1, 60
Samhain   1904, 42–4
A Selection from the Love Poetry of William Butler Yeats   128–9
'September 1913'   20–1, 104, 118–19
Synge and the Ireland of his Time   128
'That the Night Come'   126, 145
'The Theatre' (1910 lecture)   44
'These are the Clouds'   95
'The Three Beggars'   132–3, 140–1, 143
'The Three Hermits'   140–1, 143
'To a Child Dancing in the Wind'   137
'To a Friend whose Work has come to Nothing'   123, 134
'To a Shade'   117
'To a Wealthy Man who promised a Second Subscription to the Dublin Municipal Gallery if it were proved the People wanted Pictures'   112, 123
'The Tragic Theatre'   17, 26–7
'The Two Kings'   33, 130–1, 135–6, 138–42, 144, 149

'Under Ben Bulben' 94
'Under the Moon' 58, 60
'Upon a Dying Lady' 128
'Upon a House shaken by the Land Agitation' 72, 85–6, 94–5, 109, 112
The Variorum Edition of the Poems of W. B. Yeats 149
'The Wanderings of Oisin', 39, 101–2, 131–2, 173
The Wanderings of Oisin and Other Poems 29, 106

'The Watts Pictures' (1906 lecture) 48, 52
'While I, from that reed-throated whisperer' 123, 126, 132, 134
The Wind Among the Reeds 29, 34, 45, 48, 114, 129, 132, 149
'The Withering of the Boughs' 59
'A Woman Homer Sung' 72, 75, 79, 135
'Words' ('The Consolation') 73–4
1902 lectures 51–4, 66